THE COMMONWEALTH AND INTERNATIONAL LIBRARY

Joint Chairmen of the Honorary Editorial Advisory Board
SIR ROBERT ROBINSON, o.m., f.r.s., London
and DEAN ATHELSTAN SPILHAUS, Minnesota

Publisher
ROBERT MAXWELL, m.c.

BOTANY DIVISION

VOLUME 3

General Editors

G. F. ASPREY, J. BRADY, A. G. LYON

Coastal Vegetation

Coastal Vegetation

BY

V. J. CHAPMAN

M.A., Ph.D., F.L.S.

Professor of Botany
Auckland University

PERGAMON PRESS

OXFORD · LONDON · EDINBURGH · PARIS · FRANKFURT

THE MACMILLAN COMPANY
NEW YORK

PERGAMON PRESS LTD.
Headington Hill Hall, Oxford
4 & 5 Fitzroy Square, London W.1

PERGAMON PRESS (SCOTLAND) LTD.
2 & 3 Teviot Place, Edinburgh 1

THE MACMILLAN COMPANY
60 Fifth Avenue, New York 11, N.Y.

COLLIER-MACMILLAN CANADA LTD.
132 Water Street South, Galt, Ontario, Canada

GAUTHIER-VILLARS ED.
55 Quai des Grands-Augustins, Paris 6

PERGAMON PRESS G.m.b.H.
Kaiserstrasse 75, Frankfurt am Main

SET IN 10 ON 12 POINT IMPRINT AND PRINTED IN GREAT BRITAIN
IN THE CITY OF OXFORD AT THE ALDEN PRESS

Contents

Preface

THIS book is one of a series designed to give a general account of the ecology of types of British vegetation. Coastal vegetation differs greatly in various parts of the world and an author can be faced with the problem of how far afield he should wander. Bearing in mind the purpose of this volume, the text has been restricted almost wholly to the ecology of British vegetation. This has not proved difficult in the descriptive sections, but when dealing with the factors of the habitat it might be thought more reference should have been made to studies outside of Great Britain. This could have involved different climatic regions and the inevitable occasional reference to vegetation unfamiliar to residents of Great Britain, and so it has been omitted. Because it is hoped that one result of this book will be to encourage Sixth Formers and First Year undergraduates to read accounts of the local vegetation whenever it is available, every effort has been made to include at the end of each chapter all known references to specific works on that particular aspect of British coastal vegetation, whether it is referred to in the text or not.

No book of this nature could be prepared without advice and critical comment from those who have particularly worked on coastal areas. I wish, therefore, to express my sincere thanks to Professor J. A. Steers for comments on the salt marsh and shingle beach chapters, to Dr. D. S. Ranwell for criticism of the salt marsh and sand dune chapters, to Dr. M. Gillham for helpful advice on the coastal cliff chapter, and to Mr. D. J. Chapman for comments on the chapters dealing with the littoral. I am also most grateful to my colleague, Professor J. E. Morton, for reading the whole manuscript and for valuable discussions with him on problems of the littoral.

Finally, there is my deep appreciation of the advice and help given me by the series editor, Professor G. F. Asprey, and Dr. A. G. Lyon of his staff. Their comments and help have undoubtedly improved the final product, though I must remain responsible for opinions expressed and the general accuracy of statements.

Permission to reproduce the following figures is gratefully acknowledged: figs. 1.1, 1.2, 7.8—Heffer & Son; 4.1–4.4, 4.6, 4.8—Leonard Hill & Co.; 7.4, 7.10, 7.12—Bell & Co.; 7.15, 8.1—Cambridge University Press.

Auckland   V. J. CHAPMAN

CHAPTER ONE

Basic Ecological Principles

In this book coastal vegetation will be regarded as comprising (a) the marine algal vegetation of the littoral and sublittoral, (b) the phanerogamic and algal vegetation of salt marshes, (c) the vegetation of sand dunes together with that of their "slacks", (d) the specialized vegetation associated with the drift-line, (e) the vegetation of shingle beaches, and (f) the plants found on coastal cliffs.

These habitats are specialized and well defined so that they readily lend themselves to ecological study. Furthermore, such environments possess specific features that are reflected in the type of plants found growing there, so that they are of especial interest. Moreover, within at least four of these habitats one can find excellent examples of the phenomenon of vegetation *zonation*. Such zonation is invariably associated with a gradation in one or more of the environmental factors, and one of the major functions of any ecological study is to establish those factors responsible for any zonation that can be observed.

ZONATION

When any particular habitat has been selected for study, the first procedure is to become familiar with, and identify, all the plants that can be found. The next step is to determine the exact nature of any zonation that can be observed and to list the various species that are apparently typical of each zone or belt. A consideration of the habitat should then indicate whether the zoning is permanent (static) or whether it is in a state of flux (dynamic). Thus zoning of the vegetation of the littoral, of shingle beaches and less obviously, often possibly non-existent, of coastal cliffs, will be of a static nature, not changing unless there is a variation in land–sea-level relationships or a large scale change induced by a major cliff-fall or slump. The zoning of the vegetation of salt marshes and of sand dunes will be dynamic or developmental, so that in any one spot on a salt marsh, as more mud is deposited and the land level rises with consequent environmental changes, the flora also will gradually change. A similar story can likewise be observed on sand dunes as successive ridges form on the shore, the oldest dunes with the most mature vegetation being to the landward, while the youngest dunes with relatively few species and incompletely colonized are to the seaward.

The communities associated with static zonation represent what some schools of ecology term *climax* communities. There are those who believe that only one kind of climax, the climatic climax, is represented in any one area. There are others who consider that there may be more than one kind of climax in an area. In the case of the littoral and of shingle beaches it can be argued that the physiography determines the zonation, and therefore the communities represent a physiographic climax. Whilst the idea of climax vegetation, or vegetation in equilibrium with the environment, may commend itself to many, there are those who argue that there is no such thing as a climax. Until one has had an opportunity of studying and comparing many stands of vegetation from comparable habitats, it is premature to discuss the validity or otherwise of the climax concept. In the meantime, however, it is convenient for us to accept the climax as a useful concept.

SUCCESSION

Developmental or dynamic zonation is more commonly called plant succession, because starting from bare ground one can observe a series of communities that succeed one another until the final or climax community is attained. When the succession commences on bare ground not previously colonized it is known as a *prisere*. The successions that are to be observed on sand dunes and salt marshes are good examples of priseres (see Chapters 4 and 6). Should an area of dune that has developed to forest become destroyed by burning a new succession would arise, but this would be known as a *subsere*.

Subseres in coastal habitats are of rate occurrence, and the student can generally be assured that he is dealing with a prisere. The name succession implies progression to an end point—the climax. Under certain conditions, however, the succession may be halted, or it may revert to a previous stage or it may deviate through another series of communities. The advent of a dense population of browsing animals can result in the next stage of the succession not developing. Thus it is probable that excessive grazing of some of the west coast grass marshes (see p. 95) may delay or prevent the advent of the rush or *Juncus* stage. Excessive grazing on salt marsh may damage the soil surface to such an extent that the closed herb cover disappears and is replaced by annual *Salicornia* (Saltwort) or *Suaeda* (Seablite), both generally representative of an earlier stage. Over-grazing of coastal cliffs brings about replacement of Creeping fescue (*Festuca rubra*) by Sea pink (*Armeria maritima*) or Sea plantain (*Plantago maritima*) (see p. 215). Deviation of a succession is not common with coastal vegetation, but it has been recorded on Nova Scotian salt marshes where it was produced as a result of persistent mowing for hay grass.

Sand dunes, especially their damp valleys ("slacks"), can provide examples of another ecological phenomenon, namely, *cyclic change*. In this there is a build-up to a vegetation covering which then becomes destroyed, either as a result of smothering by lichens or mosses or through damage from animals or man, resulting ultimately in the complete removal of the vegetation with a new bare surface on which the succession starts afresh (see p. 155). This process differs from a halted or deflected succession in that there is a regular continuing sequence, whereas in the others the induced stages only exist so long as the factor, e.g. grazing, cutting, persists.

During the normal course of a succession, the early stages can be regarded as far removed from equilibrium with the environment or habitat, successive communities becoming more and more in harmony with it, so that when the climax state is attained the final community is in equilibrium with the environment. One function, therefore, of an ecological investigation is to determine the extent to which any community is in equilibrium with the habitat. During the course of a succession, each successive community adds to what may be called the habitat potential, or the degree to which the habitat is increasingly capable of accepting a new and perhaps wider range of plant species. This concept is illustrated schematically in Fig. 1.1, where it will be noted that each community of the succession is marked by a pioneer

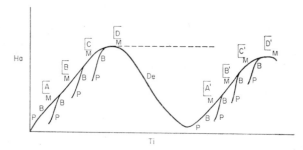

Fig. 1.1. *Build-up through successive communities to a climax. Each community passes through a pioneer* (P), *building* (B) *and mature* (M) *phase. This development is plotted in terms of build-up of habitat potential* (Ha) *with time* (Ti). *When degradation* (De) *takes place the process is repeated* (after Chapman).

or invasion stage (P), a building stage (B), and a mature (M) stage which is eventually invaded by the pioneers of the next community.

Because the study of salt marshes and sand dunes involves the study of successions, it is perhaps worth while to make brief reference to what may be called the nature of the succession.

The first stage is the existence of the bare ground which arises as deposited mud in the case of salt marshes or as blown sand in the case of dunes. The bare ground then becomes invaded by the first colonists. Invasion depends on a variety of factors and again it is the function of the ecologist to try and determine these factors and analyse their importance. Such factors include proximity of potential seed parents, method of seed dispersal (i.e. wind, animals or sea) or whether by vegetation fragments (as may be the case with *Spartina townsendii*, see p. 128) when the direction and strength of long-shore currents must be very important.

The arrival of the seeds is followed by the next stage, which is often called *ecesis*. This involves the successful germination of the seed (and the existence, therefore, of suitable temperatures and water supply and the absence of predators), successful growth of the plant to maturity (determined and controlled by the factors of the environment or habitat), flowering and the setting of seed so that the community is perpetuated.

The advent of the plants brings about changes in the habitat. Thus organic matter from dead plants is added to the soil, in the case of salt marshes and sand dunes the presence of the plants results in the former case in increased silt deposition, and in the second case in fixation of the sand so that it is no longer so mobile. The plants also bring about changes in the soil nutrients and soil water supply, and these changes may be further reflected in the soil microflora and fauna (see p. 184). If the plants happen to be of some size, they will also bring about changes in the micro-climate, e.g. air movement, surface evaporation and relative humidity, and these changes may determine the nature of other species that subsequently invade the community.

All these changes and effects upon the habitat can collectively be termed *reaction*.

Invasion and reaction result in more plants entering the former area, and usually at quite an early stage *competition* for soil nutrients, soil water and even light may become important features of the community. This competition is likely to reach its maximum for any species just around the period of flowering, when plants generally make their greatest demand on the habitat. A community could therefore be regarded as more successful if the flowering periods of its principal species do not all occur at the same time. In the case of the General Salt Marsh community (see p. 96) where there are a number of co-dominant species, the flowering times are staggered

(Fig. 1.2). This is one aspect of coastal ecology that merits much more attention, not only in respect of actual flowering periods, but in determining the demands made by the principal species at different stages of their life history.

The final stage in the succession is *stabilization*, when the climax community is reached, and with it comes dominance of the principal life-form. Earlier stages will have exhibited the phenomenon of dominance of one or more species as such, but in the climax community one has not only dominance of species but also of a particular

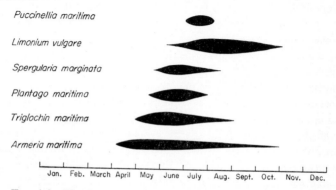

Fig. 1.2. *The flowering periods of the six species comprising the General Salt Marsh community at Scolt Head (after Chapman).*

life-form (see p. 9), which under normal, non-extreme climatic conditions is generally trees.

COMMUNITY ANALYSIS

Whether one is dealing with a static zonation, and hence climax communities, or a developmental zonation (succession), it is important to be able to describe the communities in such a way that they can be compared with similar communities elsewhere. One also needs to know the extent of variation within any given community.

One way of doing this after recognition of the community, which is generally possible by eye, is to prepare a list of the species, including if at all possible the animals. However, a species list is not of itself sufficient. We must know something of the relative frequency or abundance. This has been done by making use of terms such as dominant, abundant, frequent, occasional, rare, local, etc., but it is evident that such terms are subject to individual interpretation. Analysis of the community is therefore much more satisfactory if this kind of interpretation can be eliminated.

Some communities are very large, and whilst it may be easy to prepare a species list, detailed analysis of the entire community would take far too long. Use is made instead of samples, these being commonly contained within a square area known as a quadrat. The size of the quadrat must be such that it yields a fair statistical sample of the community. There are various ways of determining the minimal area that will give a fair sample of a particular type of community, and for those interested reference should be made to a standard ecological text[5]. Generally speaking, on sand dunes, shingle beaches and salt marshes, one square metre is likely to be sufficient, and at least ten such quadrats should be used for each community. On the rocky sea coast smaller areas may be adequate for the seaweed vegetation. Traditionally the quadrat is a square, but under certain conditions a rectangle with sides in the ratio 1:16 may be better, or a belt transect of 1 or 2 metres wide can be employed. In the succeeding chapters reference will be made to investigations that have involved use of all these variants.

With low vegetation it is also possible to make use of what is known as the "point method" where a long pin is repeatedly stuck in the ground and the species physically touched are listed. For the use of this technique, reference should be made to works by Goodall[4] and Greig-Smith[5]. With quadrats, which should normally be located at random, one can provide lists of species occurring, numbers of individuals of species, or one can map the quadrat showing the species spatially distributed. So long as the quadrats are all located in the same community, one can determine what is known as frequency, density, abundance and percentage cover:

$$\text{frequency} = \frac{\text{No. of occupied quadrats}}{\text{Total no. of quadrats}} \times 100$$

$$\text{density} \quad = \frac{\text{Total no. of individual plants}}{\text{Total no. of quadrats}}$$

$$\text{abundance} = \frac{\text{Total no. of individual plants}}{\text{No. of occupied quadrats}} \times 100 \quad \frac{\text{density}}{\text{frequency}}$$

Cover percentage = percentage of ground covered in the quadrats by a perpendicular projection of the aerial parts of the individual plants on to the quadrat.

This is not the place to enter into a discussion of the relative value and significance of the figures for frequency, abundance, density and cover, but before any of them are used, reference should be made to Greig-Smith[5].

Use can be made of some of the data in order to arrive at what is often known as a *coefficient of similarity* or *coefficient of community*, whereby two different or two apparently similar communities can be compared. There are various ways of arriving at such coefficients, and those interested should consult Greig-Smith[5]. Comparisons of this nature are only justified if one can really recognize distinct communities that are capable of analysis, and even then the methods employed are open to some criticism. Recent work has tended to throw doubt on the reality of many plant communities, and ecologists are talking today in terms of a vegetation continuum, or of a kaleidoscope of smaller patterns that make up the apparent community.

Considerable attention is being given at the present time to methods of analysis of *continua* or of vegetation patterns, and it may be that the objective approach will differ in the future. Analysis of communities is, however, only a means to an end, and provided it effectively delineates the community and enables it to be compared with another analysed by the same technique, the ecologist has a useful tool in his hand.

Quadrats are not the only means by which communities can be analysed. Life-form can and has been used successfully, and indeed can give a valuable clue to lines of further profitable study. Life-form analysis generally involves use of Raunkaier's life-form classification, the principal coastal life-forms being:

Phanerophytes (Ph).	Trees or shrubs with buds more than 25 cm above soil surface, e.g. Sea buckthorn (*Hippophäe rhamnoides*).
Chamaephytes (Ch).	Perennating buds above soil surface to 25 cm, e.g. Creeping willow (*Salix repens*).
Hemicryptophytes (H).	Plants with perennating organ at soil surface, e.g. Sea plantain (*Plantago maritima*).
Geophytes (G).	Perennating organ below soil surface, e.g. Cord grass (*Spartina townsendii*).
Hydro-helophytes (Hh).	Water plants with perennating buds in water or in mud below the water, e.g. Eel grass (*Zostera marina*).
Therophytes (Th).	Annuals, e.g. Sea rocket (*Cakile maritima*).

Stem succulents (S). Cacti,
Parasites and Epiphytes (P), } Not present in Great Britain.
etc.

When the various species have been allocated to their life-form, a biological spectrum (life-forms expressed as a percentage of the total number of species in the community) can be produced. It is desirable to make allowance for the phenomenon of dominance and so the life-form is best calculated on the frequency figures, e.g.

species a (Hemicryptophyte)   97 per cent frequency = 97 points
species b (Geophyte)   13 per cent frequency = 13 points

An example of the results that can be obtained from life-form spectra is provided in Table 1.1 and also in Table 4.3, p. 103.

There is no generally recognized life-form system for the algae, so that comparable work on a rocky shore has not been carried out. For those who might be interested in analysing seaweed communities in this fashion, the system that seems most workable at present is that of Feldmann, which can be found summarized in Chapman[3].

On the Continent, another system of vegetation analysis is employed. This is based essentially on floristics, and in particular upon

TABLE 1.1

*Life-form Spectra of Salt Marshes in different parts of the World
(from Chapman[3])*

Area	Ph.	Ch.	H.	G.	Hh.	Th.	P.
California	—	14	31	9	—	43	3
Massachusetts	3·5	3·5	60·5	11	7	14·5	—
Argentine	—	2	37·5	20	1	39·5	—
New Zealand	8	4	56	8	8	16	—
Europe	—	10	40	10	10	30	—
Hungarian inland saline marsh	—	5	40	12	5	38	—

groups of species which are termed the "faithful" species because
they are regarded as characteristic of the community[1]. Consideration
is also given to other ecological features, but association of characteristic species, and in certain cases other groups which are known as
differential species, is the main basis of the system. The floristic
composition, both qualitative and quantitative, is regarded as the
indicator of the specific environment. The vegetation is sampled
in order to determine the faithful species, and at least ten samples
should be taken. No size for the sample is set, and as the samples are
selected as being representative rather than at random, the system is
more subjective than one in which quadrats of a standard size are
employed. In each sample every species is given a value for its cover
degree-abundance and another for its sociability, and from these
values a synthetic list is prepared headed by the "faithful"
species.

One value of this system is that any community is based, like a
taxonomic species, upon a specific example which takes the name of
its original author. Subsequent workers can, if necessary, visit the
"type" community in the same way as the taxonomist can study the
"type" specimen of a given species. However, it does not always
follow that the "type" community will remain in its original condition, because if it is part of a succession it will inevitably undergo

change. Listing the "type" community is therefore really only of value in a climax or stable community.*

In many respects there is no doubt that this system has its merits. In general it can be suggested that no system of analysis is without its flaws, and great interest and value can be derived by the use of more than one system to describe the same piece of vegetation.

TERMINOLOGY

When the vegetation has been analysed, there is still the problem of how it should be classified and what terminology should be used. In this book, the ecological terms will be used in the same sense as they are by Tansley[8] in his book, *The British Islands and their Vegetation*. It is, however, important to note that the same terms have been given rather different meanings by other schools of ecology. In a climax community, regarded by Tansley as a community of relative stability, the *Association* is a major plant community dominated by distinctive species and distinctive life-forms. It is convenient to recognize such communities by use of the termination -etum. Thus for a community dominated by species of *Salicornia* one refers to the Salicornietum. The same procedure can also be used for the next smaller unit, e.g. the Salicornietum strictae is a community dominated by a single species, *S. stricta*.

Within the association, then, one may find *consociations*, each dominated by a single species, and within the consociation there can be *societies* each dominated by subsidiary species. The *associes*, *consocies* and *socies* are their equivalents in a sere (succession). It is clear, therefore, that analysis of communities should be aimed at classifying the community into one of the groups mentioned above. In carrying out such analysis, it is important to remember that the use of any of these terms can be in either of two senses. They can be used in the concrete sense to refer to a particular community, e.g. the General Salt Marsh associes of Scolt Head Island in Norfolk, or they

* Details can be found in Braun-Blanquet's *Pflanzensoziologie*, and in Poore[6, 7] or Whittaker[9].

can be used in the abstract sense, i.e. the concept of the General Salt Marsh associes, based upon a consideration of numerous samples from a very wide variety of salt marshes.

The concepts of continua or of vegetation patterns in the study of communities makes classification much more difficult, and theoretically it may turn out that the terms used above may cease to be valid. Nevertheless they have served a very useful purpose in the past, and there is no doubt that at present they can continue to do so.

THE ENVIRONMENT

After the basic steps of recognizing, analysing and classifying the communities have been carried out, attention must be directed to the habitat or environment. Here it is important to be clear from the outset what is being investigated. In the case of a community (*communal habitat*) it is possible to make measurements of the environmental features at a given date—in this case we deal with a *partial habitat*. This picture is obviously inadequate and a clearer idea will be secured by measurements obtained throughout the year. These figures can be left as they are or mean values can be calculated, and if this is then continued over a series of years it is possible to arrive at what is termed the *successional habitat*. This kind of study can be extended from a single community to include the habitat of two or more like communities. If the data is again averaged out, we shall be presented with an abstract concept of the habitat characterizing that particular community. In cases where attention is being given to the ecology of a single species (*individual habitat*) one may have the same approach—i.e. the habitat of a single individual of the species at one given moment, the habitat of the same individual over a long period, or the characteristic habitat derived from a study of the habitats of a number of individuals.

When the kind of habitat it is proposed to investigate has been determined, it will be found that the study falls into four major sections:

(a) climate
(b) physiography (including tides)
(c) soil
(d) biota

In the case of the littoral beach and the salt marsh, the tidal factor is of very great importance, whereas climate is less important. Even so, however, there are extensive periods when the vegetation is not submerged and is therefore subject to the normal climatic factors of the region. It is necessary in these two cases and also with sand dunes, coastal cliffs and shingle beaches to secure as much information as possible about the major regional climate.*

It is also highly desirable to obtain detailed information about the micro-climate, that is the climate immediately above and within the community, because this usually plays a part in determining what species may be associated with the dominants. This information can be of particular importance with tall vegetation, e.g. Marram grass, *Juncus maritimus* marsh, *Spartina townsendii* marsh.

The principal variables that require study within the community are (a) maximum and minimum temperatures, (b) precipitation (this can be done by setting up a rain gauge and taking weekly readings), (c) relative humidity (this can be carried out by using a whirling psychrometer, which gives a wet and dry bulb thermometer reading, and the R.H. is then read off from tables), (d) evaporating power of the air (achieved quite easily by the use of a simple atmometer—see Fig. 1.3), (e) wind velocity (simple portable anemometers are available for this purpose), (f) light intensity (comparative, but *not* absolute values can be obtained by the use of suitable photographic exposure meters).

Study of the tides, which is essential with littoral and salt marsh vegetation, really demands the use of a tide gauge. This is rarely available but in default useful information can be obtained by the use of a tide pole. This is a pole clearly marked in feet and inches, which is set up firmly in a sheltered spot and then the height of the tide at different times recorded from it. Such records are obtained on as many calm days as possible and preferably over a full tidal cycle. The tide pole can be related by levelling to a bench mark and hence to ordnance datum, or the help of the Navy hydrographic office can be invoked to relate the information to the nearest port of reference. In either case it will then become possible to use predicted tide curves, if wanted, from the nearest place with an official tide gauge.

* This can be obtained from the Meteorological Office.

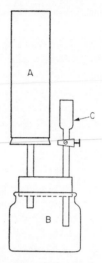

Fig. 1.3. *Simple type of atmometer. A, porous clay cylinder; B, water reservoir; C, place for addition of water. At start the whole apparatus must be full of water. The amount lost over a given period is measured by the volume of water that has to be added to bring the water up to the tap.*

Communities of sand dunes, salt marshes, shingle beach and coastal cliff require that some attention be given to the nature of the soil or substratum in which the plants grow. The features that are of greatest importance can be listed as follows:

A. *Physical*

           Pore space
           Aeration
           Temperature
           Water table movement

B. *Chemical*

           Organic matter
           Carbonate content
           Salinity

$$\left.\begin{array}{l} \text{Nitrogen} \\ \text{Potash} \\ \text{Phosphate} \\ \text{Water} \end{array}\right\} \text{content}$$

C. *Biological*

macro-organisms, e.g. crabs, worms

micro-organisms (mainly fungi and bacteria)

The significance of these various factors is dealt with in any book on ecological principles and reference will be made here only to those that can conveniently be studied in a simple fashion. Aeration in the soils of a salt marsh is an important feature and can be demonstrated readily (see p. 116). Soil thermometers are available commercially and very interesting results can be secured, especially on sand dunes (see p. 166) and shingle beaches.

In all three habitats, movement of the water table may be of very great importance. In shingle beaches and sand dunes, simple pits will yield valuable information (see p. 207), but on salt marshes another type of approach is necessary (see p. 115). In all cases, one should look for any evidence that suggests movements are determined by tidal phenomena.

After a soil has been dried in an oven at 105°C the organic matter can be determined by the loss on ignition, when the sample is heated red hot in a crucible. Very interesting results have been obtained for certain dune areas in relation to age (see p. 182) and this could be extended to other dune systems.

In coastal vegetation, salinity is of paramount importance, because there is evidence that it plays a major part in controlling some of the zonation. In this respect, the ecologist is concerned with the salinity of the soil water table and the salinity of the soil itself. Thus, with dunes and shingle beaches it is likely that a fresh water table will be found floating on a salt water one (p. 170). Samples of the water can be removed and the salinity determined by titration against standard silver nitrate (see p. 118). In the absence of any soil water table, the salinity of the soil can be determined by leaching with a known volume of distilled water and again titrating. An approximation of the nitrogen, phosphorus and potassium content of the soil can be obtained by simple spot test methods, e.g. Morgan spot tests,* which are based upon colours that are compared with standard colour charts.

The extent to which the biota is of importance varies with the community. Before the advent of myxomatosis the rabbit population of sand dunes and coastal cliffs was an important factor, and in some cases, at least, determined the stability of the dune system. On coastal cliffs the bird population can be highly significant, especially if the area is used for nesting, because of the excessive trampling and the great enrichment by nitrogenous material. On salt marshes, burrowing crabs, mollusca and annelids undoubtedly assist in aeration of the soil. The littoral, however, is the principal coastal habitat in which animals play as important a part as do the plants, so much so that the communities are in fact biomes in which sometimes animals are the dominants and sometimes plants.

AUTECOLOGY

We have concerned ourselves so far with communities. This represents what is known as *synecology*. Communities are comprised of individual species, and each species can be studied in detail. Such studies represent *autecology*, and they involve not only the same kinds of investigation outlined for the communities, but additional work as well. First of all, a taxonomic study is essential, in order to determine whether there is any evidence of ecological variation. If there is, the plants need to be grown under uniform conditions to ascertain whether such variations are "fixed" or not. Germination studies are essential, especially in relation to degrees of salinity and water content. In fact, the plant must be followed through its entire life history in relation to every possible variation in the habitat. In addition, any peculiar morphological features, e.g. existence of aerenchyma (tissue with air spaces) or succulence, should be investigated in relation to the peculiar conditions of the habitats. The

* Cf. Morgan Soil Testing System. *Bull. Connect. Agric. Expt. Station,* **541.**

species has to be studied not only under natural conditions, but it must be grown experimentally under controlled conditions. The objective in each case should be the production of an account of the type appearing in the *Biological Flora of the British Isles*[2].

Because it has been rather easier to carry out, most of the work in the past has been of a synecological nature. There is abundant scope at present for autecological studies, especially among species restricted to coastal communities.

REFERENCES

[1] BRAUN-BLANQUET J., *Pflanzensoziologie.* 2nd Ed. Vienna (1951).

[2] CHAPMAN V. J., *Suaeda fruticosa* (L.) Forsk. in *Biological Flora of the British Isles. J. Ecol.,* **35,** 303 (1947).

[3] CHAPMAN V. J., *The Algae.* Macmillan (1962).

[4] GOODALL D. W., Some considerations in the use of point quadrats for the analysis of vegetation. *Aust. J. Sci. Res.,* Ser. B, **5,** 1–41 (1952).

[5] GREIG-SMITH P., *Quantitative Plant Ecology.* Butterworths (1957).

[6] POORE M. E. D., The use of phytosociological methods in ecological investigations, I–III. *J. Ecol.,* **43,** 226, 606 (1955).

[7] POORE M. E. D., The use of phytosociological methods in ecological investigations, IV. *J. Ecol.,* **44,** 28 (1956).

[8] TANSLEY A. G., *The British Islands and their Vegetation.* Cambridge University Press (1949).

[9] WHITTAKER R. H., Classification of natural communities. *Bot. Rev.,* **28** (1), 1–160 (1962).

CHAPTER TWO

Littoral Vegetation

ALGAL COMMUNITIES

ALGAL communities are readily studied wherever there is an accessible rocky coast. A beach of small boulders or pebbles is generally too mobile to carry any extensive vegetation unless in a very sheltered locality, though even then the range of species to be found will be restricted. Estuaries with rocky shores, such as parts of the Bristol Channel, are not so rich floristically as the open coast, because the lowered salinity eliminates some algae. The silt brought down by the river and deposited continuously near the mouth probably eliminates other species, not only through the actual deposition, but also because of the greatly lowered light intensity.

Ecologically the algal communities of the sea-shore lend themselves admirably to detailed study. The principal species, together with certain marine animals, form well-marked belts on the shore and the phenomenon is not confined to any one region, but is more or less universal, though the component species obviously vary in different parts of the world. If a variety of localities is readily available, it will be found that there is a variation both in number of species and abundance of individuals, as between a rocky coast and boulder coast, and also as between a protected rocky coast and an exposed one. Comparisons of the type suggested are well worth making, since they provide information about species absent respectively from the different types of coast (Figs. 2.1 and 2.2).

LITTORAL (Rocky Shores)

On the coast the algal vegetation can be divided into that of the littoral and that of the sublittoral. We shall have to consider very briefly what is meant by the littoral, as considerable debate has taken place concerning its limits. There are two possible criteria that can be used in defining it. One is purely physical and based upon tidal phenomena. Thus it is possible to regard the littoral as extending

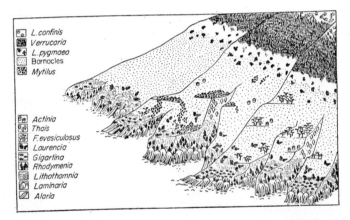

L. confinis
Verrucaria
L. pygmaea
Barnacles
Mytilus

Actinia
Thais
F. evesiculosus
Laurencia
Gigartina
Rhodymenia
Lithothamnia
Laminaria
Alaria

FIG. 2.1. *Diagrammatic representation of types of exposed shores around Anglesey. The slope on the left represents a simple extremely exposed shore with few species superimposed upon the barnacles. The other slopes show slightly less exposed shores and indicate the influence of ledges and clefts upon the distribution of* Mytilus, Fucus *var.* evesiculosus *and* Thais. *Although shown separately* Mytilus *and* Fucus *often occur together. The depth of the black zone has been considerably reduced: on these shores it would probably be at least twice as deep as the barnacle zone. Note that* Patella, Littorina neritoides, L. rudis *and* Porphyra *would also be abundant but are not shown (after Lewis).*

from mean high water (M.H.W.) to mean low water mark (M.L.W.); alternatively, it can be defined as reaching from extreme high water mark (E.H.W.M.) to extreme low water mark (E.L.W.M.). Most of the early ecological work is based upon one of these two definitions.

More recently, ecologists have come to realize that the problem is not so simple, because the zones of dominant plants and animals that are so characteristic of the littoral vary according to the influence of factors such as exposure, aspect, latitude and topography, and the tide is not necessarily paramount. For this reason, Lewis[32] urges that it would be far better to employ a biological definition based upon the distribution of major organisms. The biological criteria that he proposes are essentially founded upon the views of the Stephensons[38], which in turn were derived from surveys conducted in many parts of the world. The Stephensons recognized three major belts,* the supra-

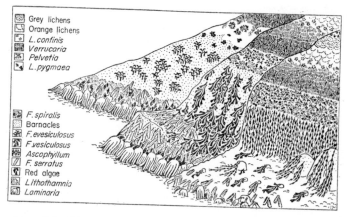

Grey lichens
Orange lichens
L. confinis
Verrucaria
Pelvetia
L. pygmaea

F. spiralis
Barnacles
F. evesiculosus
F. vesiculosus
Ascophyllum
F. serratus
Red algae
Lithothamnia
Laminaria

FIG. 2.2. *Diagrammatic representation of one semi-exposed and two sheltered shores around Anglesey, wave action decreasing from left to right. On the sheltered shores the influence of slope and substratum upon the large algae is shown. No attempt has been made to include animals other than barnacles (after Lewis).*

littoral fringe, the mid-littoral and the sublittoral fringe (sometimes called infra-littoral). The limits of these belts were determined by certain dominant groups. Thus the upper limit of the supra-littoral fringe was set by the upper limit of periwinkles (*Littorina* spp.);

* The Stephensons used the term "zone" for these belts, but since "zone" has a latitudinal or geographical connotation, it is better replaced, as here, by the word "belt".

the boundary between this belt and the mid-littoral was determined by the upper limit of barnacles (*Balanus*, *Chthalamus*), whilst the lower limit of the mid-littoral was marked by the upper limit of the oarweeds (*Laminaria* spp.). The Stephensons used extreme high and low water marks as their limits of the littoral so that their belts did not coincide with tidal levels, the supra-littoral fringe straddling extreme high water mark, and the sublittoral fringe straddling extreme low water mark. Lewis[32] suggests that it would be much

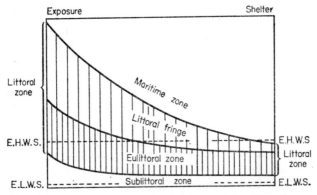

FIG. 2.3. *The proportions and positions of the littoral zones proposed as they may occur around British rocky coasts. Greater variation does exist, however, for on sheltered shores with a large tide range the eulittoral zone may be several times deeper than the littoral fringe, while on exposed shores with a very small tide range or under conditions of greater exposure on mild, northern coasts, the littoral fringe may be several times deeper than the eulittoral zone. Under special, local conditions the upper limit of the sublittoral zone may rise more steeply than that of the eulittoral (after Lewis).*

better to determine the upper limit of what he calls the *littoral zone* by the upper limit of either the *Littorina* or black lichen (*Verrucaria*)/ Myxophyceae belt, whichever happens to be uppermost. The lower limit of the littoral zone he regards as the boundary between the oarweeds and the barnacles and Fucaceae (Fig. 2.3). Above the littoral zone is the maritime zone occupied by orange and grey lichens, whilst below it is the sublittoral zone. The Stephensons' supra-littoral fringe is termed the littoral fringe, and their mid-littoral becomes the eulittoral zone.

The existence of the sublittoral fringe has been questioned by some workers, but it is quite clear that there are certain algae, and perhaps also some animals, that occupy a belt just below the eulittoral which, on sheltered coasts, straddles extreme low water mark. Whether one regards this fringe as a subdivision of the sublittoral, in the same way as different belts can be recognized within the eulittoral, or as a belt equivalent to the littoral fringe, must be a matter of opinion. In any case, it is clear that further work is necessary before it can be said that the sublittoral fringe belt is as universal as the eulittoral and littoral fringe.

In the present state of our knowledge, it would seem that the system proposed by Lewis has great merit and is the one that should be adopted. It avoids difficulties over the definition of the littoral proper and the universality of the principal demarcating organisms makes for easy recognition of the belts. It will be observed (Fig. 2.3) that the relationships between these belts and the tide marks varies depending upon the degree of exposure. On very exposed coasts the swash of the waves raises the sublittoral well above extreme low water mark of spring tides.

So far as algae are concerned, the sublittoral will extend downwards to the point where algae cease to grow. This depth varies in different parts of the world and is greatest in the clearer waters of the world, e.g. 250 m in the Adriatic, 180 m off the Balearic Isles.

Within the littoral zone one can generally find rock pools of varying size and depth. These can contain a very rich vegetation and it is well worth examining the deeper pools to see if a micro-zonation is present or not. The environmental conditions are very different from those on the rocks around and because they represent compact, self-contained units rock pools are ideal for study. It will be found that the vegetation varies with height of the pool on the shore, so that when pools are selected for study their height in relation to the tide heights must be determined at an early stage.

It will be evident that certain marine animals are equally important as dominant organisms of recognizable belts. Indeed the marine rocky coast communities are ideally biotic communities or biomes in the sense that often a plant and animal species are co-dominant. Study of such communities therefore emphasizes the importance of both kingdoms in nature.

Within the major divisions outlined above, the belts of the different communities can be recognized. The actual number of different communities or belts may vary from place to place and some of the variations in the published literature almost certainly reflect the opinions of the different authors. Whilst the zonation is essentially a static one and the dominants are to be found at all times of the year, some of the associated species may be seasonal, so that a full descriptive account requires observations made over at least twelve months. One of the major issues is the problem of how the communities comprising the belts shall be named. Should one use the terminology of terrestrial ecology as applied to static or climax communities (e.g. Formation, Association, Consociation, Society), or should a completely new set of terms be formulated? Thus it has been suggested that a group of belts that follow one another vertically should be termed an "association complex", which automatically assumes that each belt has the status of an Association as defined in terrestrial ecology. A belt may be broken horizontally by another community, especially in places where fresh water trickles over the rocks, or where there are couloirs.* The interrupting community can be termed an Association fragment. At present most marine ecologists are using the terminology of terrestrial ecology, no other alternative so far proposed having proved satisfactory. If it is considered difficult to determine the status of the belts, then one can use the non-committal term of "Community".

BELT ANALYSIS

Although it is generally easy to recognize a dominant or dominants within any belt, and hence to name the belts according to the

* A deep cleft between the rocks.

dominants, nevertheless the belts can also be analysed in terms of the Continental or Montpellier system (see p. 9).

In the past, analysis of belts has generally been carried out by listing the species that occur, and often, in addition, making an estimate by inspection of their relative frequency. If the Montpellier system is used, not only are the species listed but they are given the usual two-figure values.

Apart from the existence of the algal belts that lie within one of the major belts as delineated by Lewis or the Stephensons, the algal communities would appear capable of classification either according to their dominant(s) or on the basis of the "faithful" species, without the necessity of introducing a completely new terminology.

So far very little attempt has been made by marine botanists to use the traditional quadrat techniques of the terrestrial ecologist. Recently quadrats have been used with some success in Norway[2], especially in connection with littoral vegetation. From the quadrats the density of the brown rockweed *Ascophyllum*, in terms of fresh weight per quadrat, was obtained and the percentage occurrence (= frequency) of *Ascophyllum*, *Fucus vesiculosus*, *F. serratus* and *Codium* determined in six areas. In view of the great variation in fresh weight that can occur in algae, depending mainly upon the time after exposure, the density would have been better expressed in terms of dry weight. Quadrats should normally be located at random, but in the Norwegian study it was considered best to lay out $\frac{1}{2}$ m transects vertical to the shore-line at intervals of 5 m. Each transect was divided into metre lengths, and all quadrats containing *Ascophyllum* were sampled from the topmost one on the shore down to the lowest. As may be expected the percentage occurrence (frequency) increases with increasing size of quadrat. Mathematically the increase is not so great as it should be if the species were randomly dispersed. The conclusion therefore reached is that the plants are over-dispersed or aggregated into clumps. This raises an interesting problem because in the case of land plants, where seeds may drop to the ground around the parent plant, one can see how over-dispersion may arise; in the case of the fucoids, fertilization takes place in the water and one would have expected the fertilized eggs to settle randomly, though this possibility would be affected by the presence of other plants and local water movements.

For those who wish to try the use of quadrats, and there is no doubt that a great deal of very valuable information can be obtained from them, it is worth noting that the $\frac{1}{2}$ m^2 quadrat was found to be the best size. Quadrats very often may not do more than confirm the field observations but they have the advantage of expressing the results quite objectively. Thus in the Norwegian study the *Ascophyllum* density was less on stony shores than on rocky ones, but there was no maximum density in the middle of the zone. *Ascophyllum* and *Fucus serratus* were more frequent on rocky shores but *F. vesiculosus* was more frequent on stony ones. It also emerged that on the shores sampled, *Ascophyllum* (Fig. 2.4) and *Fucus vesiculosus* were more frequent in the upper half of the zone whereas *F. serratus* and *Codium* were more frequent in the lower half. The quadrats were also used to demonstrate the effect of shore physiography upon species frequency. With a large number of quadrats it is possible to determine the degree of association between pairs of species. There are various ways of doing this and for those who are so minded they will be found in any good book on statistics. The calculations in this particular case showed that there was a significant positive association between *Codium* and *Fucus vesiculosus* (i.e. they were likely to occur together), a negative association between *Codium* and the other two fucoids, similarly between *Fucus serratus* and *F. vesiculosus*, whilst the distribution of *Ascophyllum* was found to be independent of both *Fucus* species.

Using single transects on five different types of shore in the Isle of Wight and 25 cm^2 quadrats, Kain[24] determined the levels and occurrence of 65 macroscopic algae and 25 diatoms. This particular study was of interest because the original survey was made in April and then repeated in July. The results showed that the vertical distribution of the common species showed little change, but the existence of the fucoid belts was clearly dependent upon the slope of the substratum where fucoids are greatly restricted (Fig. 2.5).

There is no doubt that the use of quadrats can be greatly extended on the sea-shore, not only on the littoral but also in the sublittoral

B

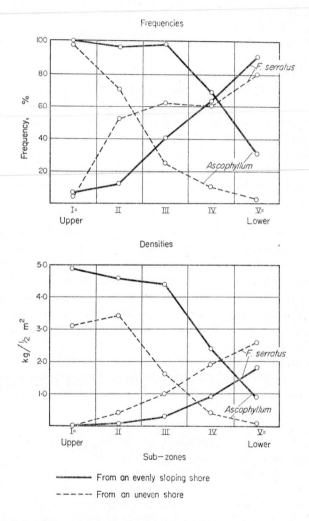

FIG. 2.4. *Frequencies and densities of* Ascophyllum *and* Fucus
serratus *on two kinds of rocky shore (after Baardseth).*

(see p. 39). It has been pointed out (p. 12) that terrestrial ecologists are moving towards the view that any piece of vegetation is either a mosaic or else part of a continuum with gradual variation in all directions towards other patterns. So far no attempt has been made

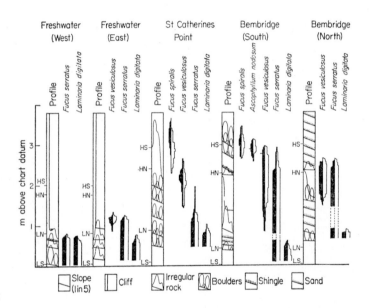

FIG. 2.5. *Diagram of the summarized profiles in five localities on the Isle of Wight, together with the limits to which the fucoids and* Laminaria *extended, in April and July. HS, HN, mean high water springs and neaps; LN, LS, mean low water neaps and springs (after Kain).*

to determine whether the vegetation patterns to be observed on the sea-shore should be interpreted as mosaics or continua, or whether the limits of the belts are so distinct that neither of these concepts is necessary.

We have seen that the ecologist can study the vegetation of the sea-shore by observation, recording his results either according to the Anglo-American system or to the Continental one. The belts can be analysed in more detail by the use of transects and quadrats when the frequency and density of species can be determined. The dry weight of the algae in a quadrat represents the algal biomass at that place at the time of sampling, so that sampling by cropping and weighing can give a picture of the vegetation. In recent years the productivity of marine crops has also been estimated in terms of the chlorophyll *a* content. This method was first applied in the marine environment to the floating phytoplankton, but more recently it has been applied to the attached or benthic algae. The gross productivity of a belt is of considerable interest, particularly when it appears that the density and occurrence of the principal species can vary so greatly in a vertical

TABLE 2.1

Average Chlorophyll a *in Four Intertidal Belts*

Belt	No. of samples	Mean g/m²	Standard deviation
1. *Littorina* ("Black") belt. 100 per cent cover *Calothrix crustacea*,	25	$0 \cdot 80 \pm \cdot 009$	0·48
63 per cent cover *Calothrix crustacea*	25	0·50	
2. Barnacle belt (+ *Gomontia* and *Rivularia*) 100 per cent cover.	52	$0 \cdot 27 \pm \cdot 001$	0·19
3. *Fucus vesiculosus, Balanus* 100 per cent cover.	50	$1 \cdot 47 \pm \cdot 051$	0·86
4. "Algae" 100 per cent cover (*Chondrus, Polysiphonia, Ceramium, Dasya*)	50	$1 \cdot 04 \pm \cdot 009$	0·68
		mean 0·82	

direction. No work of this nature seems as yet to have been done in Great Britain, but a study on the coast of Massachusetts[21] gives an indication of the kind of results that can be obtained. Areas of 25 cm[2] were sampled on the shore in four different belts, the samples ground up, extracted with acetone, which was then filtered and centrifuged, and the chlorophyll *a* determined spectrophotometrically. The results are given in Table 2.1.

Rather surprisingly it will be seen that under comparable conditions of cover *Calothrix* in the "Black" belt contains over half the chlorophyll *a* content of the *Fucus* and "algal" belts. Although there are differences in chlorophyll content, they may not be ecologically significant, but a final answer to this problem will not be forthcoming until physiological studies have been undertaken on the principal algae during submergence and exposure (see p. 56).

PHYSIOGRAPHIC FEATURES

Rock Pools

We have been directing our attention up to the present to the main ecological features of the vegetation that can be observed on rocky and boulder shores, whether exposed, sheltered or estuarine. On the shore there are other physiographic features that lend themselves to ecological study, and which merit further comment. Such features comprise the rock pools, couloirs and caves.

Rock pools may conveniently be grouped into three major categories: those of the lower eulittoral (often never uncovered during neap-tide periods), the pools of the middle eulittoral (covered once or twice every day) and the pools of the upper eulittoral and littoral fringe, which may remain exposed for several successive days during neap-tide periods. In these upper pools the conditions can become extreme, particularly in summer. These pools have an interesting counterpart in the pans of the salt marshes (see p. 47), and, providing both are accessible, comparisons could prove extremely interesting. The elements comprising the flora of rock pools can be grouped as follows: (a) species characteristic of the sublittoral, (b) species from the sublittoral fringe or lower eulittoral that reach their upper limit on the shore in the pools, (c) eulittoral species, (d) species wholly confined to pools. Any study made of rock pools should, therefore, be related to the position of the pools on the shore, and the analysis of the vegetation should be considered in relation to the occurrence of the species elsewhere.

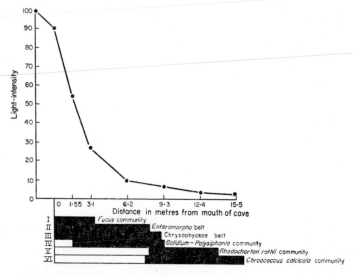

FIG. 2.6. *Graph showing the relation between light intensity and the distribution of algal communities in a long cave at various distances from the opening. The shaded areas indicate the extent of the various communities inside the cave (after Anand).*

Caves and Couloirs

Some shores are characterized by deep couloirs and caves. Both these physiographic features provide environments that are very different to the open rock surface and, as such, are worthy of independent study. In the case of caves the principal phenomenon is the change in vegetation with diminishing light intensity. It is now quite easy to make simple light measurements and the vegetation of a cave or couloir can be plotted in relation to the light intensities (Fig. 2.6). In doing such work it must be remembered that the intensity of the light will vary with the time and kind of day and also with the season of the year, so that extended observations are essential if they are to mean anything. It may safely be assumed that those species which penetrate into caves and occur low down in couloirs are fundamentally "shade" species, whereas those that occur on open rock surfaces are "sun" species. In a cave on Stronsay, Sinclair[34] recorded on walls or in pools, *Odonthalia dentata, Lithothamnion* (two species), *Plumaria elegans, Lomentaria articulata, Cryptopleura variosum* and *Rhodochorton purpureum*. The same or similar species were recorded[33] for cave vegetation at Lough Ine in Ireland. *Plumaria elegans* appears capable of the deepest penetration, whilst other cave species not recorded at Stronsay were *Phyllophora epiphylla* and *Hildenbrandtia*. Sixteen species are listed from the sublittoral of the cave.

BIOTIC RELATIONS

Another feature that lends itself to study on the sea-shore is the relationship between certain animals and plants. One can, for example, make a study of the algae that occur on the shells of some of the larger mollusca or on barnacles. This is a field that has not been greatly investigated and would well repay investigation. The algal population on barnacles has been described by den Hoek[23] and studies have been undertaken[13, 35] in respect of the browsing habits of limpets (*Patella*) in relation to the presence of algae. *Fucus, Ascophyllum* and *Pelvetia* are commonly absent or scarce on exposed coasts and these two facts have in the past been regarded as related. The common limpet (*Patella vulgata*) is very frequent on exposed shores and it now appears that the absence of the fucoids may be closely related to the limpet population. Clearing areas completely of algae and limpets resulted in a colonization sequence of diatoms—filamentous algae—sheet algae (*Porphyra, Ulva*)—fucoids. Within two years a dense growth of algae develops but underneath limpets can be found, often in great numbers. With their appearance, there is little further successful establishment of algae and old plants begin to disappear. With the gradual elimination of the algae the limpet food

supply becomes reduced and they too decrease and the bare area
becomes colonized by barnacles (Fig. 2.7). It will be observed that
the limpet maximum occurs a year behind that of the *Fucus* maxi-

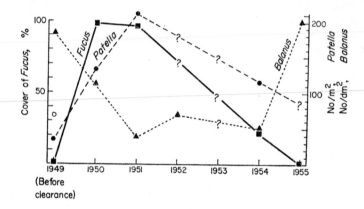

FIG. 2.7. *Fluctuations in the abundance of* Fucus vesiculosus,
Balanus balanoides *and* Patella vulgata *at Mean Tide Level on
the area cleared of limpets in 1949 (after Southward).*

mum. Further work of this nature is greatly to be desired because
there are almost certainly other local factors that can become
involved.

VEGETATION PATTERN

Rocky Shores

We are now in a position to outline the general pattern of algal
vegetation to be found on the rocky shores of Great Britain, and it is
convenient to commence with the upper sublittoral (= sublittoral
fringe). The upper limit of the fringe is generally set by the upper
limit of the laminarian zone. In most parts *Laminaria digitata* or
L. cloustoni (*L. hyperborea*) are the species involved, but on exposed
coasts, particularly of the north and west, they are replaced by
Alaria esculenta with its characteristic mid-rib and lateral reproductive appendages. Where rock and sand are mingled or in quieter

localities *Laminaria saccharina* may be the principal species, whilst in south and west Ireland and south-west England *Saccorhiza polyschides* with its bulbous base and twisted stipe mingles with the other laminarians or may be the sole dominant. As Lewis[30] has pointed out, there are two types of locality in which it may be difficult to recognize the upper limit of the sublittoral. One is where there is excessive exposure, when no laminarian is present and its place is taken by the encrusting red *Lithothamnia*, but since these are capable of extending into the eulittoral they do not provide a means of demarcating the sublittoral. Accessible shores of this type are very rare but they clearly merit further study.

The second case is provided by sheltered bays and lochs where the substratum changes to pebbles or gravel. In such places there is sufficient water movement from time to time to move the stones with the large laminarians so they are replaced by a great variety of smaller algae. The composition of this algal population varies with turbidity and water movement. In the south-west, species of *Cystoseira* may dominate, in other places *Stilophora*, *Spermatochnus* and *Laurencia obtusa* form the major components. Where the stones are so small as to be regarded as shingle, *Rhodochorton* and *Cladophora* may be the predominant algae. Transitional floras on more stable stones can include *Laminaria saccharina* with fucoids (*Himanthalia*, *Halidrys*) mixed with *Codium* and *Chorda*. From accounts that have been published for different parts of the world, it is evident that small algae, albeit different species, behave in a similar manner elsewhere, though such shores cannot be regarded as wholly typical, at least in the Northern Hemisphere.

The lower limit of this fringe belt is not at present well understood. It would seem that there are certain species which are limited to a region just above and below extreme low water mark. Until these species have been listed for the different types of coastline, it will not be possible to set any lower limit, nor is it possible to say whether the lower limit will be set by organisms or by reduction in light quantity or quality. The use of the aqualung (p. 39) will undoubtedly facilitate research in this particular field.

The lower eulittoral is commonly occupied by *Fucus serratus*, with

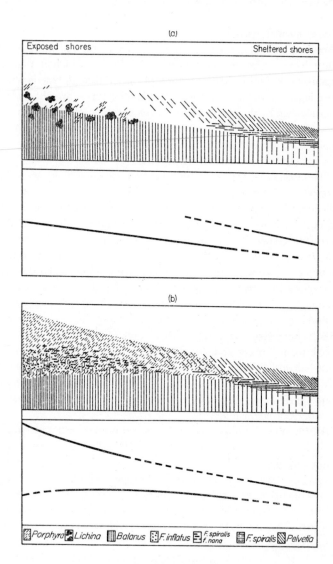

Fig 2.8 (See opposite).

which is often associated *Himanthalia*, though in exposed places these disappear and are replaced by red algae, such as *Chondrus*. Above *Fucus serratus* one finds *F. vesiculosus* and *Ascophyllum nodosum*. Sometimes *Fucus vesiculosus* occurs below the *Ascophyllum* whilst in other places the situation is reversed, and there are also regions where both species occur mixed together. On exposed coasts these algae disappear and the belt is essentially demarcated by the barnacles. The upper limit of the barnacles was postulated by the Stephensons[38] as representing the upper limit of the eulittoral (mid-littoral). This upper limit may be set by either *Balanus balanoides* or by *Chthalamus stellatus*. One complexity that arises by making use of these two indicator species is that *Chthalamus* generally rises to a slightly higher level on the shore than *Balanus*. As a result, depending on which genus is present, the upper limit of the eulittoral can change its level from one part of the British Isles to another. Furthermore since *Pelvetia canaliculata* commonly grows above the uppermost *Balanus* but below the upper limit of *Chthalamus*, it will belong to the littoral fringe in the former case and to the eulittoral in the latter. It is evident that the upper limit of the barnacles is not an absolutely constant feature because it fluctuates[30] within a narrow belt located approximately between high water of spring and neap tides.

The typical *Balanus* type of zonation (found mostly around the

---

Fig. 2.8. *The* Balanus *pattern of zonation,* (a) *shows the typical pattern, while* (b) *shows the modified form which occurs on the exposed shores in Caithness. The upper part of each figure shows the distribution of important species, and the lower part shows the position of the most conspicuous landmarks (clear upper limits) of the upper shore. On some Caithness shores* Fucus spiralis *and* F. spiralis f. nana *are linked by intermediate forms, while on others two distinct communities exist.* Enteromorpha, *which is usually mixed with the* Porphyra, *has been omitted from the diagram. (N.B. To avoid confusion the Littorinae have been omitted from this and the succeeding figure, and no attempt has been made to show the* Mytilus, Fucoids *or* Rhodophyceae *which may overlie the barnacles to a greater or lesser extent) (after Lewis, 1955).*

North Sea and in parts of the Irish Sea) is depicted in Fig. 2.1, where it will be seen that in sheltered places it or the *Ascophyllum/ Fucus vesiculosus* belt gives way to *F. spiralis* and *Pelvetia* of the littoral fringe plus, in places, *Catenella, Bostrychia* and *Calothrix*. With increasing exposure these algae gradually disappear, and are replaced by the black lichen *Lichina pygmaea* and the red laver, *Porphyra umbilicalis*, both of which, together with the Littorinids, lie astride the upper barnacle limit.

In Caithness, a modification of this zoning has been recorded[29] on exposed shores where the balanoid belt gives way to a growth of *Porphyra, Enteromorpha, Fucus inflatus, F. distichus* and *F. spiralis* f. *nana*. (Fig. 2.8).

The *Chthalamus* (barnacle) type of zonation as it is found on exposed coasts of west Scotland and Ireland contains *Balanus* as

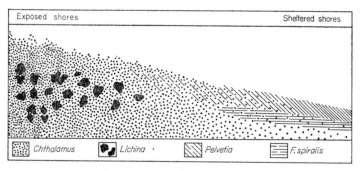

Exposed shores   Sheltered shores

☐ *Chthalamus*   ☐ *Lichina*   ☐ *Pelvetia*   ☐ *F. spiralis*

Fig. 2.9. *The* Chthalamus *pattern of zonation as it usually occurs in south-west England. In south-west Ireland,* Porphyra *and* Fucus spiralis f. nana *frequently mingle with or lie just above the uppermost patches of* Lichina *(After Lewis)*.

well, though the latter occurs essentially below the upper limit of the *Chthalamus*. Exposure is generally too severe for *Pelvetia* to occur and, because of the higher level attained by *Chthalamus* in relation to *Balanus*, the lichen *Lichina* lies wholly within the barnacle zone and is therefore a mid-littoral plant. In south-west England, *Balanus* is less common and in sheltered places *Pelvetia* and *Chthalamus* jointly provide the upper limit (Fig. 2.9). With extreme shelter the barnacle limit descends farther together with the *Fucus spiralis* belt.

Between the two types of zonation described above (*Balanus* and *Chthalamus*) it is only to be expected that varying degrees of transition will exist. The essential feature of these transitional zonations is the existence of a well-marked *Balanus* upper limit with, in exposed places, *Chthalamus* above. The latter species is found either just below or in the *Pelvetia* belt, but with increasing exposure it extends farther up the shore. In places there may even be a gap of some inches between the two barnacle belts. As Lewis[30] points out, the first appearance of the *Chthalamus* may be gradual or it may occur quite suddenly. On such transitional shores, the upper limit of *Chthalamus* (where present) must be regarded as the limit of the eulittoral, leading in more sheltered places to a lower limit that is demarcated by *Balanus*.

In sheltered places the littoral fringe is occupied at its lower levels by *Pelvetia*, *Fucus spiralis*, accompanied perhaps by *Catenella*, *Bostrychia* and Myxophyceae (*Calothrix*). Above this is a zone of black lichens dominated by *Verrucaria marina* and *V. maura*. Still higher it may be possible to recognize orange and grey lichen zones. Some workers regard these as still within the littoral fringe, but others, including the present writer, regard them as outside but in a maritime zone (p. 21) because the littorinids do not penetrate them under normal conditions. With increasing exposure the fucoids are replaced by *Porphyra* and *Lichina* and the littorinids increase in number[28]. The black lichen zone also may increase in importance (Fig. 2.1).

It will be found that the general arrangement of the principal algal belts around the rocky shores of Great Britain will fit into the broad framework that has been outlined above. In any given area there will be other seaweed species that are sufficiently prominent to justify inclusion in a local schema. Thus around the shores of north and west Scotland *Rhodymenia*, *Gigartina*, *Laurencia*, *Corallina*, *Leathesia*, *Cladophora*, may all become significant. Where fresh water runs down the shore or where streams spread out over the shingle *Fucus spiralis* is generally replaced by *F. ceranoides* and there is an abundant growth of green algae such as *Enteromorpha intestinalis*,

Monostroma grevillei and *Cladophora rupestris*. Where slopes become very steep and there is considerable water movement the usual algae may be more or less completely absent, being replaced by small turfy algae, which are better enabled to find lodgement in the small cracks and crevices and with small thalli are better able to withstand the conditions.

Once the principal belts have been recognized, further detailed study may lead to the recognition of smaller, less extensive, secondary communities. A number of such communities have been recognized from different areas: they include the *Enteromorpha intestinalis* community, *Porphyra-Urospora-Ulothrix* community, *Laurencia* community or association, *Gigartina-Cladophora* community, *Ulva linza* community, *Porphyra* association, *Bangia-Urospora* society, *Callithamnion-Ceramium* association, *Nemalion* society, *Gigartina* association, *Lomentaria* society and so on. From the nomenclature that has been used by different workers and repeated above, it is clear that a wide divergence of opinion exists as to the status of the particular communities. For school work it is almost certainly better not to apply status to these smaller groups and the non-committal name of community meets the circumstances admirably.

What has been said so far essentially concerns the large benthic (attached) algae. Beneath them or growing on substrate not occupied by other algae one can find growths of diatoms. A study of these[1] has shown that the communities vary with substrate (concrete piles, rocky reef or pool) and also with the geological nature of the substrate, whether calcareous or otherwise. There is, as may be expected, very much more variation in seasonal aspect than with the larger algae. These communities can be sought for and after collection examined under the microscope, but since diatom taxonomy is a difficult field, and because ecologically the communities are not very important, they can perhaps be neglected here.

SUBLITTORAL

Whilst we may neglect the diatomaceous communities, we cannot overlook the major communities of the sublittoral. The sublittoral fringe where present is represented by a specialized group of algae (see p. 33) which occupy a narrow belt around mean low water mark of spring tides. Below this belt, and extending down to a varying depth, there is a collection of algae which comprise the sublittoral flora proper. The principal components of this flora around most of Great Britain are the oarweeds *Laminaria cloustoni* (*L. hyperborea*) and *L. digitata*. The first-named species is often very heavily epiphytized and on one plant washed ashore at Stronsay[34] no less than 14 other species of algae were attached. Indeed, a study of the epiphytic flora of *L. digitata*, *L. cloustoni* and species of *Fucus* would form an admirable ecological exercise, because it would be concerned not only with the species that occur but also with attempting to determine the conditions under which they are found.

Up to fairly recently the only effective method of securing information about the sublittoral was by means of standard zoological trawls. Since the war, however, new techniques have been developed, but whilst all these may not be readily available to schools and universities, the potentialities are now much greater. Among these newer techniques is the combination of aerial photography, grab sampling and the echo-sounder as a means of mapping entire submarine beds and recording the composition of the major species (Fig. 2.10).

Another means of studying the sublittoral is by use of the aqualung, which enables the investigator to collect carefully and to observe the distribution of the various species (Fig. 2.11). This technique is likely to be used with increasing success and value because one can then employ traditional ecological sampling methods such as the transect and quadrat. It is also possible, if water and light conditions are suitable, to secure photographs of the vegetation being studied. The aqualung should not, however, be used except by persons who have undergone a course of training in it.

The detailed survey of the Scottish submarine beds[8, 39–49] covered 80,000 acres, and was carried out over a period of seven years so that sampling included seasonal and perennial changes. The survey was mainly restricted to the zone between low water mark and 10 fathoms, the dominant species being *Laminaria cloustoni* (*L.*

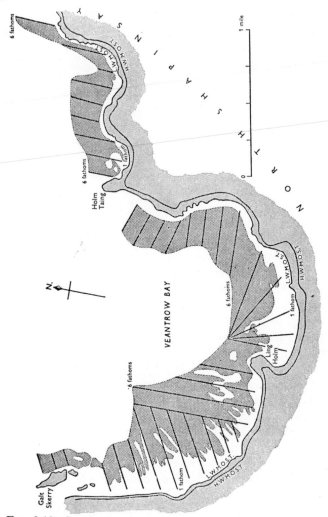

FIG. 2.10. *Correlation of seaweed cover by sampling and aerial photography. Straight lines indicate the measured transects (1–6 fathom) along which sampling was carried out by boat during May 1947, and the shaded areas show the algal cover photographed from the air two years later. The cover was 78 per cent by both methods (after Walker).*

hyperborea), *L. digitata* and *L. saccharina*. At the conclusion of the survey the master means (= mean of the means) for 59 surveys were determined for both density (based on wet weight rather than the more desirable dry weight) and cover (Table 2.2).

TABLE 2.2

Oarweed density and cover in relation to depth

Depth L.W.M.O.S.T. (fathoms)	Density lb/yd^2	Cover per cent	$\dfrac{\text{Density}}{\text{Cover}} \times 100$
1	11·0	76	14·4
2	10·3	72	14·3
3	8·8	65	13·2
4	7·5	57	13·1
5	6·2	48	13·0
6	5·3	44	12·0
7	4·7	35	13·4
8	3·3	28	11·7
9	2·7	21	12·9
10	2·3	18	12·8

It will be seen that the density/cover values approximate to a constant so that the fresh weight is proportional to the percentage cover. A relationship was also established between both cover and density, and depth of occurrence, all of them decreasing exponentially. The decrease in density appears to be more a result of reduction in the actual number of plants per unit area rather than in size (or weight). It has been argued from the results that with increasing depth the total spore production is decreased, dispersion of spores reduced and also fertilization reduced and plant cover limited.

Spore production of these algae is colossal, one plant of *L. digitata* producing over eleven million zoospores, so that even if spore production is reduced there should be more than sufficient spores to provide a deep-water population. There is no published evidence that fewer gametophytes are produced at greater depths or that fertilization is reduced. Whilst the results of this extensive survey cannot be ignored, there may be other hypotheses that could account for the facts.

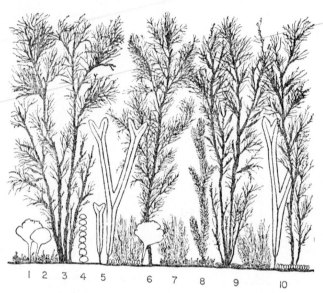

FIG. 2.11. *Profile of a* Cystoseira discors *stand in the Adriatic.* 1, Udotea petiolata. 2, Rytiphlaea tinctoria. 3, Cystoseira discors. 4, Halimeda tuna. 5, Dictyopteris membranacea. 6, Cystoseira barbata. 7, Cladophora prolifera. 8, Digenea simplex. 9, Peyssonelia squamaria. 10, Valonia utricularis (*after Ernst*).

The seasonal and perennial changes in beds of this nature can be quite extensive but until we have more information, particularly in relation to gale incidence and changes of sea temperature, it would be premature to suggest any causes. As may be expected, the perennial changes exceed the seasonal ones (Figs. 2.12, 2.13).

A combination of glass-bottomed view box, grab and aqualung has been used to study the sublittoral algal populations of the Isle of Man[5, 25]. Two types of substrate were encountered; continuous

rock and sand with shells, or stones and small boulders. The use of
the grab was checked by a diver and it was found that it did not
always give a complete sample of all species in the area. The use of

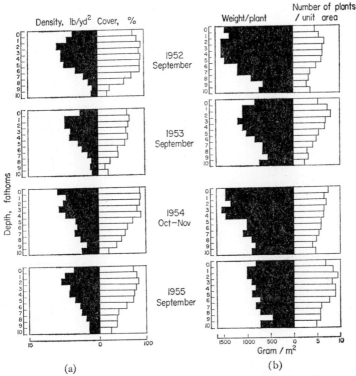

FIG. 2.12. (a), *Fraserburgh-Rosehearty*. Density (based on
quadrats with algae) and cover of Laminariaceae at 1 fathom
intervals of depth. (b), Fraserburgh-Rosehearty. Fresh weight of
plants of Laminaria cloustoni at 1 fathom intervals of depth
(after Walker and Richardson).

the aqualung is, in fact, the only effective means of sampling. On
the rock surface the large Laminarians form the perennial underwater
forest with smaller algae growing below or as epiphytes on the oarweeds. On the sandy floor of the bay there was a more or less loose-

lying flora dominated by *L. saccharina*, *Saccorhiza polyschides*, *Chorda filum*, and *Desmarestia aculeata*. These algae must all have started life as attached forms and with increase in size have become

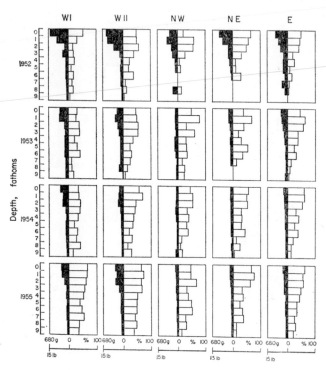

FIG. 2.13. *Seaweed density (black histograms), fresh weight, based on quadrats with Laminariaceae; seaweed cover (white histograms), at fathom intervals of depth in 5 sub-areas, during the winters of 1952, 1953, 1954 and 1955 (after Walker and Richardson).*

detached. Smaller algae such as *Dictyota* and *Plocamium* were also present in tangled masses. The loose-lying population is essentially seasonal, occurring during the summer months and decreasing in winter when much is washed up on to beaches by storms. How far such detached algae are effectively living and growing and capable of reproduction, has yet to be studied.

In muddy bays and estuaries, one can find an association of sub-merged marine phanerogams, though such communities are by no means so extensive as they used to be because of the incidence of an epidemic disease. The principal plant is the Eel-grass, *Zostera*, but in parts of Europe this may be accompanied by equally abundant growths of the plant *Ruppia maritima*. Although such fields are generally exposed at low water, in some regions they extend into the sublittoral. *Zostera* can indeed be regarded as a plant of the sublittoral fringe. This community also represents one in which the aqualung has been used as a means of studying the perpetually sub-merged vegetation. The principal study has been in the Bay of Gdansk (Danzig, Poland) where, in addition to the marine phanerogams a number of algal communities, e.g. *Fucus–Furcellaria*, *Enteromorpha compressa*, have been described. The distribution of the phanerogamic vegetation extends down to about 5 m, but the *Fucus–Furcellaria* community descends even deeper. The distribution appears to depend upon the depth of the water and the degree of exposure to water current. A similar study has been carried out in Denmark[22], where the amount of the standing crop has been determined during periods of maximum and minimum growth. Studies of standing crop, in terms of dry weight, for unit areas over the seasons would be extremely valuable and would not be beyond the resources of a school located near a coastline with *Zostera* beds.

SALT MARSH ALGAE

In areas that possess beds of *Zostera* it is likely that there will be salt marshes (see p. 94). Whilst the main interest of salt marshes will tend to centre around the phanerogams, nevertheless there is also a distinct algal vegetation. As one might expect, the nature of the vegetation on salt marshes is very different to that on rocky coasts. On the latter we have seen that it is static though there is a well-marked vertical zonation. On the salt marsh the perpetual accretion of mud brings about a steady rise in soil level so that conditions change and the vegetation changes[9] (see p. 94). Both phanerogamic and algal vegetation are therefore dynamic in character, changing with the years, and the changes may be quite rapid. For this reason, therefore, it is legitimate to use successional terminology, e.g. associes, consocies. At any given moment in time, however, a zonation of algae can be observed stretching from the lowest salt marshes up to the highest, and belts exist, though their existence may be masked by the vast horizontal extent of the marshes.

On low marshes, at a level below that of the phanerogams, one can find a mat of green algae (mainly species of *Enteromorpha* and some *Cladophora*) on the more sandy flats, whilst on mud flats the firmer areas often bear a green covering of the xanthophycean (yellow-green alga) *Vaucheria thuretii*. This alga, particularly, tends to form a community on the banks of creeks at low tidal levels. On the south coast of England in the *Spartina* (Cord grass) zone one can also see a blue-green soil covering, comprising species of *Lyngbya*, *Oscillatoria* and *Phormidium*. With the advent of phanerogamic vegetation, green algae such as *Enteromorpha* (especially *E. prolifera* and *E. prolifera* var. *tubulosa*) and *Lola* persist, but on the plants themselves there is often a green mat of the small *Enteromorpha nana* (= *Blidingia minima*). On the east coast of England these low marshes are characterized by a dense covering of the remarkable free-living salt marsh fucoids[3, 7, 10]. At the lowest level one finds the spirally twisted thalli of *Fucus vesiculosus* ecad* *volubilis*. Higher up it is replaced by the partially embedded *F. vesiculosus* ecad *caespitosus* whilst around it can be found masses of the free-living *Pelvetia canaliculata* ecad *libera*† with which in places may be associated the red *Bostrychia scorpioides*. These algae are particularly abundant in the Salicornietum (p. 95). Along the creek banks, where *Halimione* predominates, *Catenella repens* and *Bostrychia scorpioides* form a red algal community on the stems (sometimes also on *Spartina*) and extending up on the fringes to form a mud community beneath bushes of the Shrubby seablite, *Suaeda fruticosa*. In the Spartinetum of the

* Signifies an ecological variant.
† This occurs also on East Lothian marshes in Scotland.

Essex marshes, another free-living fucoid, *Ascophyllum nodosum* ecad *scorpioides* is to be found, and it, together with *A. nodosum* ecad *mackaii*, also occurs on the salt marshes of the western Scottish lochs. Scattered around Great Britain a smaller fucoid, *Fucus vesiculosus* ecad *muscoides*, can be found on some of the higher marshes, whilst in East Anglia the General Salt Marsh community and Plantaginetum (see p. 96) bear a green covering dominated by *Enteromorpha clathrata* f. *prostrata*. Most of the marshes have salt pans scattered over them and here, with conditions comparable to those of rock pools (p. 76), one can find an algal flora composed of species from the adjacent marsh together with other species that clearly survive because of the particular environment. Some of these other species may be naturally free living whilst others are attached to the plants or roots around the edges of the pans, e.g. *Striaria attenuata, Sphacelaria radicans*[6]. Apart from the salt marsh fucoids, the algae of the salt marshes are not so spectacular as those of rocky coasts. In addition to the larger algae extensive diatom communities exist in the different habitats[33a*] but this is a field that has not received much study. Despite the drawbacks, these salt marsh algae are equally worthy of study, in some ways more so because so much less work has been carried out upon them.

REFERENCES

1 ALEEM A. A., Distribution and ecology of British marine littoral diatoms. *J. Ecol.*, **38** (1), 75 (1950).
2 BAARDSETH E., A statistical study of the structure of the *Ascophyllum* zone. *Norsk. Inst. for tang-og tarefons. Rept. II.* 1–34 (1953).
3 BAKER S. M. and BOHLING M. H., On the brown seaweeds of the salt marsh. I. *Journ. Linn. Soc. Bot. Lond.*, **40**, 275–291 (1912); II. *Journ. Linn. Soc. Bot. Lond.*, **43**, 325–380 (1916).
4 BLACKLER H., An algal survey of Loch Foyle, North Ireland. *Proc. Roy. Irish Acad.*, **54**, B, No. 6. 97–139 (1951).
5 BURROWS E. M., Sublittoral algal population in Port Erin Bay, Isle of Man. *J. Mar. Biol. Ass. U.K.*, **37**, 687–703 (1958).
6 CHAPMAN V. J., A revision of the marine algae of Norfolk. *Journ. Linn. Soc. Bot. Lond.*, **51** (338), 205–263 (1937).

* See also Chapter 4, ref. no. 5.

[7] CHAPMAN V. J., Studies in saltmarsh ecology. Section IV. *J. Ecol.*, **27** (1), 160–201 (1939).

[8] CHAPMAN V. J., Seaweed resources along the shores of Great Britain. *Econ. Bot.*, **2** (4), 363–378 (1948).

[9] CHAPMAN V. J., Studies in salt marsh ecology. Section IX. *J. Ecol.*, **47** (2), 619–639 (1959).

[10] CHAPMAN V. J., The Plant Ecology in *Scolt Head Island*. Ed. J. A. Steers. 2nd Ed. Cambridge. pp. 85–163 (1960).

[11] COTTON A. D., Clare Island survey. 15. Marine algae. *Proc. Roy. Irish Acad.*, **31**, 1–171 (1912).

[12] DUNN M. D., The marine algal associations of St. Andrews district. I: the dominant associations of the spray and littoral regions. *Trans. Bot. Soc. Edin.*, **33** (2), 83–93 (1941).

[13] EBLING F. J., SLEIGH M. A., SLOANE J. F. and KITCHING J. A., The ecology of Lough Ine. *J. Ecol.*, **48** (1), 29–54 (1960).

[14] EVANS R. G., The inter-tidal ecology of Cardigan Bay. *J. Ecol.*, **34**, 273–309 (1947).

[15] EVANS R. G., The inter-tidal ecology of selected localities in the Plymouth neighbourhood. *J. Mar. Biol. Ass. U.K.*, **27**, 173 (1947).

[16] EVANS, R. G., The inter-tidal ecology of rocky shores in south Pembrokeshire. *J. Ecol.*, **37**, 120–139 (1949).

[17] GOULD D. T., BAGENAL T. B. and CONNELL J. H., The marine fauna and flora of St. Kilda, 1952, *Scot. Nat.*, **65**, 29 (1953).

[18] GIBB D. C., The marine algal communities of Castletown Bay, Isle of Man. *J. Ecol.*, **26**, 96–117 (1938).

[19] GIBB D. C., Some marine algal communities of Gt. Cumbrae. *J. Ecol.*, **27** (2), 364–382 (1939).

[20] GIBB D. C., A survey of the commoner fucoid algae on Scottish shores. *J. Ecol.*, **38** (2), 253–269 (1950).

[21] GIFFORD C. E. and ODUM E. P., Chlorophyll *a* content of intertidal zones on a rocky seashore. *Limn. and Oceanog.*, **6** (1), 83–85 (1961).

[22] GRONTVED J., Underwater macrovegetation in shallow coastal waters. *J. cons. Intern. L'Expl. Mer.*, **24** (1), 32–42 (1958).

[23] HOEK C. VAN DEN, The algal microvegetation in and on barnacle shells, collected along the Dutch and French coasts. *Blumea*, **9** (1), 206–214 (1958).

[24] KAIN J. M., Observations on the littoral algae of the Isle of Wight. *J. Mar. Biol. Ass. U.K.*, **37**, 769–780 (1958).

[25] KAIN J. M., Direct observations on some Manx sublittoral algae. *J. Mar. Biol. Ass. U.K.*, **39**, 609–630 (1960).

[26] KITCHING J. A., An introduction to the ecology of inter-tidal rock surfaces on the coast of Argyll. *Trans. Roy. Soc. Edin.*, **58**, 351 (1935).

[27] KORNAS J., Sea bottom vegetation of the Bay of Gdansk off Rewa. *Bull. Acad. Pol. Sci., Cl. II.,* **7** (1), 5–10 (1959).

[28] LEWIS J. R., The ecology of rocky shores around Anglesey. *Proc. Zool. Soc. London,* **123** (3), 481–549 (1953).

[29] LEWIS J. R., The ecology of exposed rocky shores of Caithness. *J. Ecol.,* **62** (3), 695–723 (1954).

[30] LEWIS J. R., The mode of occurrence of the universal inter-tidal zones in Great Britain. *J. Ecol.,* **43** (1), 270–290 (1955).

[31] LEWIS J. R., Inter-tidal communities of the northern and western coasts of Scotland. *Trans. Roy. Soc. Edin.,* **63** (1), 185–220 (1957).

[32] LEWIS J. R., The littoral zone on rocky shores—a biological or physical entity? *Oikos, Fasc.* **11, 12,** 280–301 (1961).

[33] REES T. K., The marine algae of Lough Ine. *J. Ecol.,* **23** (1), 70–133 (1935).

[33a] ROUND F. E., The diatom flora of a salt marsh on the River Dee. *New Phyt.,* **59,** 332–348 (1960).

[34] SINCLAIR J., The marine algae of Stronsay. *Notes Roy. Bot. Gard. Edin.,* **20,** No. 99, 160–179 (1949).

[35] SOUTHWARD A. J., The population balance between limpets and seaweeds on wave-beaten rocky shores. *Rep. Mar. Biol. Sta. Port Erin.,* **68,** 20 (1952).

[36] SOUTHWARD A. J., The ecology of some rocky shores in the south of the Isle of Man. *Proc. & Trans. Liverp. Biol. Soc.,* **59,** 1–45 (1953).

[37] SOUTHWARD A. J. and ORTON J. H., The effects of wave action on the distribution and numbers of the commoner plants and animals living on the Plymouth Breakwater. *J. Mar. Biol. Ass. U.K.,* **33,** 1 (1953).

[38] STEPHENSON T. A. and STEPHENSON A., The universal features of zonation between tidemarks on rocky coasts. *J. Ecol.,* **37,** 289–305 (1949).

[39] WALKER F. T., Sublittoral seaweed survey. *J. Ecol.,* **35** (1), 166–185 (1947).

[40] WALKER F. T., Sublittoral seaweed survey of the Orkney Islands. *J. Ecol.,* **38** (1), 140–165 (1950).

[41] WALKER F. T., Sublittoral seaweed survey: Dunbar to Fast Castle, East Scotland. *J. Ecol.,* **40** (1), 74–83 (1952).

[42] WALKER F. T., Distribution of Laminariaceae around Scotland. *J. Cons. Intern. L'Expl. Mer.,* **20** (2), 160–166 (1954).

[43] WALKER F. T., A sublittoral survey of the Laminariaceae of Little Loch Broom. *Trans. Proc. Bot. Soc. Edin.,* **36** (4), 305–308 (1955).

[44] WALKER F. T., The Laminaria cycle. *Rev. Algol. N.S.,* **3,** 179–181 (1956).

[45] WALKER F. T. and RICHARDSON W. D., The Laminariaceae off North Shapinsay; Changes from 1947–1953. *Ann. Bot. N.S.*, **18** (72), 483–494 (1954).

[46] WALKER F. T. and RICHARDSON W. D., An ecological investigation of *Laminaria cloustoni* Edin. (*L. hyperborea* Fosl.) around Scotland. *J. Ecol.*, **43** (1), 26–38 (1955).

[47] WALKER F. T. and RICHARDSON W. D., The Laminariaceae of North Shapinsay, Orkney Is., changes from 1947–1955. *J. Mar. Res.*, **15** (2), 123–133 (1956).

[48] WALKER F. T. and RICHARDSON W.D., Survey of the Laminariaceae off the Island of Arran: changes from 1952–1955. *J. Ecol.*, **45** (2), 225–232 (1957).

[49] WALKER F. T. and RICHARDSON W. D., Perennial changes of *Laminaria cloustoni* on the coasts of Scotland. *J. Cons. Intern. L'Expl. Mer.*, **22** (3), 298–308 (1957).

CHAPTER THREE

Algal Vegetation—The Environment

In the previous chapter we have seen that on most coasts it is possible to observe a zonation of plants and animals. Certain indicator species dominate the different belts and it is only natural to ask what are the factors[3, 8, 11] that determine the upper and lower limits of the major belt-demarcating species. Once these have been established, then the same question can be asked for other seaweeds that occur on the shore. In trying to arrive at an answer to the problem it should be realized that more than one factor may be involved, though it is not unlikely that at one time of the year or at a certain phase in the life history of the alga, one factor may be paramount. We shall see that the environmental factors must exercise an influence upon the physiological behaviour of the plants, and therefore a full understanding cannot be achieved without a study of algal physiology accompanied by the necessary experimentation. In fact, proof that any particular factor determines either the upper or lower limit of a species must depend ultimately upon experiment.

GEOGRAPHICAL DISTRIBUTION

The geographical distribution of any species is probably determined by the temperature of the sea water, though in many cases we do not know whether it is the mean temperature, the maximum summer temperature or the minimum winter temperature. It must be this factor that controls the northern limit of Mediterranean plants, e.g. species of *Cystoseira*, that reach the shores of Great

51

Britain. More recently, however, evidence has come forward to show that another factor may operate, namely day-length or photoperiodism. A very large body of information about this phenomenon is available for terrestrial plants but practically nothing is known for the algae. There is, however, sufficient to show that some algae are long-day plants (requiring 16 hr or more) and others are short-day plants (8–10 hr). Thus sporelings of some *Enteromorpha* species are essentially long-day whereas those of some *Monostroma* species grow best under short-day conditions[9]. In Europe the northern *Ulva lactuca* is reported[31] to be a long-day plant whilst the southern *U. thuretii* is a short-day plant. Certain algae may then be limited to particular latitudes where the correct day-length or photoperiod will be available for some of the year at least. The failure of species of *Laminaria* to penetrate the warmer waters of the globe has usually been regarded as a temperature phenomenon, but it may turn out to be one of photoperiodism, growth of the adult plants being dependent upon long-day conditions. Here then is a whole new field awaiting urgent investigation. Green algae such as *Enteromorpha* and *Ulva* are not difficult to culture in the laboratory and it should be quite possible, using fluorescent lights, to grow such plants under different day-lengths and determine rates of growth.

FACTORS

Some years ago I suggested[8] that the environmental factors operating on the sea-shore could be divided into those that are (1) causal, i.e. directly responsible for determining the upper and lower limits of species, (2) presence or absence factors that determine whether a species shall be present or not in the area provided it is within its geographical range, (3) modificatory. The last group comprises those factors that result in an elevation or depression of the upper or lower limits of species, such as heavy spray, much shade, etc. Any study of the shore should therefore aim at trying to evaluate the factors into these three groups. In addition it is also convenient to divide the environmental factors into four main categories, (1) physiographic,

(2) physical, including the regional climate, (3) chemical, (4) biological. In the following pages it is proposed to consider these one by one, indicating their behaviour in controlling the limits of species.

PHYSIOGRAPHIC FACTORS

The Tides

The principal physiographic factor is the tide, though it operates in a number of directions. Tides differ from place to place and in any study of zonation it is important to acquire a knowledge of the kind of tide in the area. If there is only one high and one low water per 24 hr the tide is said to be diurnal. In most places there are two high and low waters and such tides are called semi-diurnal. In the case of semi-diurnal tides, if successive high and low waters are different in height the tides are said to be mixed. In a few localities, where there are two separate entrances, such as Southampton Water, one can have four high and low waters in every 24 hr. Figure 3.1 illustrates some of these different tides and it will be noticed that over a neap- and spring-tide cycle the nature of the tide may change.

Information about the tides can be obtained from simple float gauges or from pressure gauges. If such are not available, useful though not extensive information can be secured from marked tide poles (see p. 13). The main disadvantage of tide poles is the necessity to have records of tides over spring- and neap-tide cycles at different times of the year, and securing this information is laborious.

Submergence and Exposure

One of the most important effects of the tide relates to submergence and exposure, which in turn have a profound influence upon the physiological activities of algae (see p. 70). Two kinds of exposure exist in so far as effects on algae are concerned. There is first the exposure that occurs between two successive semi-diurnal or diurnal tides: the second is the exposure at upper levels that occurs during neap tides. The former is of relatively short duration, but in this time excessive water loss or a major effect upon photosynthesis, which in some seaweeds falls to zero soon after exposure, or upon respiration, may operate as a causal factor. During the period of exposure the seaweeds are subject to ordinary climatic conditions and these may be so severe as to restrict their extension upwards on the shore. The high temperatures of the midday tropics probably prevent most algae from occupying the littoral, whilst the high humidities of many higher latitude regions may well enable algae to extend high up on

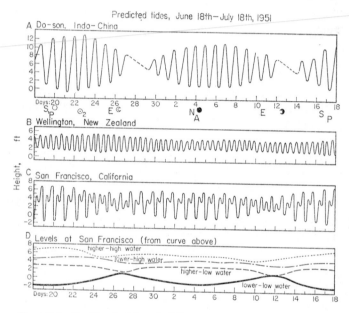

FIG. 3.1. *Predicted tides of different types plotted for 30-day periods at the designated localities. Compiled from the U.S.C. and G.S. tide tables (after Doty).*

the shore because water loss is reduced. At the other extreme very low temperatures can result in the death of algae, whilst the formation of ice can bring about a complete clearing of rocks when the ice is torn bodily from the rock at the time of spring melt (see p. 66).

The inter-tidal exposure also affects conditions in the tide pools, particularly those at higher levels. In the summer the temperature of the water in the shallow upper pools may rise considerably: increased evaporation then takes place and salinity will also change. It can be seen from Fig. 3.1 that a very slight change in elevation can result in the inter-tidal exposure being doubled, e.g. above and below the lower high tide mark of a pair.* At low-tide levels exposure is replaced by submergence, and whilst it may be very difficult to

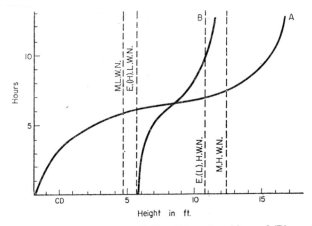

FIG. 3.2. *Hours of exposure during* (A) *spring tides and* (B) *neap tides at Wembury* (*after Colman*).

separate the two phenomena, nevertheless there are levels below which the submergence period can be trebled. Such changes, which occur between low water mark of neap and spring tides and between high water mark of neap and spring tides, may well determine the existence of certain critical levels (see p. 77).

In Fig. 3.2, which depicts the differences in hours of exposure between neap and spring tides, it will be seen that above mean high water mark of neap tides there will be levels that do not get a daily submergence and this period of continuous exposure (the second kind of exposure) increases in length with increasing height on the shore. Similarly below low water mark of neap tides there will be

* San Francisco, curve C.

levels that do not become exposed at all during the day and such periods will be more and more extensive as one descends towards low water mark of spring tides. These periods of prolonged exposure or submergence for several days will be more profound in their effects than the inter-tidal periods and equally may determine the existence of critical levels. In particular these periods have a direct effect upon water loss, thallus temperature and salinity changes. The periods are probably of greater significance to the sporelings of the algae than to the adult plants but we possess remarkably little information on this subject. It is a matter of observation that fucoid sporelings rarely occur outside the belts the species occupy as adults and injurious exposure may be responsible. Injurious exposure permits of various possibilities: in some algae it may be water loss:

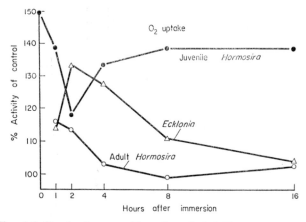

FIG. 3.3. *Respiration rate of juvenile and adult* Hormosira banksii *and* Ecklonia radiata *after desiccation and reimmersion. Note that the adult* Hormosira *and* Ecklonia *return to the control value (non-dehydrated plants) but the juvenile* Hormosira *does not (after Bergquist).*

in the case of at least one alga (*Hormosira banksii* of New Zealand) it is known that the respiration rate of the juvenile is affected to such an extent (Fig. 3.3) that after a few such exposures the plants would surely respire to death: in other algae it may be the effect upon photosynthesis. In those cases where there are seasonal changes of level (particularly tideless seas) the long periods of exposure may result in the appearance of a special algal community or the development of a bare zone in the summer.

Emphasis has been laid upon the changes that take place at different tide levels, and it might be supposed that algae affected by such changes would reach their limits (upper or lower) at the same tidal levels in all the regions where they occur. This does not prove to be entirely the case (Fig. 3.4) thus showing that other local factors

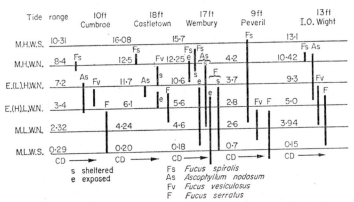

FIG. 3.4. *Showing the relation of the principal known fucoids (at five localities) to the important tidal levels. The tide levels are represented by the horizontal lines. Underneath each locality the vertical extent of the principal fucoid zones is shown by the dark lines. Where exposure or shelter make a difference there are two lines, labelled* e *and* s *respectively. On the left of each locality the tide-table level (chart datum) for the six tidal levels is placed opposite the respective line. Above each locality is noted the maximum tidal range (based on Admiralty tide-tables) (after Chapman).*

may intervene. One of the principal local factors intervening in this manner is the degree of wave action, which is itself dependent on the degree of physiographic exposure or shelter. On a very exposed coast the elevation of the algal zones can be quite considerable, e.g. North Gavel on Fair Isle[40] (see p. 62 and Fig. 3.5), whilst exposure commonly brings about a difference in the composition of the vegetation

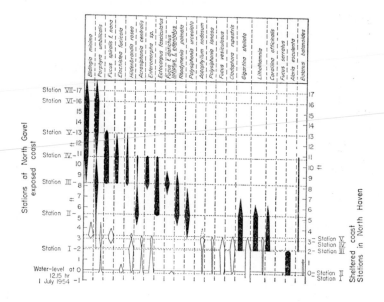

FIG. 3.5. *Comparison of the distribution of inter-tidal algae in relation to tide levels. Fair Isle, June–July 1952. Dark bands for exposed coast, plain for sheltered coast (after Burrows et al.).*

(see p. 36 and Figs. 2.1, 2.2). There is also the effect of latitude, operating through other factors, such as temperature, humidity, etc., which may result in the elevation of species on the shore with increase of latitude. This has been demonstrated for *Fucus serratus*[28] in Great Britain and for some algae in other parts of the world.

Water Loss

The principal phenomenon associated with tidal exposure is that of daily water loss, especially if it occurs during the heat of the day. Various workers[23, 24, 25, 39] have directed their attention to this problem and much of the work has been performed with the fucoids that occur on British shores. In the case of the highest fucoid on the shore (*Pelvetia canaliculata*) the major loss occurs in the first 3–6 hr, whereas with other fucoids (Fig. 3.6) the loss is spread over as much

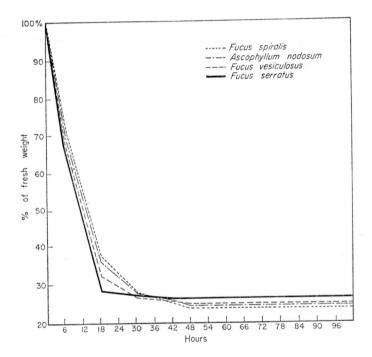

FIG. 3.6. *Loss of water in fucoids during exposure. The curves show the percentages of fresh weight in relation to the time of desiccation. The higher a fucoid is growing the slower it loses its water and the greater is its total percentual water content (after Zaneveld).*

as 18 hr. Figure 3.6 shows that *Fucus spiralis* (= var. *platycarpus*) loses water more slowly than the other three fucoids, and that the rate of water loss with the various species increases in relation to their successively lower positions on the shore. Although *F. spiralis* loses its water at a slower rate than the other three species, nevertheless it eventually suffers a greater water loss. Some evidence has been produced[20] to show that the rate of water loss is related to the fat content, and that this in turn is related to the thickness of the cell walls.

It can be demonstrated that water moves readily out of these cell walls when they are placed in sea water of increasing concentration. The walls also decrease in thickness during periods of desiccation, the

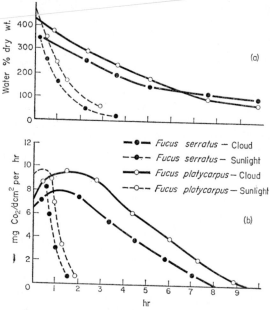

FIG. 3.7. (a), *water loss, and* (b), *assimilation of* Fucus serratus *and* F. spiralis *var.* platycarpus *in relation to exposure (drying) on sunny and cloudy days (after Stocker and Holdheide).*

higher the species is growing the greater is the ultimate shrinkage. Species which lose water more slowly take longest to reabsorb it, and, water being necessary for growth, species highest on the shore (which lose and reabsorb water most slowly) will have the slowest growth. The rate of water loss in these fucoids must influence their upper limits, though before this could be said with certainty one would need information on the effect of desiccation on metabolism both during exposure and on subsequent re-immersion.

Water loss in algae cannot be studied without considering the weather conditions. The effect of cloud or unrestricted sunlight upon water loss (and also assimilation) in *F. serratus* and *F. spiralis* var. *platycarpus* is strikingly demonstrated in Fig. 3.7. Drying of the thallus may also, in some forms, affect the respiration rate of the plant. In *F. vesiculosus* the respiration rate decreases steadily with increasing water loss[25].

It is possible to investigate water loss on other species of algae, particularly those that form mats, such as *Enteromorpha*. In these cases portions of the mat are cut out and fitted into waterproof paper dishes which are then replaced in position on the shore. In this way it was found[1] that an *Enteromorpha* mat lost 25 per cent of its moisture in the first three hours of exposure as compared with a mat of Chrysophycean (golden-brown) algae that lost only 8·4 per cent. The reduced loss by the latter algae, whether through evaporation or drainage, is due to the gelatinous nature of the Chrysophycean algae which aids water retention. In these experiments the evaporating power of the air over the Chrysophyceae was 1·41 units as against 1·1 over the *Enteromorpha*.

Wave Action

Other physiographic factors include the degree of shelter or exposure to waves. This is essentially a presence or absence factor and the absence of *Ascophyllum* on exposed coasts is an example of its operation[2]. Extreme exposure to wave action may operate mechanic-ally in preventing swarmers or fertilized eggs from becoming attached to the rocks. In the case of successful species one must suppose that attachment is very rapid. We still, however, know very little about this process.

Apart from operating as a presence or absence factor, wave action may also act as a modifying factor. The important feature of wave action is related to the mean average height of prevailing waves or the height of storm waves if they are of any frequency. Big waves commonly result in much splash and spray and as a result of large waves and spray the upper and lower limits of algae and animals, mainly of the upper eulittoral and littoral fringe, can be elevated to a height of many feet. This elevation forms what is known as the *"Splash zone"*. When the coast is very exposed and waves generally large, the splash zone can be subdivided into (a) the swash zone, which is the height the actual waves wash up the rock face (this will, of course, depend upon the slope of the rocks themselves), (b) the splash zone, which is that part of the shore actually splashed by the waves (this tends to be greater the more the rocks are inclined to the vertical), (c) the spray zone which can often be very extensive, particularly on the west coast of the Outer Hebrides and western Eire (see Chapter 2, p. 36).

Tidal range acts as a modifying factor because the vertical height of a belt is related to the maximum tidal range. Even regions with a very small tidal range, e.g. the Gulf of Mexico and the Caribbean, possess a distinct zonation of marine organisms. It is true that such shores do not provide the great variety of rock pools to be found on shores with a large tidal range.

Tide Currents

Strong tidal currents can affect the growth and size of plants. On the east coast of Scotland the strength of the current determines in large measure whether *Laminaria saccharina* or *L. cloustoni* (*L. hyperborea*) is the dominant, the latter occurring with the stronger currents. Currents also tend to vary with the state of the tide. Thus at high and low tide, when one talks of "slack water", there is commonly little or no current, whereas between these periods, when the rise or fall may be rapid, currents tend to be strong. It is interesting to note that high water of neap tides marks the lower limits of *Fucus spiralis* in certain places, e.g. Castleton, Isle of Wight (Fig. 3.4), and low water mark of neap tides is closely associated with the lower limits of *Ascophyllum*, whilst *Fucus vesiculosus* generally lies within this zone of stronger currents. On another type of shore, the salt marsh shore, the strength of the current flowing up and down the creeks largely determines the degree of erosion and upon this depends the extent to which characteristic creek bank communities can develop.

PHYSICAL FACTORS

Substrate

We can conveniently include here the nature of the substrate, i.e. whether it is rock, boulders, stones, mud or peat. In determining the effectiveness of anchorage, this factor must operate as a presence or absence one. Larger algae obviously cannot grow or survive on stones and small pebbles. Mud demands especial adaptations as shown in the embedded salt marsh fucoids (see p. 46). The angle of slope of rock faces and the presence of cracks and crannies affects the occurrence of some species, and can either operate as a presence or absence factor or as a modifying factor (Fig. 2.5).

Temperature

During the period of tidal exposure temperature affects the algae, high temperatures causing loss of water from the thallus together with the consequent effect this loss has upon photosynthesis and respiration (see p. 73). It has already been noted that sea temperatures affect biogeographic distribution and may set the limits of species. Gradual changes of sea temperatures over a number of years can bring about the appearance of species from warmer or colder waters depending upon the direction in which the temperature is changing. Seasonal changes of temperature may even change the composition of the flora. A classical example here is Cape Lookout in North Carolina where the winter sea temperatures result in a flora of essentially northern species, whilst in the summer the temperatures rise to the point that enables a well-marked group of southern species to appear.

On upper levels of salt marshes where the phanerogamic vegetation may be of low stature, i.e. General Salt Marsh or Plantaginetum (see pp. 96–97), evaporation may be so severe that salt crystallization takes place on the soil and only gelatinous algae, e.g. *Rivularia atra*, *Phaeococcus adnatus*, can grow successfully in such places.

The effect of temperature upon algal metabolism needs further study. Temperature changes can affect both photosynthesis and respiration during submergence and exposure. Photosynthetic activity is generally low or absent during the periods of exposure. A balance sheet between net gain during submergence and net loss during exposure therefore needs to be compiled.

Some very interesting results have been obtained[25] for the effect of temperature on respiration of *Fucus vesiculosus*, the respiration rate dropping sharply below 0°C. Very similar results were also found for *Chondrus crispus* and *Ulva lactuca*. In Europe Ehrke[15] found that for *Delesseria* the optimum temperature for photosynthesis was 0°C, and that maximum growth took place in winter and early spring when sea-water temperature was nearest 0°C. For *Fucus* and *Enteromorpha*, however, the optimum temperature for assimilation is 17°C, and maximum development occurs in August or September when sea temperatures are around 17°C.

Seaweeds appear to fall into four groups[34] in their temperature responses during exposure periods:

(1) Algae of the upper littoral of protected bays or of upper tide pools. These are resistant to air temperatures up to 35–37°C.

(2) Algae of the upper littoral of open coasts which are resistant to air temperatures up to 32°C.

(3) Winter and spring annuals of the upper littoral. These resist air temperatures up to 30–32°C.

(4) Sublittoral algae which are intolerant to air temperatures above 30°C.

While smaller algae can be studied as a whole, larger algae may need to be studied organ by organ. Thus the main frond of *Alaria esculenta* probably behaves very differently to the lateral reproductive leaflets. The same may be true of the lateral vegetative, fertile, and vesicular appendages of *Ascophyllum*. This is certainly the case on the Pacific Coast of North America where the various organs of deep water plants of *Egregia laevigata*[10] behave quite differently in relation to temperature (Table 3.1).

TABLE 3.1

Photosynthesis (μl. O_2 g dry wt/5 min) of organs of deep water plants of Egregia laevigata

Organ	10°C	15°C	20°C	25°C	Temp.
Dissected "leaves"	130	375	1175	630	
Juvenile "leaves"	670	725	700	965	
Basal "leaves"	530	540	265	145	

In the sea itself, changes of temperature can affect both photosynthesis and respiration. The point at which these two processes exactly balance, and where oxygen content remains stable, is called the *compensation point*. The effect of temperature upon the compensation point has been worked out for the Southern Hemisphere fucoid, *Hormosira banksii* (Fig. 3.8). At temperatures around 15°C, the compensation point occurs at a much lower depth than it does at 20°C. The compensation point must set the lower limit to which an alga descends and this point is not only related primarily to available light but is also presumably related to the mean sea temperature or possibly to the mean summer temperature.

In confined spaces such as rock pools or salt pans (p. 93) temperature fluctuations can bring about considerable changes[35].

Elevation of the water temperature affects metabolism, and the increase in salinity through evaporation may be very considerable in pools high up on the littoral. Rise of water temperature probably does not cause damage at moderate or high latitudes, but daylight respiration may be so speeded up that the overall metabolism no longer permits growth. Biebl[5] devoted some time to the study of rock pools on the south coast of England, and he found that temperature increases up to 26°C over a period of 24 hr had no effect on most red algae and, further, that rapid changes of as much as 12°C, when the incoming tide flooded a pool after a hot day, could occur without causing any damage.

In arctic waters very low temperatures are commonplace in winter and algae may be frozen for many weeks. In *Fucus vesiculosus*, as much as 80 per cent of the contained water can be frozen[25], yet upon thawing out there is no impairment of metabolism. It is for this reason, of course, that the algae are able to survive in the Arctic.

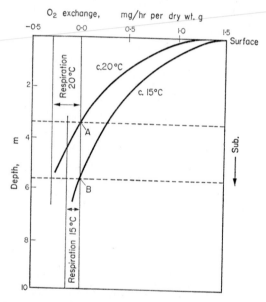

Fig. 3.8. *Variation of compensation point with depth and sea temperature in* Hormosira banksii (*after Trevarthen*).

Similar behaviour has been recorded for the cold water plants of *Ascophyllum nodosum, Chondrus crispus* and *Ulva lactuca*.

Humidity

Humidity may be significant on a rocky coast (see p. 61), and there is no doubt it is very important on a salt marsh. Within a stand of tall plants, such as Sea rush (*Juncus maritimus*) or *Spartina townsendii*, the relative humidity can be high whilst outside it may be much lower.

It is possible that certain salt marsh algae associated with these phanerogams, e.g. *Enteromorpha nana* (*Blidingia minima*) on Cord grass (*Spartina*) or Sea purslane (*Halimione*), or *Bostrychia* and *Catenella* under *Halimione* or Shrubby seablite (*Suaeda fruticosa*), are able to survive at these levels because of the maintenance of high humidities. Some useful facts on this problem could easily be obtained: thus, wet and dry bulb thermometers give the relative humidity, and water loss of algae maintained in desiccators over solutions that provide a given humidity should not prove difficult to measure.

Pressure

An ecological factor that has received very little attention is that of pressure. Certain species develop bladders which commonly contain a gas[12], and such bladders are normally regarded as a flotation mechanism. Speculation as to the function of bladders is complicated in that some have extremely thick walls; in one species, *Pelagophycus porra*, the gas pressure is less than 1 atmosphere and the gas contains carbon monoxide. In another species, *Egregia laevigata* (this and *Pelagophycus* occur in the Pacific) many of the bladders in deeply submerged plants are full of liquid.

Light

The most important physical factor is that of light, because of its necessity for photosynthesis. Light, however, is not an easy factor to measure. There are also problems with lower littoral algae, connected with daily and seasonal variation in light intensity, the former obviously being related to tide height provided the tidal range is large[31, 33, 36]. Finally, there are all the problems associated with the changes of light intensity and the varying spectral composition of light at different depths (Fig. 3.9). From the point of view of photosynthetic efficiency, one needs to know not only the quantity of light reaching any given depth of water, but also its quality (spectral composition). The combination of light intensity and clarity of water will determine the maximum depth to which seaweeds can descend (see p. 22). At such depths, the amount of light penetrating is a very small proportion of the incident surface light. Experiments on a few deep-growing algae have shown that they can be fully light-saturated at very low values, though much more information is needed. We also know that certain algae when submerged, rapidly cease to

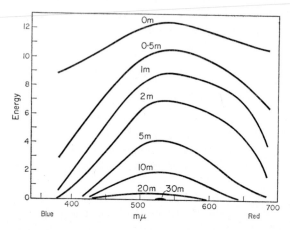

FIG. 3.9. *Spectral distribution of radiant energy (in relative units) at different depths (after Levring).*

photosynthesize at a rate in excess of the respiratory rate, and hence their compensation point is quickly reached[27]. Such algae obviously cannot descend to any great depth.

The extent to which the incident light is cut down in passing through a body of water depends, among other things, upon water turbidity, which in turn depends on quantity of plankton, "yellow" material,* and the amount of silt carried. Coastal waters are particularly variable in this respect, as may be seen from some data for the Californian coast[9] (Fig. 3.10). This variation in absorption coefficient

* Found mainly in coastal waters and derived from algal exudates.

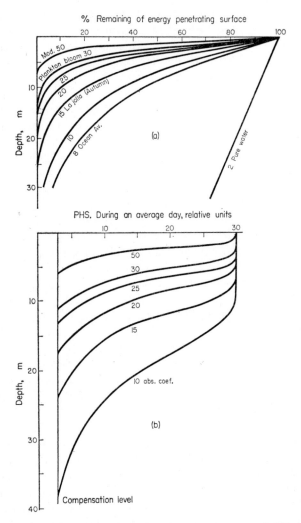

FIG. 3.10. (a), *per cent light absorption in sea water of different absorption coefficients*, (b), *relative photosynthesis in* Macrocystis *on an average day in waters of different absorption coefficients* (*after North*).

for the different waters will affect the relative photosynthesis of the algae. Again using the data from California, the likely variation in photosynthesis and the resulting variation in depth of the compensation point has been calculated for the dominant sublittoral alga, *Macrocystis pyrifera* (Fig. 3.10).

With the sublittoral algae, especially those near the low tide mark, there are changes in quantity and quality of light with rise and fall of the tide, but with the littoral algae there are in addition the effects of light intensity during the periods of exposure[37]. This varies, at least to some extent, with humidity, which itself may be affected by sun and cloud, because the more rapidly the thalli dry up the more rapid is the fall-off in assimilation rate. Under extreme conditions level on the shore does not seem to make much difference, but when the rate of water loss is not so great then an upper belt alga, such as *Fucus platycarpus*, has a slower fall off in assimilation rate than a low level alga such as *F. serratus* (Fig. 3.7). The same kind of effect has been found for the fucoid *Hormosira banksii* in New Zealand, whilst in another New Zealand littoral alga (*Scytothamnus*) it seems likely that net assimilation gain is restricted to the periods of submergence, and this probably sets the upper limit to which the alga can grow.

When an alga has been exposed, one needs to know how rapidly it returns to the normal assimilation rate after the reduced exposure rate[7]. Delicate plants such as *Ulva* and *Porphyra* recover very rapidly, while the behaviour of the tougher fucoids varies with position on the shore (Table 3.2).

With algae that are permanently submerged, the rate of photosynthesis depends, as we have seen, upon the amount and quality of penetrant light. Apart from considerations mentioned earlier, this may be affected by the degree of wave action or choppiness of the water and the angle of the sun. Thus Tschudy[38] found that on choppy days maximum photosynthesis occurred at the surface, but that on calm days it occurred at about 5 m down. With the brown fucoid *Hormosira* the rate of photosynthesis during exposure and submergence was related to light intensity, and under supra-optimal light conditions (unclouded sky, midsummer and calm water)

TABLE 3.2

Percentage of Normal Assimilation re-attained on Flooding after Exposure

Level	Species		After 5 hr exposure at 90 per cent R.H. and 4 hr after flooding
Upper littoral	*Pelvetia canaliculata*	70–80 per cent 9 hr after flooding. 11 days exposure	
Top of mid-littoral	*Fucus spiralis*	49 per cent 8–9 hr after flooding. 3 days exposure	97 per cent
Mean sea level	*F. vesiculosus*	20 per cent 8–9 hr after flooding. 3 days exposure	72 per cent
Lower littoral	*F. serratus*	Cannot tolerate 3 days exposure	42 per cent
Sublittoral fringe	*Laminaria digitata*	—	Cannot tolerate 2 hr exposure

maximum photosynthesis took place at 1 m below the surface (Fig. 3.11).

When the photosynthesis of algae is studied in relation to different light intensities, it is found that the littoral algae have an optimum

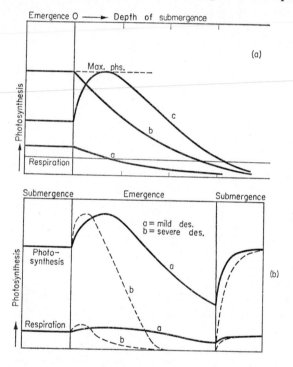

Fig. 3.11. (a), *effect of light intensity upon photosynthesis of exposed and submerged* Hormosira banksii *in relation to depth. a, low light intensity; b, optimum light intensity; c, supra-optimum light intensity.* (b), *effect of desiccation upon photosynthesis (full line) and respiration (broken line) of* H. banskii *when exposed (after Trevarthen).*

light intensity around 50,000 m candles (= 5000 foot candles), which is in the same region as that for many terrestrial plants. This is certainly true of *Fucus, Ulva linza* and *Porphyra atropurpurea.* In the sublittoral alga, *Laminaria saccharina*, the optimum is much lower. In extra-European waters where there are algae with distinct appendages the efficiency of the different organs may vary, particularly with the brown Pacific laminarian *Egregia laevigata*[10], where there are differences between the entire and dissected appendages and the axis. For every sublittoral alga there must be a minimum light intensity below which there is no growth. The depth at which this occurs is known as the compensation point so far as light intensity is concerned (there is also one for temperature, see p. 66). This minimum light intensity may sometimes be very low, e.g. at 15°C it is 32 foot candles for *Laminaria saccharina* and 38 foot candles for *Fucus serratus*. An indication of the light compensation depth can be obtained quite readily by the Winkler technique for determining oxygen content in water. Round-bottomed flasks are completely filled with sea water. Some have seaweed added and after being stoppered one or more of these are covered effectively with black cloth, whilst one or more remain without seaweed as a control. All are attached to a metal ring and if several such rings are set up they can be lowered from a boat or wharf to different depths in the sea for an hour. At the end of the period the oxygen in the flask water is determined and in the case of littoral algae it is generally not difficult to find a depth above which an oxygen gain is recorded and below which there is an oxygen loss.

In so far as both temperature and light exert an effect upon assimilation it is most desirable to devise experiments involving both factors, as Lampe[30] has done for *F. serratus* and *Porphyra*. With *Fucus serratus* the assimilation rate increases in sunlight with increasing temperature; with *Porphyra*, on the other hand, when the temperature is raised above 15°C the rate of photosynthesis is lowered with low light intensity. Very similar results for *Fucus serratus* were also obtained by Hyde[22], except that above temperatures of 25°C there was a decrease in photosynthesis with increasing light intensity. *F. serratus*, therefore, can be regarded as a *eurythermal* species, tolerating a wide range of temperature, whilst *Porphyra* would have to be regarded as *stenothermal*, tolerating a much narrower temperature range.

Most work relating temperature and assimilation has been carried out with the experimental material submerged in water. Temperature, however, can be very important during the periods of exposure in its effects after re-submersion.

It has been shown[33] that, in general, littoral algae exhibit an increase in photosynthesis on submersion after exposure to high temperatures whereas sublittoral algae show a decrease. Among the algae studied, *Fucus serratus* was the only lower littoral species showing any tolerance towards high temperatures.

Today no really effective work can be carried out on photosynthesis of algae without a consideration of the absorption curves[21] in relation to light of different wave-lengths (Fig. 3.12). Quite a number of years ago the German physiologist Englemann put forward the view that the colour of an alga, particularly those growing in the sea, was complementary to that of the available light: maximum assimilation in Chlorophyceae occurs in red (long waves) and blue-green light, and as the former are rapidly absorbed such algae generally grow at the upper levels. This is not invariably true as many Siphonales, such as *Caulerpa* and *Udotea*, can grow at considerable depths.

In the brown seaweeds maximum absorption occurs in the blue and blue-green region which assists them in growing at medium depths; similarly the red algae with their capacity to absorb light of the short wave-lengths can also grow at great depths.

Although the different parts of the light spectrum are absorbed differentially this does not mean that they are equally efficient in photosynthesis. The absorption spectrum needs, therefore, to be complemented by the action spectrum (Fig. 3.12) which indicates the degree of efficiency of the different wave-lengths. Levring[31] has pointed out that for any given species the pigments, which determine absorption and utilization of light, can vary depending on locality, depth and season. This means that the spectral absorption and action curves will also vary and that a single determination is not sufficient. He further points out that Englemann's complementary theory is mainly valid for "shade" or "weak light" algae, whereas with "sun" algae light intensity determines their lower limit, because a shallow depth of water is sufficient to reduce their assimilation rate and this involves very little change in quality of the light.

CHEMICAL FACTORS

The major factor here is salinity which may be particularly important in estuaries, where red and brown seaweeds tend to disappear.

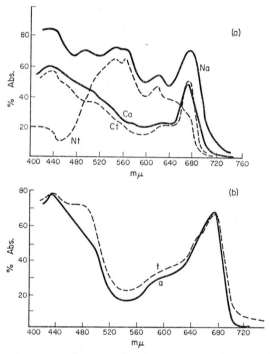

Fig. 3.12. *Absorption* (a) *and action* (t) *spectra of marine algae.* (a), Coilodesme californica (Ca, Ct) *and* Smithora (Porphyra) naiadum (Na, Nt). (b), Ulva taeniata (a, t) (*after Haxo and Blinks*).

Changes in salinity may also be very significant in rock pools and salt pans[6]. Internal salinity changes also take place in algae when they are exposed and this can affect their assimilation rate[23].

Biebl[6], who has done much work in this field, believes that algae can be placed in one of three groups according to their behaviour on exposure:

(1) Deep-growing algae: resistant to a concentration 1·4 times that of sea water.

(2) Algae of L.W.M. and lower littoral tide pools: resistant to a concentration 2·2 times that of sea water.

(3) Littoral algae: resistant to a concentration 3 times that of sea water.

Generally the physical nature of the substrate, i.e. rough or smooth, with cracks or without, is more important than its chemical composition. A comparison of the algal flora of chalk cliffs, such as those on the south coast and East Anglian coasts, reveals differences which are probably due to the excess chalk. This must be regarded as a presence or absence factor.

In rock pools and salt pans pH (acidity or alkalinity) and oxygen can change very greatly during a day, particularly in summer, but there is no evidence that such changes inhibit or prevent the growth of algae. Most marine algae that have been investigated tolerate a wide range of pH. Shade appears to be a much more important factor in the case of rock pools, where depth of water and overhang of ledges may determine the type of vegetation that occurs.

With some salt marsh fucoids the existence of thallus twisting has been linked with stimulus from soil nutrients promoting extra growth in that part of the thallus that is currently in contact with the soil. In *Ascophyllum nodosum* ecad *mackaii*, Gibb[18] has shown that its development from normal plants of *A. nodosum* is promoted by either darkness or lowered salinity. Nutrient variations in sea water are mainly of concern in the development of plankton and need not interest us here.

BIOLOGICAL FACTORS

Animals may often operate as presence or absence factors, e.g. the presence of abundant *Patella* (limpets) generally prevents the establishment of *Fucus* sporelings and the sea urchin, *Paracentrotus lividus*, rapidly clears areas of algae[26]. The mollusc *Helcion pellucidum* is also responsible for the detachment of plants of *Laminaria saccharina*, whilst on salt marshes the small snail *Hydrobia ulvae* can damage beds of *Ulva* species. Grazing by marine animals is a field in which many more observations are needed, especially at dusk or dawn, and at night.

Plants of course may exhibit host-parasite relations, e.g. the parasite *Harveyella* on species of *Rhodomela*, and *Holmsella pachyderma* on *Gracilaria confervoides*, and host-epiphyte relations where there is some restriction of host (this may include *Polysiphonia fastigiata* on *Ascophyllum*). In another direction there is the dependence of *Fucus* sporelings upon the presence of an existing *Enteromorpha* felt. On salt marshes there is the restriction of certain algae to the neighbourhood of phanerogamic plants, e.g. *Bostrychia* and *Catenella* to *Suaeda fruticosa* and the base of *Juncus maritimus* tufts (p. 97).

SUMMARY

It can be seen that there is a great complex of factors operating on the sea-shore. Nevertheless there is a remarkable uniformity in the belts to be observed. When the upper and lower limits of algae occurring at different levels are calculated, it is found that there are certain levels at which there are more algae reaching their limits than elsewhere. These are termed *critical levels*. At these levels there are presumably changes in a factor or factors that affect a number of organisms. The following critical levels appear to be fairly general, which suggests that the tidal factor is probably paramount:

(a) Around extreme high water mark of neap tides.
(b) Around mean low water mark of neap tides.
(c) Between mean and extreme low water marks of spring tides.

Clearly the major belt algae must continue to be investigated in the fullest possible manner. A prerequisite to any such study is an analysis of the various ecological forms, because all work must be based upon taxonomically properly understood plants. In the Southern Hemisphere, *Hormosira banksii* exists in a number of forms and statistical methods were used[4] to show that populations could be

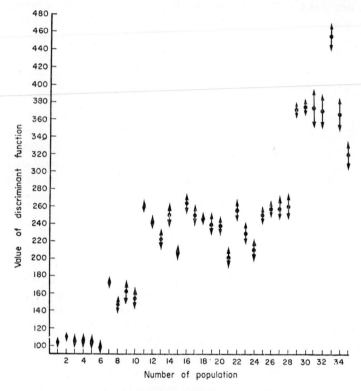

FIG. 3.13. *Plot of discriminant function with standard deviation for all open rock populations of* Hormosira banksii. *The populations fall into five distinct groups (after Bergquist).*

clearly delimited (Fig. 3.13). In a study of *Egregia laevigata* on the Pacific coast of North America, I[10] found that there were distinct deep and shallow water forms.

In a similar detailed study of *Ascophyllum nodosum* Baardseth[2] has shown that there may be giant and dwarf races. Furthermore, in this seaweed vesicle formation takes place at different times of the year in different regions, and varies between basal and lateral shoots. Basal shoot vesicles do not appear in under $1\frac{1}{2}$ years ($\frac{1}{2}$ year for lateral shoots) or before they have reached a weight of 50 mg (5 mg for

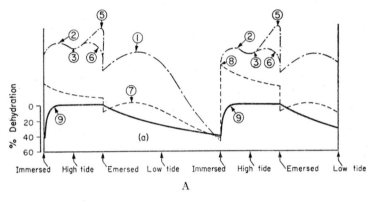

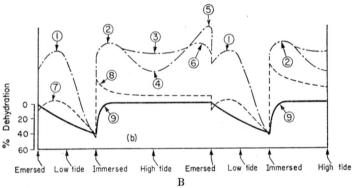

Fig. 3.14. *Schematic diagram showing variation in major factors for* Hormosira banksii *at* A, *its upper limit,* B, *its lower limit. 1, dehydration photosynthesis rise; 2, reimmersion photosynthesis rise; 3, high tide depression of photosynthesis from reduction of light; 4, further depression under suboptimal light conditions or in presence of turbid water; 5, photosynthetic elation as tide starts to rise on dehydration; 8, enhanced respiration stimulus on reimmersion; 9, tissue rehydration (after Bergquist).*

lateral shoots). Such developmental aspects must always be kept in mind in any detailed study of a major species.

When an alga has been carefully studied, we may attempt a first approximation to understanding its behaviour, and the factors responsible. In *Hormosira banksii* this has been done, and Fig. 3.14 compares the response of plants at the upper and lower limits. Further modification is necessary in order to allow for the additional effect of varying times during the day of high and low water. These schemas are deficient in neglecting annual temperature variations in sea water, and air temperatures during exposure. In spite of this they point the way in which ecological problems will ultimately have to be attacked on the sea-shore.

REFERENCES

[1] ANAND P. L., An ecological study of the algae of the British chalk cliffs. *J. Ecol.*, **25**, 344–367 (1937).

[2] BAARDSETH E., Regrowth of *Ascophyllum nodosum* after harvesting. *Inst. for Indust. Res. & Stand. Rept.*, Eire. (1955).

[3] BAKER S. M., The causes of zoning of brown seaweed. *New Phyt.*, **8**, 196–202, (1909); **9**, 54–67 (1910).

[4] BERGQUIST P. L., A statistical approach to the ecology of *Hormosira banksii*. *Bot. Marina*, **1** (1), 22–53 (1959).

[5] BIEBL R., Ökologische und zell physiologische Studien an Rotalgen der englische sudküste. *Beih. Bot. Cent.*, **57**, 381 (1937).

[6] BIEBL R., Trochenresistenz und osmotische Empfindlichkeit der Meeresalgen verschieden tiefer standorte. *Jahr. Wiss. Bot.*, **86**, 350 (1938).

[7] BIEBL R., Lichtresistenz von Meeresalgen. *Protoplasma*, **46**, 1/4, 63 (1956).

[8] CHAPMAN V. J., Zonation of marine algae on the sea-shore. *Proc. Linn. Soc. Lond.*, **154**, 239–253 (1943).

[9] CHAPMAN V. J., *The Algae*. Macmillan (1962).

[10] CHAPMAN V. J., A contribution to the autecology of *Egregia laevigata* Setch. Parts I–III. *Bot. Marina*, **3**, 33–55, 101–122 (1962).

[11] COLMAN J., The nature of the inter-tidal zonation of plants and animals. *J. Mar. Biol. Ass. U.K.*, **18**, 435–476 (1933).

[12] DAMANT G. C. C., Storage of O_2 in the bladders of the seaweed *Ascophyllum* and their adaptation to hydrostatic pressure. *J. Exp. Biol.*, **14**, 198 (1937).

[13] DAVID H. M., Studies in the autecology of *Ascophyllum nodosum* (L.) La Jol. *J. Ecol.*, **31**, 178–198 (1943).

[14] DELF E. M., The significance of the exposure factor in relation to zonation. *Proc. Linn. Soc. Lond.*, **154**, 234 (1943).

[15] EHRKE G., Über die Wirkung der Temperatur und des Lichtes auf die Atmung und Assimilation einiger Meeres und Süswasser algen. *Planta*, **13**, 221 (1931).

[16] EHRKE G., Über die Assimilation komplementär färbter Meeresalgen in Lichte von verschiedenen Wellenlängen. *Planta*, **17**, 650 (1935).

[17] GESSNER F., *Hydrobotanik*. Vol. I. Berlin (1955).

[18] GIBB D. C., The free-living forms of *Ascophyllum nodosum* (L.) La Jol. *J. Ecol.*, **45** (1), 49–84 (1957).

[19] GRUBB V. M., Marine algal ecology and the exposure factor at Peveril Point, Dorset. *J. Ecol.*, **24**, 392–423 (1936).

[20] HAAS P. and HILL T. G., Observations on the metabolism of certain seaweeds. *Ann. Bot.*, **47**, 55–67 (1933).

[21] HAXO F. T. and BLINKS L. R., Photosynthetic action spectra of marine algae. *J. Gen. Physiol.*, **33**, 389–422 (1950).

[22] HYDE M. B., The effect of temperature and light intensity on the rate of apparent assimilation in *Fucus serratus*. *J. Ecol.*, **26**, 118–143 (1938).

[23] ISAAC W. E., Some observations and experiments on the drought resistance of *Pelvetia canaliculata*. *Ann. Bot.*, **47**, 343–348 (1933).

[24] ISAAC W. E., A preliminary study of the water loss of *Laminaria digitata* during inter-tidal exposure. *Ann. Bot.*, **49**, 109–117 (1935).

[25] KANWISHER J., Freezing and drying in inter-tidal algae. *Biol. Bull.*, **113** (2), 275–285 (1957).

[26] KITCHING J. A. and EBLING F. J., The ecology of Lough Ine. XI. *J. Anim. Ecol.*, **30** (2), 373–383 (1962).

[27] KLUGH B. and MARTIN J. R., The growth rate of certain marine algae in relation to depth of submergence. *J. Ecol.*, **8**, 221 (1927).

[28] KNIGHT M. and PARKE M., A biological study of *Fucus vesiculosus* and *F. serratus*. *J. Mar. Biol. Ass. U.K.*, **29**, 439–514 (1950).

[29] LAMI R., Sur les conditions d'éclairement de quelques algues vivant dans les grottes et anfractuosites littorales de la région malouine. *C.R. Acad. Sci. Paris*, **208**, 764 (1939).

[30] LAMPE R. H., Die Temperatureeinstellung des Stoffgewinns bei Meeresalgen als plasmatische Anpassung. *Protoplasma*, **23**, 534 (1935).

[31] LEVRING R., Submarines licht und die Algenvegetation. *Bot. Marina.*, I (3/4), 67–73 (1960).

[32] MACFARLANE C. and BELL H. P., The effect of salinity of water on algal assimilation. *Proc. Trans. Nova Scotia Inst. Sci.*, **18**, 27 (1932).

[33] MONTFORT C., Assimilation und Stoffgewinn der Meeresalgen bei Ausüssung und Rüchversalzung. *Ber. Deut. Bot. Gesell.*, **55**, 85 (1937).

[34] MONTFORT C., RIED A. and RIED I., Abstufeungen der funktionellen Wärmresistenz bei meeresalgen in ihren Bezeihungen zu Umvelt und Erbgut. *Biol. Zentrl.*, **76** (3), 257 (1957).

[35] NICHOL E. A. T., The ecology of a salt marsh. *J. Mar. Biol. Ass. U.K.*, **20**, 203–261 (1935).

[36] SEYBOLD A., Über die Lichtenergiebalanz submerser Wasserpflanzen, vornehmlich der Meeresalgen. *Jahr. Wiss. Bot.*, **79**, 593 (1934).

[37] STOCKER, O. and HOLDHEIDE W., Die assimilation Helgoländer Gezeitenalgen ährend die Ebbezeit. *Zeit. Bot.*, **32**, 1 (1938).

[38] TSCHUDY R. H., Depth studies on photosynthesis of the red algae. *Amer. J. Bot.*, **21**, 546–566 (1934).

[39] ZANEVELD J., The littoral zonation of some Fucaceae in relation to desiccation. *J. Ecol.*, **25**, 431–468 (1937).

[40] BURROWS, E. M., CONWAY, E., LODGE, S. M. and POWELL, H. T., The raising of Inter-tidal algal zones on Fair Isle. *J. Ecol.*, **42** (2), 283–288 (1954).

CHAPTER FOUR

Salt Marshes

SALT marshes are tracts of land covered with phanerogamic vegetation and subject to periodic flooding by the sea. During the flooding mud is deposited on the marsh as the water movement slows down. Salt marsh areas can be either coastal or inland, but the latter have little or no mud deposition and are of no consequence in Great Britain.

OCCURRENCE

Maritime salt marshes are found on coastlines that are stable, sinking or rising, though on submerging coasts they will form only if the rate of sedimentation is greater than that of subsidence. On these coasts marshes can be found if any one of the following physiographic conditions is fulfilled: the presence of estuaries, the shelter of spits, off-shore barrier islands, and large or small protected bays with shallow water. Some of the finest salt marshes in Great Britain have developed behind Blakeney spit in Norfolk and in the protection of Scolt Head Island[53]. Extensive estuarine marshes are to be found in the Humber, Solway Firth, the Thames and Southampton Water. Bay marshes occur in Morecambe Bay and in the Wash. In this last example although there is some exposure to wave action nevertheless the off-shore region is so shallow that large destructive waves are very infrequent.

All these physiographic situations provide admirable conditions for salt marsh formation, though the extent of marsh formed depends on the slope of the land. If it comes down steeply into the sea, as in the Scottish lochs, the strip of salt marsh will be narrow. When the slope is gradual and the beach shelves gently, the marshes can become very wide. In estuaries, where the final fall is also usually very

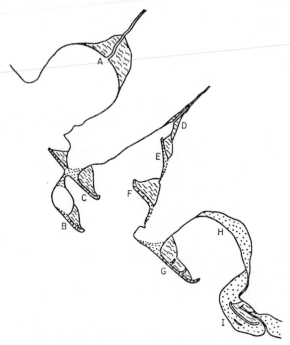

Fig. 4.1. *Diagram illustrating marsh formation behind various types of spits and bars. Marsh areas are indicated by fillings of short wavy lines. A, bay estuary marsh; B, marsh behind simple spit; C, marsh behind bay mouth bar; D, estuary marsh in narrow valley; E, marsh behind bay head bar; F, marsh behind mid-bay bar; G, marsh behind complex spit; H, sand beach; I, off-shore barrier island and marsh.*

slight, the rivers which often bring down much silt, are checked in flow by the estuarine plain and by the tide backing up the water. Silt is hence deposited, the greater its amount the more extensive are

the marshes. In estuaries, therefore, the banking up of the tide raises
the marsh level from the mouth of the estuary up to the limit of tidal
influence. There is a similar lateral rise of level from the banks of the
river to the upland on either side.

Spits or barrier islands can be built of many different materials,
including shell or shingle, and may be simple, double, recurved or
complex. When spits extend across from one headland to another
they are known as bars. The various types of spit can be near the
mouth, near the centre, or at the head of a bay (Fig. 4.1). Their

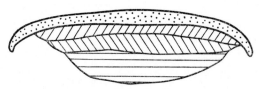

Fig. 4.2. *Diagram showing marsh development behind a small and
single off-shore barrier island. Three successive vegetation zones
are shown, the oldest being next to the bar (after Chapman).*

position and extent is primarily dependent on long-shore movement
influenced by currents, the angle of wave approach, and other
factors (see p. 193)[28]. During the growing period occasional storms
may turn the growing point, more or less at a right angle, so that the
mature structure exhibits a series of laterals[46, 53] (Fig. 4.1G).

In other regions, the spit may grow without the formation of
numerous laterals, as appears to have occurred at Romney where
marsh developed in relation to a cuspate foreland (see Fig. 8.4).
Similarly in the early stages of marsh formation behind a small
barrier island there is no evidence of any lateral (Fig. 4.1I), and
several vegetation zones may develop before the first lateral is
formed (Fig. 4.2).

Where we have spits or barrier islands with laterals, increasing rise
of level of the sand or mud will eventually cause salt marsh to
develop between the laterals. At this stage we can recognize two
types of marsh (Fig. 4.3): one (a) will have a wide mouth with silt
being deposited over a wide area, whilst the other will have a narrow
mouth (b) with silt being deposited almost wholly on the enclosed

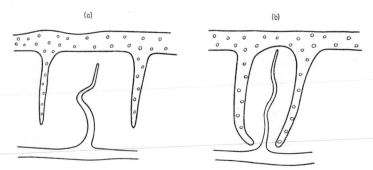

FIG. 4.3. (a), *open marsh;* (b), *closed marsh. Each is bordered by shingle laterals on which sand dunes may develop. Note wide mouth to* (a) *and narrow mouth to* (b) *(after Chapman).*

marsh with the result that growth in height takes place much more rapidly. The former are known as *open marshes* and the latter as *closed marshes.* Vegetation change on the former is relatively slow whereas with the latter, because of the rapid rise of land level, vegetation change is much quicker.

Where there are a series of laterals, and marshes form between them, the oldest marshes will naturally be those near the proximal

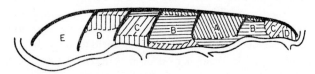

FIG. 4.4. *Later stages in marsh development behind a complex off-shore barrier island growing from right to left. The oldest marsh type is* A. E *is a mud or sand flat as yet uncolonized.* D *represents the youngest marsh association and is the primary colonizing community (after Chapman).*

end and the youngest, generally bare mud or sand flats, nearest the distal end (Fig. 4.4), though closed marshes at any place will upset the general sequence for the reasons given above. Whilst much valuable information can be gained by investigation of the area, the

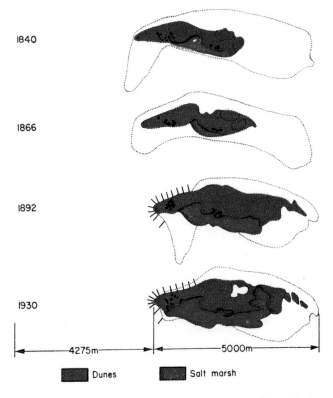

1840

1866

1892

1930

|←————4275m————→|←————————5000m————————→|

Dunes   Salt marsh

FIG. 4.5. *Stages in the development of Baltrum Island (after Tüxen).*

full story is only revealed by a study of old maps over a period of years. Excellent examples of this use of maps can be seen for the development of the closed marsh at Gore Point in Norfolk[48], Scolt Head Island and for the Island of Baltrum in Friesia (Fig. 4.5).

Whilst growth of spits or barrier islands takes place laterally, strong on-shore winds from time to time can cause the spit or island to move landward and in that event former salt marsh mud may be exposed from time to time on the fore-shore, e.g. Scolt Head in Norfolk[15].

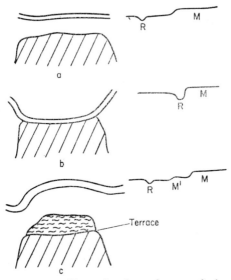

FIG. 4.6. *Diagrams illustrating how changes of river channel could result in the establishment of an erosion cliff and the development of a new marsh, which, if removed by land elevation from tidal influence, will give rise to terraces. Hatching, old marsh; waves, new marsh at lower level (after Chapman).*

As we have pointed out, salt marshes can develop on rising, stable or submerging coastlines. On rising coasts there is usually only a narrow belt of marsh, unless the sea is extremely shallow so that with elevation a large area of mud or sandy mud becomes continually exposed. If the rate of rise is considerable, the upper zones of the salt marsh soon pass into a fresh water condition which may be reed swamp (p. 98) or grassland (p. 97). It seems likely that the present salt marshes in Scotland are forming on an emerging coastline. On

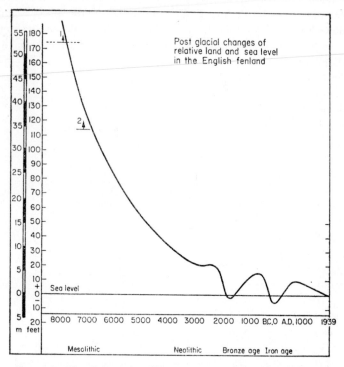

Fig. 4.7. *The thick curve represents the relation of land level to sea level in the Fenland throughout the period indicated on the base-line. The diagram is meant to imply nothing of the absolute movement of land and sea level: sea level has been regarded as constant only as a convention (modified after Godwin).*

the Solway marshes one can generally recognize two or three distinct terraces, probably a result of land elevation with concurrent changes in the channel of the Solway (Fig. 4.6). Other evidence of elevation is the existence of obvious invasion by glycophytic* species at the higher levels, e.g. White clover (*Trifolium repens*), Tormentil (*Potentilla erecta*) associated with Sea plantain (*Plantago maritima*) and Sea pink (*Armeria maritima*), etc. The upper marshes are only flooded by storm tides so that they are used extensively for grazing. Unexpected storm tides have on isolated occasions in the past caused stock loss.

If the level is stable, then the development of salt marsh will be dependent upon the slope of the fore-shore and the rate of silting. On a sinking coastline marsh will form only if the rate of sedimentation exceeds the rate of sinking.

In Great Britain the south-east coast marshes and possibly some south coast marshes are developing upon a subsiding coastline. By making use of pollen analysis, Professor Godwin of Cambridge has suggested the course of land/sea level changes in East Anglia since the end of the Ice Age (Fig. 4.7). The successive heights of the enclosing sea walls[3] of locally reclaimed marshes confirm such subsidence, and there is further evidence† from the tide gauge and levels at Newlynn in Cornwall which over the years of operation indicate that subsidence is occurring.

It should be evident from what has already been said that a knowledge of the rate of sedimentation is, then, very important in any study of salt marshes. The sediments may be of silt or of sand blown up from the beach; the latter can provide complications since it is dependent upon the intensity of prevailing on-shore winds and the incidence of gales.

We may study sedimentation by laying down on the soil a layer of a distinctive sand (the coloured sands from Alum Bay in the Isle of Wight are very suitable) or of iron filings. A continuous band may be used or else patches at measured intervals. The line should be well marked by stout posts. After twelve months small sections can be removed and the depth of mud above the marker layer measured. The method has been used successfully on the Scolt and Dovey

* Non-halophytic.

† Some doubt has been cast upon the conclusions derived from the tide gauge and geodetic levelling data.

D

marshes in England and elsewhere[43, 49]. From the observations, the sedimentation is greatest on the lowest plant-covered marshes, which are the first to be flooded and also the ones that are flooded most frequently, and also it is greater nearer the major creeks and decreases with distance from them. Because more of the material in suspension, particularly the coarser particles, is deposited along creek banks as the tide spills over, a natural revetment to the creeks is produced.

Other factors involved in sedimentation include:

(1) Tidal currents during ebb and flood tides, which may be considerable in the middle periods (see p. 62), so that the mud may be removed after deposition.

(2) Physico-chemical deposition due to the flocculating action of sodium on suspended soil colloids.

(3) The physical effect of fresh water overlying salt water.

(4) Vegetation, which slows down water movement so that the burden of silt is deposited.

As an example of what has been found, the mean annual accretions on the mud marshes of East Anglia are given in Table 4.1[52].

TABLE 4.1

Mean Annual Accretion Rate (1935–1947) on Scolt Head Marshes
(After Steers)

Marsh	Vegetation (see p. 96)	141 months (cm)	45 months (cm)	Mean ann. (cm)
Missel marsh	Asteretum	10·6	5·33	0·87
Lower Hut marsh	Halimionetum	7·5	2·67	0·71
Golf Links marsh	Puccinellio-Halimionetum	6·4	2·16	0·57
Aster marsh	Asteretum	5·25	1·74	0·45
Upper Hut marsh	Suaedeto-Halimionetum	2·8	0·81	0·20 ↓
				increasing height above sea level

The Welsh marshes are very much more sandy and the rate of growth seems to be rather less, because although sand can accumulate more rapidly than mud, it can also be rapidly removed before being fixed by the arrival of plants (Table 4.2).

Before considering the vegetation of the marshes there are two important physiographic features which must be described. The first of these are the *creeks*. In early stages of marsh development the future course of the creek probably depends on minute irregularities of the ground. As soon as the first channels are formed, they are enlarged by the scouring action of the water as it runs off after each

TABLE 4.2

Accretion on Dovey Marshes (after Richards, 1934)

Vegetation	Mean annual			
	Line I (cm)	Level (ft)	Line II (cm)	Level (ft)
Puccinellietum	0·78	1·65	0·44	1·15
Puccinellio-Armerietum ecotone	0·66	1·53	0·83	1·64
Armerietum	0·42	2·13	0·48	1·67
Armerio-Festucetum ecotone	0·24	2·85		
Festucetum	0·21	3·24	0·4	2·31
Juncetum	0·24	2·69	0·27	3·0

tide. On sandy marshes the head of the creek may also start to erode backwards. The advent of the vegetation increases the rate of deposition along the banks, so that we have a stream becoming deeper simultaneously by scour and by building up of its banks.

Sooner or later the banks reach a height where miniature waterfalls arise as the water pours off a marsh after a flooding tide. The creek thus commences to widen by the erosion of its banks. Erosion of the creek banks leads to undercutting and collapse of the walls (Fig. 4.8c), and often one finds secondary marsh developing at a lower level (Fig. 4.8d, e). On high marshes, where flooding is not so frequent, the vegetation may succeed in growing over the creek (Fig. 4.8f, g), or else a succession of pans are formed (see below). The earlier stages in creek formation with rapid accretion and head extension with bed deepening is seen in Fig. 4.8a, b.

I have previously[14] classified marsh creek systems into three main groups. On very sandy marshes, the creek system is very simple and drainage channels are not numerous. Such systems are characteristic of the Welsh, Lancashire and Solway marshes. On more muddy marshes, minor branches are more numerous, and the whole system has a tree-like appearance when seen from the air. This type of

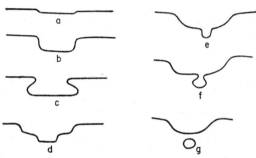

FIG. 4.8. *Stages in the undercutting and collapse of creek walls* (a–e), *followed by overgrowth of vegetation* (f, g) (*after Chapman*).

drainage system is found in the Humber and Wash marshes. On the south coast of England where *Spartina* (Cord grass) vegetation is dominant, the growth habit of this plant appears to favour the development of extremely tortuous and intricate drainage creeks.

Tidal range can also be important in relation to creek pattern. Thus in the Bristol Channel (tidal range 40 ft), *Spartina* marshes have simple creek systems with small, branched, parallel creeks running normal to the shore-line. In Poole Harbour (tidal range 6 ft) there are the complex dendritic tree-like creeks referred to above.

The second feature of salt marshes remaining to be described is the *salt pan*. These are the marsh equivalent of rock pools (p. 29) and they may contain an algal vegetation that is quite distinct from that of the adjacent marsh. Pans develop in a variety of ways that were first clearly enumerated by Yapp *et al.*[60]. Most pans fall into the category of *"primary"* pans, which means that they have developed along with the marsh. In the early stages of primary colonization, bare areas become cut off and surrounded by vegetation. When this happens, water can no longer escape after a flooding tide, and this discourages any plant colonization. In summer, when the water evaporates, the area becomes highly saline, which may again inhibit plant growth. Where a creek cuts back into such a pan, normal drainage is established, and the bare area rapidly becomes colonized.

On the Solway, Lancashire and Welsh marshes the seaward edges may suffer erosion and a low cliff then forms. Below and in front of such a cliff, new secondary marsh may form, not only from new colonists but also from the spread of plants eroded off from the primary marsh. In such conditions *"secondary"* pans may develop. The third type of pan is known as the *"creek"* pan, and is derived from the tributary ends of older creeks as a result of vegetation growing across and forming a dam. Such pans tend to be elongate in shape and are perhaps more frequent on sandy than on muddy marshes because of the greater preponderance of grasses that are the principal dam formers. At times a series of dams can give rise to pans so that the former course of the creek can be readily traced. The fourth type of pan to be found on British and European salt marshes is the *"residual"* pan. This arises from subdivision of any of the other three types of pan, either as a result of colonization or as a result of vegetation slowly growing across and breaking up the bare area. This is especially to be found on marshes where the plant species are grasses and rushes that propagate vegetatively. A fifth type of pan occurs on eastern American marshes but is not found on European marshes.

THE VEGETATION

Sufficient should now have been said to indicate that as accretion takes place, the land gradually rises and the numbers of floodings become fewer and fewer. This decrease in floodings brings about other changes (see p. 110), so that, as the environmental conditions alter, one vegetation type is replaced by another. On the rocky sea-shore, the algal belts remain constant, and represent the climax vegetation. On the salt marsh, the vegetation is dynamic and the zonation to be observed in going from the seaward edge to the upland behind is a developmental zonation or *succession* (see p. 2). The succession is initiated on bare mud or sand that has not previously borne vegetation, and the whole sequence therefore forms an excellent example of a prisere. Because of the dynamic nature of the vegetation, normal seral terminology must be used in describing the different communities. One may therefore distinguish associes, consocies, socies, etc., among both the phanerogamic and crypto-gamic vegetation.

Since the deposition of mud depends on tidal flooding, accretion ceases when the land level is raised to extreme high tide mark. In fact it probably ceases slightly below this level, where the sub-mergences are so few that mud deposition is negligible. At this level in Europe, there is generally a community dominated by the Sea rush, *Juncus maritimus*. Provided the land is not sinking and there is no influx of fresh water, further change will not take place. The *Juncus* represents the regional climatic climax, though it is potenti-ally capable of further development. For this reason, it is best termed the sere climax. Should a fresh water stream or river enter the marsh area, it will be found that the salt marsh passes imperceptibly into fresh water reed swamp (see p. 98).

SALT MARSH COMMUNITIES

The lowest phanerogam community (Zosteretum) is that of the Eel-grasses, *Zostera marina* and *Z. nana*, which occur on mud-flats that are exposed at low tide. These flats, and also those higher ones that are submerged daily by the tides flowing over them as a con-tinuous sheet of water, have been termed "sloblands". Associated with the *Zostera* will be found a number of algae, and in some parts of Europe, where the water is rather more brackish, *Ruppia maritima* may also occur. Some years ago, the eel-grass beds were very much more extensive but they were then decimated by a disease[58]. Since the attack, some of the beds have recovered. If *Zostera* beds are present, there will usually be a bare zone above them before the next phanerogam is able to colonize the ground although *Spartina townsendii* can invade at the *Zostera* level. On the sandy soils of the west coast, the primary community is likely to be either a Salicornietum or a Puccinellio-Salicornietum. The former will be dominated by annual species of Glasswort or Marsh samphire, (*Salicornia herbacea*, *S. stricta*, and *S. ramosissima*) and there may also be many plants of the unbranched Seablite, *Suaeda maritima* var. *flexilis*, which in places can become the dominant. This is particularly likely to happen on disturbed soil. On the Norfolk coast this community will be intimately associated with two algal communities, one a pure sward of the embedded *Fucus vesiculosus* ecad *caespitosus*, the other a dense community of *Pelvetia canaliculata* ecad *libera* with which may be associated the red alga *Bostrychia scorpioides*. The Puccinellio-Salicornietum is dominated by the Sea poa, *Puccinellia maritima*, and species of *Salicornia*, whilst the Sea aster, *Aster tripolium*, which has also a ray-less variety var. *discoideus* that reaches its northern limit on the west coast in Lancashire, is either scattered throughout or in places may be associated with the Glassworts as the co-dominant in an Asteretum tripolii. On the Norfolk coast near the dunes, a variant of this community with *Puccinellia* and *Limonium bellidifolium* may be found. This appears to be associated with the very sandy nature of the soil. Another variant of the *Puccinellia* community is found on creek banks where Seablite (*Suaeda maritima*) may be more abundant than the *Salicornia*.

The Salicornietum is a primary community, not only on sandy marshes but also on muddy flats as well. On the south and south-east coasts it is commonly replaced by the hybrid Cord grass, *Spartina townsendii* which forms a Spartinetum[14, 26a].

On the sandy marshes of the west coast, much of the marshland is covered by two grass-dominated communities, the Puccinellietum and Festucetum rubrae. Workers on these marshes have sometimes divided both into upper and lower communities. Thus the lower

Puccinellietum can be characterized by the presence of *Aster*, Sea arrow-grass (*Triglochin maritima*) and Sea lavender (*Limonium vulgare*), whilst the upper Puccinellietum possesses Sea pink (*Armeria maritima*), *Limonium*, Creeping fescue (*Festuca rubra*), Sea milk-wort (*Glaux maritima*), Sea plantain (*Plantago maritima*) and Long-leaved scurvy-grass (*Cochlearia anglica*). The lower Festucetum often contains abundant *Armeria*, and at higher levels Fiorin (*Agrostis stolonifera*), Mud rush (*Juncus gerardi*), Buck's-horn plantain (*Plantago coronopus*) are very common. On the rising (see p. 88) marshes of the Solway, glycophytes such as White clover (*Trifolium repens*), Tormentil (*Potentilla erecta*), and Autumnal hawkbit (*Leontodon autumnalis*) indicate the very rare flooding undergone by the Festucetum.

On the south coast, this zone is still occupied by *Spartina townsendii*, but, until this species effectively invades areas in the future, one finds on the East Anglian coast an Asteretum with which is associated the embedded *Fucus* and free-living *Pelvetia* (see above). A variant of the community occurs along creek banks, where the annual species of *Salicornia* (Glassworts) are replaced by perennial *S. lignosa* and *S. perennis*, together with another larger free-living form of *Fucus vesiculosus* ecad *volubilis*.

A community that is particularly abundant on the east coast but restricted elsewhere, is the one known as the General Salt Marsh community (G.S.M.). On the south coast it has been very largely ousted by the ubiquitous *Spartina* whilst the regular grazing of the sandy grass marshes of the west also restricts it. The co-dominants of the community are Sea pink (*Armeria*), Sea lavender (*Limonium*), *Spergularia marginata*, Sea plantain (*Plantago maritima*), *Triglochin* and at high levels Sea hard-grass (*Parapholis strigosa*). *Glaux maritima* (Sea milkwort) may also occur, especially with *Triglochin* (Arrowgrass) in the wetter depressions.

From the Asteretum stage to higher levels on the east coast, from the Spartinetum stage on the south coast, and from the Puccinellietum stage on the west coast, the Sea purslane (*Halimione portulacoides*) forms a fringe along the banks of creeks, a fringe that becomes generally wider with age, unless the marshes are grazed. There is reason to believe that *Halimione* is restricted to places where drainage is good, hence it occurs along creek banks and along the edges of shingle laterals (p. 199). At high levels it may spread over the marshes and be associated with the Sea poa, *Puccinellia maritima*. On the Norfolk coast at Scolt Head, a peculiar variant of this community is found near the sand dunes: this has been termed the Sandy Halimionetum and in such places *Halimione portulacoides* var. *parvifolia* tends to replace the common var. *latifolia*.

A high-level community common on some European marshes but not so frequent on British marshes is the Agrostidetum dominated by Fiorin (*Agrostis stolonifera*). A more frequent high-level community, especially on the muddy east coast marshes, is the Plantaginetum maritimi dominated by the Sea plantain, *Plantago maritima*, with *Agrostis*, *Festuca*, *Glaux* and *Armeria* commonly associated with it.

The uppermost levels of the marshes, where there is no influx of fresh water, are usually occupied by either a Juncetum gerardii or a Juncetum maritimi or the two together: where both occur, local conditions seem to determine whether or not the *Juncus gerardi* occupies a higher or lower level than *J. maritimus*. Both species have certain salt marsh plants associated with them, essentially species that must be able to tolerate considerable reduction of light. In some cases, at least, the associated plants tend to be spindly. *Glaux*, *Plantago maritima* and *Triglochin* are common associates together with Creeping fescue (*Festuca rubra*) and Sea poa (*Puccinellia maritima*), the two latter particularly on the more sandy western marshes. In the Solway area, where these upper levels only become flooded by extreme or storm tides, other plants such as Lesser spearwort (*Ranunculus flammula*), Brookweed (*Samolus valerandi*), Parsley water dropwort (*Oenanthe lachenalii*), Bird's foot trefoil (*Lotus corniculatus*) and Yorkshire fog (*Holcus lanatus*) enter the community and can clearly tolerate the brackish conditions. It is in the Sea rush (*Juncus maritimus*) zone that the debris of the drift-line is generally to be found, and this can often be characterized by a zone of *Atriplex patula* var. *hastata* or a belt of Sea wormwood (*Artemisia maritima*) and occasional plants of the beet, *Beta vulgaris* ssp. *maritima*. These are probably nitrophiles and occur there for that reason and the fact that their seed is distributed by the tide along the drift-line (see also p. 133).

In other areas where fresh water streams or rivers pass through the marshes, a transition to fresh water swamp can be observed. A common transitional community is the Phragmitetum dominated by the tall reed *Phragmites communis,* and there seems little doubt that the Phragmitetum of the East Anglian fen country was the normal successor to a salt marsh community. It can also be seen occupying the same position on the south coast. Where conditions have a tendency to be brackish throughout, one can find Sea club-rush (*Scirpus maritimus*) as a primary colonist, or it may occur in depressions at high levels where there is standing brackish water. In the Scirpetum maritimi one can particularly find the Glaucous bulrush (*Schoenoplectus tabernaemontani*), the Bulrush (*S. lacustris*) and Broad blysmus (*Blysmus compressus*).

No single marsh area will provide an example of every one of the communities that have been briefly described. The student must study each marsh area and try and determine which major communities are present and whether there are any variants.

The communities on any marsh are related to each other in space and time, and one of the problems of the ecologist is to try and work out these relationships. They can be expressed in terms of successional diagrams which are by no means as simple as earlier workers believed. It is possible to summarize such successional diagrams and indicate in a broad manner how communities on sandy marshes, on muddy English east coast marshes, and on south coast marshes, may be related to each other. For any given marsh area, only some of the stages in the succession will be represented. The following schemes indicate the kind of inter-relationships it is believed may exist in various regions of the British Isles.

The succession on lower marshes can take place relatively rapidly and vegetation maps prepared over quite a short period of years can indicate the rapidity of the changes. Such vegetation maps are therefore well worth making[13].

Apart from describing the various communities, it is possible on any salt marsh area to make use of life-form spectra as a means of

GENERALIZED SUCCESSION—SOUTH COAST

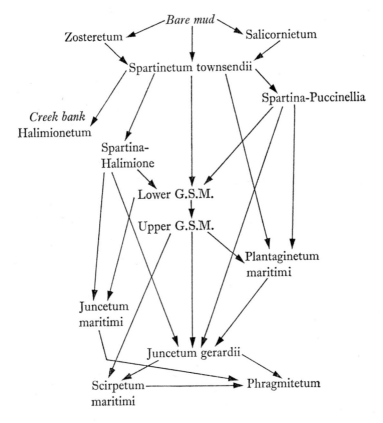

Note. In regions of reduced salinity one can have a direct transition from the Spartinetum to either a Phragmitetum or Scirpetum maritimi, e.g. Poole Harbour, Lytchett Bay.

comparison. In comparing the spectra, the values should be determined preferably on a frequency basis in order to allow for the significance of dominance (see p. 9). Whilst no figures are

GENERALIZED SUCCESSION—EAST COAST

Increasing silt ⟶

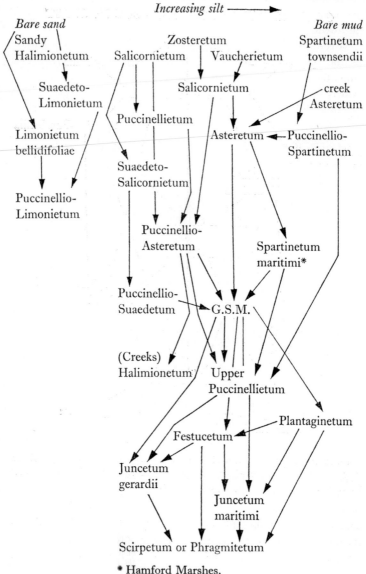

* Hamford Marshes.

immediately available for Great Britain, the kind of results that can be obtained are indicated (p. 103) for the salt marshes of the Öresund in Sweden[14].

It is evident from these figures that the hemicryptophyte element is the dominant, with the therophytes forming the next most important group. This appears to be general over salt marshes from widely different parts of the globe.

For those who wish to compare communities objectively from

GENERALIZED SUCCESSION—WELSH MARSHES

* Morfa Harlech.

different areas, there are various mathematical methods by which this can be done (see p. 8). If any of these are used, their limitations should be borne in mind, and also the fact that different methods may yield different results. It may, however, well prove instructive to carry out such exercises; salt marsh communities, because of their definiteness of character and the relatively few species involved, form very suitable communities for analytical studies and consideration of the value of quadrats and other means of sampling vegetation (see Chapter 1).

Apart from the algae[2, 5, 9] (and p. 45), very little work has been done on the thallophyte flora of salt marshes. Recently, however, studies have been made of the fungal and bacterial flora including the rhizosphere populations, of a Lincolnshire salt marsh[40, 41, 42, 56, 57]. As might be expected, the greatest number of fungi and bacteria

GENERALIZED SUCCESSION—WEST COAST

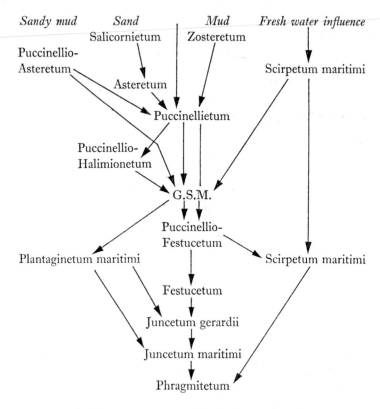

were recorded from mature marsh. An interesting feature was a decrease in number of both organisms in the *Spartina* zone as compared with the lower mud flats on the one hand and the higher

TABLE 4.3

Percentage of Life-forms

Community	Chamae-phyte	Hemi-crypto-phyte	Geo-phyte	Hydro helo-phyte	Thero-phyte
Salicornietum	—	57·5	11·5	—	31
Scirpetum maritimi	—	33	22·5	11·5	33
G.S.M.	5	52	10	—	32
Plantaginetum	6	57·5	12·5	—	24
Juncetum gerardii	4	58	8	—	30
Artemisietum maritimae	3·5	49	11	—	36·5
Suaedetum maritimae	—	50	17	—	43

marsh on the other. At present, the significance of this is not known. It is evident, however, that this rather difficult field of study, as the organisms are not well known, presents considerable opportunities for future investigation.

REFERENCES

[1] BARNES F. A. and KING C. A. M., A preliminary survey at Gibraltar Point, Lincolnshire. *Bird Obs. & Field Res. St. Gib. Pt. Lincs. Rept.*, 41–59 (1951).
[2] BLACKLER H., An algal survey of Loch Foyle, N. Ireland. *Proc. Roy. Ir. Acad.*, **54** B (6), 97–139 (1951).
[3] BORER O., Recent coastal changes in south-eastern England. IV. Changes in the Wash. *Geog. J.*, **93** (6), 491–496 (1939).
[4] BRACHER R., The ecology of the Avon banks at Bristol. *J. Ecol.*, **17**, 35–80 (1929).

[5] CARTER N., A comparative study of the algal flora of two salt marshes. *J. Ecol.*, **20**, 341–370 (1932); **21**, 128–208, 385–403 (1933).

[6] CHAPMAN V. J., A note upon *Obione portulacoides* (L.) Gaert. *Ann. Bot. N.S.*, **1** (2), 305–310 (1937).

[7] CHAPMAN V. J., Marsh development in Norfolk. *Trans. Norf. Norw. Nat. Soc.*, **14** (4), 394–397 (1938).

[8] CHAPMAN V. J., Studies in salt marsh ecology. Sect. I–III. *J. Ecol.*, **26** (1), 144–179 (1938).

[9] CHAPMAN V. J., Studies in salt marsh ecology. Sect. IV, V. *J. Ecol.*, **27** (1), 160–201 (1939).

[10] CHAPMAN V. J., Studies in salt marsh ecology. Sect. VIII. *J. Ecol.*, **29** (1), 69–82 (1941).

[11] CHAPMAN V. J., Some vegetational changes on a shingle off-shore bar at Thornham. *Trans. Norf. Norw. Nat. Soc.*, **24**, 273–278 (1948).

[12] CHAPMAN V. J., *Halimione portulacoides* (L.) Aell., *in* Biological Flora of the British Isles. *J. Ecol.*, **38** (1), 214–222 (1950).

[13] CHAPMAN V. J., Studies in salt marsh ecology. Sect. IX. *J. Ecol.*, **47** (2), 619–639 (1959).

[14] CHAPMAN V. J., *Salt Marshes and Salt Deserts of the World*. Leon. Hill, London. (1960).

[15] CHAPMAN V. J., The Ecology in *Scolt Head Island*. Ed. J. A. Steers. Heffer, Camb. (1960).

[16] CHATER E. H., Recent changes in the halophytic vegetation of the Rye coastline. *Hastings Nat.*, **5** (1), 3–20 (1934).

[17] CHATER E. H. and JONES H. Some observations on *Spartina townsendii*. H. and J. Groves in the Dovey estuary. *J. Ecol.*, **45** (1), 157–167 (1957).

[18] CONWAY V., Further observations on the salt marsh at Holme-next-the-Sea. *J. Ecol.*, **21**, 263–267 (1933).

[19] COTTON A. D., Clare Island survey. Part 15: Marine algae. *Proc. Roy. Ir. Acad.*, **31**, 1–178 (1912).

[20] DAVIES M. R. and LAMBERT J. M., A sandy area in the Dovey estuary. *J. Ecol.*, **28**, 453–464 (1940).

[21] DIXON E. E. *et al.*, The geology of the Carlisle, Longtown and Silloth districts. *Mem. Geol. Surv. U.K.* (1926).

[22] GILLHAM M. E., Vegetation of the Exe estuary in relation to water salinity. *J. Ecol.*, **45** (3), 735–756 (1957).

[23] GILLHAM M. E., Coastal vegetation of Mull and Iona in relation to salinity and soil reaction. *J. Ecol.*, **45** (3), 757–778 (1957).

[24] GIMINGHAM C. H., Contributions to the maritime ecology of St. Cyrus, Kincardineshire. III. The salt marsh. *Trans. Bot. Soc. Edin.*, **36**, 137–164 (1953).

[25] GODWIN H., Studies of the post-glacial history of British vegetation. III–IV. *Phil. Trans. B.*, **230** (570), 239–343 (1940).

[26] GOOD R. D'O., Contributions towards a survey of the plants and animals of South Haven Peninsula, Studland Heath, Dorset. II. General ecology of the flowering plants and ferns. *J. Ecol.*, **23**, 361–405 (1935).

[26a] GOODMAN F. J., BRAYBROOKS E. M. and LAMBERT J. M., Investigations into "die-back" in *Spartina townsendii* agg. I. *J. Ecol.*, **47**, 651–677 (1959).

[27] HESLOP-HARRISON J. W., A survey of the lower Tees marshes and of the reclaimed areas adjoining them. *Trans. Nat. Hist. Soc. Northumb.*, N.S. **5** (1) (1918).

[28] KING C. A. M., *Beaches and Coasts.* Arnold (1959).

[29] LINDER E., Red hill mounds of Canvey Island in relation to subsidence in the Thames estuary. *Proc. Geol. Ass.*, **51** (3), 283–290 (1940).

[30] MARSH A. S., The maritime ecology of Holme-next-the-Sea. *J. Ecol.*, **3**, 65–93 (1915).

[31] MORSS W. L., The plant colonization of merselands in the estuary of the River Nith. *J. Ecol.*, **15**, 310–343 (1927).

[32] MOSS C. E., Geographical distribution of vegetation in Somerset. *Roy. Geog. Soc. Spec. Publ.* (1957).

[33] NEWMAN L. F. and WALWORTH G., A preliminary note on the ecology of part of the S. Lincolnshire coast. *J. Ecol.*, **7**, 204–210 (1919).

[34] OLIVER F. W., Some remarks on Blakeney Point, Norfolk. *J. Ecol.*, **1**, 4–15 (1913).

[35] OLIVER F. W., Blakeney Point reports. *Trans. Norf. Norw. Nat. Soc.*, 9–12 (1925–29).

[36] O'REILLY H. and PANTIN G., Some observations on the salt marsh formation in Co. Budlin. *Proc. Roy. Ir. Acad.*, **58** B (5), 89–128 (1957).

[37] PERRATON C., Salt marshes of the Hampshire–Sussex border. *J. Ecol.*, **4** (2), 240–247 (1953).

[38] PRAEGER R. L., Phanerogamia and Pteridophyta *in* Clare Island survey. Part X. *Proc. Roy. Ir. Acad.*, **31** (1911).

[39] PRIESTLEY J. H., The Pelophilous formation on the left bank of the Severn estuary. *Proc. Bristol. Nat. Soc.*, 4th ser. 3 (1911).

[40] PUGH G. J. F., The fungal flora of tidal mud flats, in *The Ecology of Soil Fungi.* Liverpool Univ. Press (1960).

[41] PUGH G. J. F., Fungal colonization of a developing salt marsh. *Nature*, **190**, 1032–1033 (1961).

[42] PUGH G. J. F., Studies in fungi in coastal soils. I. *Trans. Brit. Mycol. Soc.*, **45** (2), 255–260 (1962).

[43] RICHARDS F. J., The salt marshes of the Dovey estuary. IV. The rates of vertical accretion, horizontal extension, and scarp erosion. *Ann. Bot.*, **48**, 225–259 (1934).

[44] SLATER L., Sedimentation on the salt marsh on Scolt Head Island. *Trans. Norf. Norw. Nat. Soc.*, **13** (2), 133 (1931).

[45] SMITH W. G., Botanical survey of Scotland. III–IV. Forfar and Fife. *Scot. Geog. Mag.*, **73**, (1905).

[46] STEERS J. A., The East Anglian Coast. *Geog. J.*, **69**, 24–48 (1927).

[47] STEERS J. A., Scolt Head Island. *Geog. J.*, **83** (6), 479–502 (1934).

[48] STEERS J. A., Some notes on the north Norfolk coast from Hunstanton to Brancaster. *Geog. J.*, **87** (1), 35–46 (1936).

[49] STEERS J. A., The rate of sedimentation on salt marshes on Scolt Head Island, Norfolk. *Geol. Mag.*, **75** (883), 26–39 (1938).

[50] STEERS J. A., *The Coastline of England and Wales*. C.U. Press (1946).

[51] STEERS J. A., Accretion on Scolt Head Island marshes. *Trans. Norf. Norw. Nat. Soc.*, **24**, 279 (1948).

[52] STEERS J. A., Twelve years measurement of accretion on Norfolk salt marshes. *Geol. Mag.*, **85** (3), 163–166 (1948).

[53] STEERS J. A., The Physiography in *Scolt Head Island*. Ed. J. A. Steers. Heffer, Camb. (1960).

[54] TANSLEY A. G., *The British Islands and their Vegetation*. C.U. Press (1939).

[55] THOMPSON H. S., Changes in the coast vegetation near Berrow, Somerset. *J. Ecol.*, **10**, 53–61 (1922).

[56] TURNER M. and GRAY T. R. G., Bacteria of a developing salt marsh. *Nature, London*, **194**, 559–560 (1962).

[57] TURNER M. and PUGH G. J. F., Species of *Mortierella* from a salt marsh. *Trans. Brit. Mycol. Soc.*, **44** (2), 243–252 (1961).

[58] TUTIN T. G., The autecology of *Zostera marina* in relation to its wasting disease. *N. Phyt.*, **37** (1), 50–70 (1938).

[59] WIEHE P. O., A quantitative study of the influence of the tide upon populations of *Salicornia europaea*. *J. Ecol.*, **23**, 323–333 (1935).

[60] YAPP R. H. *et al.*, The salt marshes of the Dovey estuary. II. The salt marshes. *J. Ecol.*, **5**, 65–103 (1917).

CHAPTER FIVE

The Salt Marsh Environment

THE TIDES

JUST as the tides and tidal phenomena form the principal environmental feature in marine algal ecology, so the tides represent the major phenomenon of the salt marsh habitat. The vegetation of salt marshes is subject to periodic inundation by sea water, the lower the marsh the more frequent the inundation. During the periods of flooding in daylight, photosynthesis of phanerogamic plants will be reduced because the supply of carbon dioxide is diminished and silt in the water reduces the light supply. Irrespective of when the flooding occurs, the environment of the root may also be altered and the oxygen supply reduced so that respiration is affected. In the case of the seaweeds, the reverse phenomena are likely to occur, photosynthesis and respiration being reduced during the periods of exposure. There is also the effect of saline water on the metabolic plant processes, especially those of the phanerogams.

At low tide the vegetation will be subject to the normal regional and local climate. Thus a flooding tide may leave the marsh and be followed by a heavy downpour, resulting in a rapid change of salinity in the soil water. In summer, when the tide leaves the marsh the vegetation may become exposed suddenly to high temperatures. On the other hand, the vegetation does not suffer from drought conditions even in the driest summer. It must be evident, therefore, that the periods of submergence and exposure are of profound significance to the plants, both phanerogams and algae. In addition to all these effects, there is also a purely mechanical effect exerted by the tide.

The tide is generally responsible for the conveyance of seeds over the salt marsh. At middle and high levels, these seeds become trapped in the vegetation, and are left when the tide recedes. Success in germination and growth depends here, as in any other phanero-gamic community, on the environment, availability of space and competition. At the lower levels where there may be much open ground, the problem is essentially one of successful establishment before the seedling can be washed away by the tide. We know very little about establishment on low marshes and it is a problem that does not present any great difficulties in investigation. Wiehe[22] used the density of *Salicornia* seedlings on low marsh in relation to

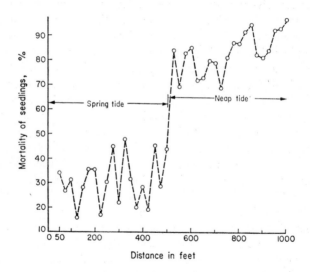

FIG. 5.1. *Percentage mortality of* Salicornia *seedlings along a transect (after Wiehe).*

frequency of flooding tides, and his data suggest that the lower limit of the plant is set by the mechanical removal of seedlings. In Fig. 5.1 it will be seen that there is a sharp rise in disappearance (mortality rate) at the level where there is daily flooding (neap-tide zone). Field observations such as the above, however, need to be coupled with germination and growth studies under controlled conditions in order to determine rate of root and shoot growth. It would thus seem that with the annual species of Glasswort (*Salicornia*), seedlings need to be left uncovered for 2 to 3 days, and this will only happen during neap-tide periods above the level of mean high water mark of neap tides (see p. 111); in that period, the root can penetrate the soil to a sufficient depth to anchor it when the marsh is next flooded and so prevent it being swept away. It would therefore be most desirable to have information on root growth and soil penetration for primary colonists such as the various species of Glasswort (*Salicornia*), Seablite (*Suaeda maritima*), Sea poa (*Puccinellia maritima*) and indeed all salt marsh species.

It is not, however, sufficient to determine the minimum period of continuous exposure required for successful anchorage. It is essential that the period must occur at the normal time for germination, which will be some time in the spring. For this reason, the lower limit of an annual *Salicornia* may fluctuate from year to year depending on the period when neap tides coincide with germination. The present writer has shown that Sea aster (*Aster tripolium*) seedlings normally need 5 days before they are properly anchored. This, therefore, represents the minimum exposure time required. On the Norfolk marshes, the lower limit of abundant *Aster* is at +7·5 ft O.D.*, whilst the lowest is at +6·4 ft O.D. The maximum period of continuous exposure is 7 days at the former level and it occurs in February. At the lower level, the period is 5 days and it occurs in March. It is true there is still a 5-day exposure at +6·1 ft O.D., but it occurs in April and May, after the normal germination time. It seems, therefore, that the lower limit of *Aster* on the Norfolk marshes may be determined by the establishment period and the time of its occurrence at the lower levels.

From the above, it is evident that much valuable information can be secured by carrying out levelling surveys on the marshes and finding the vertical ranges of major species and the principal

* Ordnance Datum.

communities. If the levels are related to the nearest tide levels, it is then possible to determine not only the maximum periods of continuous exposure at each level, but also the expected number of submergences per annum and the average number of hours submerged each day during daylight.

On this basis[7] the marshes fall into upper and lower marshes, the principal feature separating the two being the period of continuous exposure, which increases greatly in passing from the top of the lower marshes to the bottom of the upper marshes. It appears that the boundary between these two groups lies near mean high water. At present the only set of British data refer to the Scolt marshes in Norfolk[7], and it would be highly desirable to obtain more information for other salt marsh areas. Using Scolt data, the lower marshes there commonly undergo more than 360 submergences per annum, though this value for other places may well depend upon tidal range and the character of the tides (see p. 54). The maximum period of continuous exposure never *exceeds* 9 days and the mean daily submergence in daylight is more than 1·2 hours. So far as the period of continuous exposure is concerned, it may change from a maximum of 8 days on lower marshes to one of 16 days on higher marshes, with change of level of only 0·2 ft. It is easy to see that such a change could be of profound importance to many plants, not only in respect of germination and establishment, but also in the effect it could have during a hot, dry summer.

Phanerogams and algae appear about equally affected by this division into upper and lower marshes. Thus, twelve phanerogamic species occur wholly on one type or the other, whilst six are common to both: among the algae, twenty-seven species are restricted, and nine are common to both. This result only applies to East Anglia and will differ in other regions: the vertical distribution of species requires to be worked out for many more areas before arrival at any general conclusions. The algae restricted to the upper marshes are mostly members of the Myxophyceae which, as a group, are well adapted to withstand long periods of desiccation. It seems that very few phanerogams are able to tolerate more than 3 hours' submergence in daylight. This, however, is an aspect that requires further study with detailed

measurements of photosynthesis and respiration under conditions of
submergence and exposure.

After a levelling survey has been carried out, it is possible to plot
the continuous exposure periods for individual species at the upper
and lower limits (Fig. 5.2). For a given species one would expect the
diagrams to be comparable for different salt marsh areas, particularly
if the tidal phenomena represent the principal causal factors. This

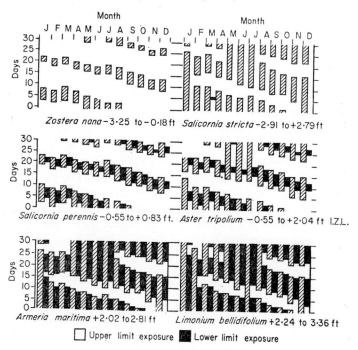

FIG. 5.2. *Charts indicating features of continuous exposure for
salt marsh plants at the upper and lower limits of their vertical
range at Scolt (after Chapman). I.Z.L.=Island Zero Level.*

aspect needs much further study, since at present comparable data
are only available for Scolt and Massachusetts, and the species concerned, though listed as taxonomically identical, may belong to
different physiological races and thus account for the present

differences. It can, however, be noted that Sea purslane (*Halimione portulacoides*) appears to be a species limited by tidal phenomena since the number of submergences per annum at its upper level on both Scolt and Dublin marshes is between 100 and 104.

Certain algal species have representatives common to both salt marsh and rocky coast. No detailed work has as yet been undertaken to ascertain if such plants occupy comparable levels on the two types of shore in relation to the tides. Thus *Pelvetia canaliculata* and its ecad *libera* would be ideal to study in this respect, as also *Fucus vesiculosus* and its salt marsh ecads *volubilis*, *caespitosus* and *muscoides*.

WATER TABLE

Apart from the major effect of periodic floodings and the intervening periods of exposure and the indirect effect of these phenomena upon water loss and basic metabolic processes of the plants, there is the influence of the tides upon the soil water table, an influence which can be counteracted or complemented by the incidence of rainfall. The movement of the water table can be of profound significance should it result in water-logging of the roots for any appreciable period, and furthermore, variation in water movements with distance from major creeks may result in a vegetation zonation correlated with it. Indeed there seems little doubt that the zone of Sea purslane (*Halimione portulacoides*) found along creeks is related to the better drainage conditions[5, 10].

Water table conditions on a marsh are related not only to the proximity of creeks, but also to soil structure. For this reason a study of the soil is an essential feature of any salt marsh investigation. In so far as the soil water table is usually not far below the surface, the soil study can generally be prosecuted effectively by digging pits.

SOIL STRUCTURE

The broad features of salt marsh soils have already been indicated. It is apparent that they are formed generally on a sand base, more rarely on a rocky one, and that the deposited material is either wind-blown sand, water-borne clay and silt, plant remains or a combination of any of these.

A study of the geological structure of salt marshes requires amplification by the carrying out of simple mechanical analyses using a standard sedimentation technique that will be found in any book on soil analysis. The result of such an analysis reveals essentially the proportions of coarse sand, fine sand, clay and silt that are present. Marshes with a high proportion of the first two will possess good drainage and will generally carry a grass-dominated vegetation. Marshes with a high proportion of clay and silt will tend to be poorly drained, except near creeks, but such marshes have a much higher agricultural potential when they have been reclaimed by the building of sea walls.

The relative proportions of the sand fractions to those of clay and silt largely determine the pore space of the soil, and this affects the drainage conditions. The pore space of a peat soil may vary between 75 and 90 per cent, whereas that of a clay soil will range between 50 and 65 per cent and that of a sandy soil will be rather less. Although the sandy soil may have the lowest pore space, water movement will be rapid because there is a low proportion of soil colloids to which water can become tenaciously bound. The actual spaces, though fewer than the numerous minute capillaries of a clay soil, are probably larger, and hence offer less resistance to water movement.

In addition to the above features, the height of the marsh itself plays a part in determining the depth of the water table, because the higher the marsh, the less frequent the submersions and the lower will be the water table, though the marsh is potentially more influenced by heavy rainfall than is a lower marsh. The higher marshes also have a greater depth of surface mud which will impede water movement and for this reason is of great importance (see p. 116).

WATER MOVEMENT

The access of water to a marsh and its subsequent removal after high tide have been summarized in Fig. 5.3. As the tide begins to rise, water commences to seep laterally into the creek, the rate of such lateral seepage depending on the nature of the soil strata. Where there is a deposit of mud on the banks, as in older creeks, the rate of seepage may be reduced. Seepage will not, of course, commence until the level of water in the creek exceeds that of the soil water table in the adjacent marsh. As the tide rises, the amount of seepage increases, though when the surface mud layer is reached, a back pressure is set up due to air trapped in the soil (see later). So far as the soil water table is concerned, the extent of the tidal influence upon it will depend on the distance apart of the creeks, the size of the creek and the height of the marsh. As water movement is greatest nearest the creek, close proximity of creeks will increase the movement of the

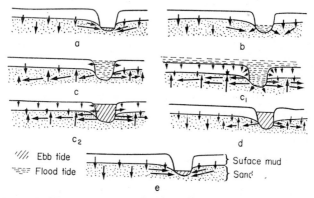

Fig. 5.3. *Water movements during a diurnal tidal cycle.* a, b, c, d, e, *non-flooding tide,* c-c$_1$-c$_2$-d, *flooding tide. Surface mud remains as an aerated layer (after Chapman).*

water table. The larger and deeper the creek, the greater the water pressure and again the greater will be the lateral soil water table movement. Eventually flooding of the marsh will occur, this happening more frequently with the lower marshes, and seepage then takes place vertically into the surface soil layers.

When the tide turns the flooding surface water is removed first of all and as it pours over the creek edges erosion slowly but surely takes place. Shallow pools of water persist in the slight irregularities of the marsh surface, and slowly disappear by seepage and evaporation. These shallow pools do, however, make it difficult to determine exactly when a marsh is re-exposed. Such pools disappear more rapidly in summer than winter and also more rapidly at the commencement of a spring tidal cycle rather than at the end when the soil may be approaching saturation. The entry of water by gravita-

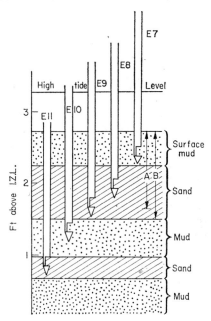

FIG. 5.4. *Plover marsh, Scolt Head Island, away from a creek. Morning tide, 28 June 1934.* E 10, E 11 *flooded;* E 11 *recorded,* E 7 *to* E 9 *no record.* A, *definite aerated layer;* B, *probable extent of aerated layer.*

tional and lateral seepage results in the gradual elevation of the soil water table over a spring tidal cycle, whilst during the neap-tide cycle the water table slowly falls. Superimposed upon this cyclic movement will be the effect of each single tide, though the effect here is likely to be restricted to a zone adjacent to each creek. Water will not effectively start to drain out of the soil into the creeks until the

water level in the creeks is below that of the soil water table in the
adjacent marsh. Because of the occlusion of air in the surface mud
layer, it is not really possible to follow water table movements by
digging pits in the soil. The movement can be followed by using
tubes perforated in the lower portion, the bottom opening being
closed by a wooden plug, and employing a graduated stick to determine the water level in the tubes. Between measurements the upper
opening is kept closed by a cork. An electrical circuit recording
technique has also been used[8] with success on marshes, though it
cannot be used where there is a peat soil, which tends to remain
saturated.

AERATED LAYER

Use of tubes and recorders has shown quite clearly that the soil
water table never rises completely to the surface, even during a
flooding tide[7]. Therefore there is always an aerated layer just below
the surface. How the recorders and tubes demonstrate the existence
of this layer is illustrated in Fig. 5.4. Further evidence of the
aerated layer can be obtained by plunging a stick into the soil when
the tide is covering it, and then on withdrawing the stick bubbles of
gas emerge. This gas can be collected over a glycerine–sea water
mixture and analysed. As may be expected, the composition is quite
different from that of the atmosphere, the oxygen content being
greatly reduced and the CO_2 content greatly increased (Table 5.1).

TABLE 5.1

Per cent composition of Salt Marsh Gas

	Asteretum				Limonium bellidifolium	
	a	b	c	d	a	b
$CO_2 + H_2S$*	2·99	2·55	3·26	4·22	1·46	0·93
O_2	1·61	0·82	0·71	1·42	10·5	17·5

* This is present in small amounts.

This gas must have an influence upon root respiration and the low
oxygen may account for the development of aerenchyma* that seems
to have occurred with many salt marsh species.

The composition of this gas varies considerably over a single
marsh and from marsh to marsh, and probably seasonally as well.
Manometers which can be carefully inserted into the soil at different
depths also demonstrate the existence of the aerated layer, and

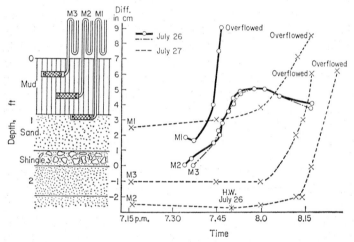

FIG. 5.5. *Effect of rising tide on aerated layer in a* Juncetum.
Manometers during evening tides, 26 and 27 July 1934 (after
Chapman).

confirm that during a flood tide the rising water table exerts a
pressure upon the occluded gas (Fig. 5.5). When the distribution of
roots in the various soil strata is studied, the great majority are found
to be in the surface mud layer, which is mostly occupied by the
aerated zone. The great importance of this aerated layer to the plants
cannot be over-estimated, and it is likely that many species would not
be able to grow at low levels on the marshes without it.

* Tissue with numerous large air spaces: usually cortex and pith.

SOIL SALINITY

Of the chemical constituents in the soil, the chloride and sodium ions are by far the most important.* They determine the salinity of the environment, and the amount present is dependent upon a number of factors first enunciated by Morss[16]. Some of these factors have already been mentioned in connection with other aspects of the habitat: such factors are height of the preceding tide, i.e. whether flooding or restricted to creeks; rainfall, which can bring about downward leaching of salts; proximity to creeks (drainage); mechanical composition of the soil, the soil colloids of a clay soil binding sodium ions more strongly than in a sandy soil; height of marsh in relation to frequency of flooding; slope of ground and its effect on rate of run-off after flooding; proximity of any fresh water inflow; depth of water table, as the nearer this is to the surface the more constant will be the soil salinity; presence of vegetation and the type of vegetation. The plants reduce evaporation from the soil surface and their transpiration is responsible for a continual rise of soil water from the lower layers.

It is very difficult to distinguish between the effect of the tides (through submergence and emergence) and of salinity in determining the zonation that can be observed on salt marshes. One answer to this problem rests with experimental work on the salinity tolerance of the dominant species, associated with extensive field sampling of soils over extended periods of time. Any experimental work on salinity tolerance must take into consideration the age of the plant, because it seems likely that adult plants are very much more tolerant than seedlings. Seedling establishment is the first essential, and it is therefore of greatest importance to study the effect of salinity on germination and early stages of growth.

Salinity and Germination

The results obtained to date indicate that the great majority of

* In the following pages, salinity studies have been expressed in terms of osmotic pressure, percentage of NaCl, or percentage of soluble chloride.

salt marsh plants show maximum germination under fresh water conditions. It will be indicated later (p. 124) that germination time for many species on salt marshes is correlated with a period of minimum surface soil salinity, and it is this that enables some species, at least, to occur where they do. So far as germination is concerned, the effect of high salinity is essentially to inhibit the process, because if ungerminated seeds are transferred to fresh water they will then

TABLE 5.2

Percentage Germination after 28 Days

	*Spartina townsendii**	*Phragmites communis*	*Aster tripolium*	*Spergularia marginata*	*Salicornia stricta*	*Suaeda maritima*	*Juncus maritimus*	*Artemisia maritima*	*Halimione portulacoides* ecovar latifolia	*H. portulacoides* ecovar. parvifolia
Tap water	80	4	45	66	93	4	50	86	83·3	25
1 per cent NaCl	21	32	25	4	45	0	18	8	50	8·3
2 per cent NaCl	15	16	10	0	36	4	5	0	8·3	0
Sea water	3	0	0	0	38	0	0	0	0	0
5 per cent NaCl	0	0	0	0	36	0	0	0	0	0
10 per cent NaCl	0	0	0	0	12	0	0	0	0	0

* Jacquet, 1949.

germinate. There is evidence that the prehistory of the parent plants may play some part in growth of the seedlings of some species.

There is, however, very little information available and further studies of this nature, as well as more work on the effect of salinity on germination, would be very welcome. Some typical germination results that have been obtained are set out in Table 5.2.

It is evident that very few species will tolerate more than 2 per cent sodium chloride, and that of the species tested the annual *Salicornia stricta* is the only one with any real tolerance and this explains why it is such a successful colonist, not only at low levels but also on salt pans at high levels where soil salinity can rise to very high values. There is also some evidence[9] that lowering the temperature enables germination of certain species to take place at increased salinities. This is certainly the case with *Spergularia marginata*, but it is an aspect which requires much more experimental work in relation to concurrent field studies. It has also been reported that light intensity affects the germination of seeds of Sea arrow-grass (*Triglochin maritima*), *Spergularia marginata* and Sea milkwort (*Glaux maritima*). Since plants from inland salt regions of Europe were used for this work, its repetition and extension, using maritime plants, is essential. Suitable simple experiments would not be difficult, using lattice screens to provide different degrees of light intensity.

Salinity and Growth

Once the seeds have germinated, subsequent growth is also affected by soil salinity. Thus with Annual glasswort (*Salicornia stricta* = *S. europaea*) optimum growth occurs between 1·5 and 2·5 per cent NaCl[2, 11, 14], whereas with Sea aster (*Aster tripolium*) it lies between 0·5 and 1·0 per cent. This, however, is a field in which much more experimental information is required, correlated with salinity determinations from the marshes. Ultimately it will be necessary to try and relate growth phenomena to either the sodium or chloride ions, since there is no doubt that the effect of these two ions is quite different on the development of morphological features such as succulence. In the meantime, the operation of NaCl upon growth needs much more investigation. The general effect appears to be one of dwarfing of plants, such reduction being commonly ascribed to the high osmotic pressures engendered in the cells. There are, however, other possibilities, such as the water-logging of very clayey soils through the effect of sodium on soil colloid dispersion, with the result that reducing conditions inimical to plants are produced. Other possibilities involve ion antagonism and the effect of sodium on the calcium metabolism. Salinity as such cannot be the only factor affecting growth and it must need be studied in relation to other factors of the environment, such as light intensity and drainage. In the case of adult plants, there is evidence that *Salicornia* spp., *Spergularia marginata*, Sea aster (*Aster tripolium*), *Glaux*, Sea plantain (*Plantago maritima*), Sea poa (*Puccinellia maritima*), Sea lavender (*Limonium vulgare*) and *Spartina* spp., are all tolerant of high salinities, so that their occurrence in an area may well depend upon the tolerance of the seedlings. On the other hand, Mud rush (*Juncus gerardi*), Fiorin (*Agrostis stolonifera*) and *Scirpus* spp. are intolerant of high salinity. More work has been done in the United States on this aspect than in Europe and further work on European species is much to be desired.

In some of the work in this field, the salinity of both soil solution and of the plants growing in the soil has been expressed in terms of osmotic pressures, the argument being that because of the high excess of sodium chloride the osmotic pressures will be proportional to the amount of NaCl present. This, however, is not always true, because in the Shrubby seablite (*Suaeda fruticosa*) only 42 per cent of the osmotic pressure is due to the chloride ion, whereas in *Salicornia stricta* it is 91 per cent. Further examples of such variations are given in Table 5.3.

A further complication is that the osmotic pressures of different parts of the plant can vary, that of leaf cells commonly being much higher than those of roots or stem. This means that a great deal of the earlier work will need to be repeated.

Salinity Variations

A detailed study by the present writer[8] of the Scolt marshes indicated that a fairly regular horizontal gradient in the soluble chloride could be observed in the 3 in. and 9 in. soil layers of the principal prisere communities. The same gradient existed in the surface layer during the winter, but evaporation during the hot summer months

E

exerts a profound effect upon bare soil and upon high marshes with low vegetation, such as the General Salt Marsh and Plantaginetum maritimi (p. 97). In the Juncetum the tall character of the vegetation lowers evaporation and hence surface salinity does not rise in the

TABLE 5.3

Osmotic Pressures of Cell-sap of Various Halophytes and Proportion Due to Chloride Ion (after Arnold)

Species	No. of determinations	O.P. sap (atm)	Proportion O.P. sap due to Cl⁻ (atm)	Cl⁻ as per cent O.P. sap.
Atriplex patula var. *hastata*	6	31·6	13·3	42
Suaeda fruticosa	15	35·2	15·3	43
Glaux maritima	2	14·6	7·4	51
Juncus gerardi	3	27·8	15·5	56
Triglochin maritima	10	24·6	16·1	66
Scirpus maritimus	2	14·7	10·4	71
Salicornia rubra	11	44·3	31·5	71
Spartina patens	4	20·9	15·7	75
Salicornia ambigua	6	42·5	34·1	80
S. stricta (*herbacea*)	10	39·7	35·9	91
S. mucronata	3	34·0	31·5	93
		Av. 32·6		

summer. In the Phragmitetum the habit of the dominant species (*Phragmites communis*) and also the influence of fresh water modify the salinity.

While some workers[19, 21] have recorded salinity gradients with increasing soil depth, irregularities have been recorded elsewhere. During parts of the year there may be a gradient with depth but on English marshes studied[8] there is a lack of regularity. Rainfall can have a marked temporary effect upon the salinity gradient, particularly at the higher levels on a marsh. The lower communities show the least effect of rainfall whilst the higher communities exhibit the greatest influence of rainfall and tidal inundation. One may expect to find some form of salinity gradient with depth, but it is likely to be

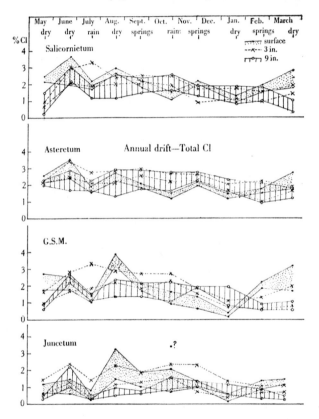

FIG. 5.6. *Annual drift at surface, 3 in. and 9 in. levels of the total chloride in four Norfolk salt marsh communities. The widths of the bands indicate the degree of variation found at each soil level (after Chapman).*

more pronounced in summer on high marshes with low vegetation, and it also can be subject to modification by excessive rainfall and abnormal tides.

The seasonal changes in salinity on salt marshes are perhaps of most importance because they affect germination and seedling establishment (p. 118). On the Norfolk marshes, the principal feature is an early spring fall in the soluble chloride of the surface soil (Fig. 5.6). This spring fall has been recorded for salt marshes in the U.S.A. and New Zealand, and it is this lowering of the surface salinity that permits the germination of salt marsh species. The extent to which the salinity is lowered must vary from year to year and hence the occurrence of annuals for any year will vary somewhat from marsh to marsh.

Sodium Ion

A similar study has been made of the exchangeable sodium present in these soils. Since the sodium ion is adsorbed to the clay particles, it will not always be present in the exchangeable form in a molecular ratio to the soluble chloride. In fact, the exchangeable sodium at Scolt only accounted for a fraction of the total soluble chloride in the surface and 3 in. layers. In the more sandy subsoil at 9 in. there is less adsorption of the sodium and the values obtained frequently equalled those expected on a molecular ratio basis. There is, however, no comparable seasonal drift with a January–February minimum as is found with the soluble chloride, nor was there any real correlation between the behaviour of the soluble chloride and exchangeable sodium. This, however, is by no means universally true and the Norfolk phenomena may be associated with the considerable variation exhibited by the different salt marsh soils. It is possible that on the sandy marshes of the west coast, where the soil is more uniform, that a correlation between the behaviour of the two ions would be found.

It is interesting to compare the variations that occur in the chloride and sodium of plants growing on salt marsh soils with the corresponding values for the soils. This has been done for the annual *Salicornia stricta* (Fig. 5.7), and it will be seen that for this species, at least, there is no correlation between the amounts absorbed by the plants and those present in the soil. This, however, is only an isolated investigation and other species may behave quite differently, but at present we have no data.

There is still plenty of scope for further studies on all aspects of salinity and salinity tolerance of salt marsh species, as also on the control of high osmotic pressures arising from habitats rich in sodium chloride and also on the effect of high salinities upon transpiration, though this last probably plays little or no part in controlling zonation on marshes. So far as osmotic pressure control is concerned, salt marsh plants can be grouped into three classes:

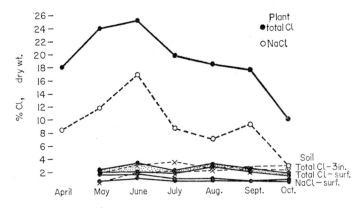

Fig. 5.7. *Relation of total chloride and chloride equivalent of the exchangeable sodium in plants of* Salicornia stricta *compared with the amounts in the surrounding soil (lower bands) (after Chapman).*

(a) Succulents, in which salt uptake is compensated for by water intake, though at the end of the season the succulent portion may dry up and be sloughed off, e.g. *Salicornia* species.

(b) Salt excreting forms, e.g. *Limonium, Spartina, Glaux,* where special glands remove salt to the exterior, though the extent to which the amount of salt removed prevents the osmotic pressure from rising is not known.

(c) No special mechanism other than leaf death at the end of the season. If the leaves contain much accumulated salt, their death and decay removes the salt from the plant.

Salinity and Transpiration

Studies on the effect of salinity upon transpiration are difficult to interpret because of the various criteria used to express the transpiration rate, e.g. dry weight, surface area, fresh weight. There seems little doubt that halophytes have a lower number of stomata per unit area than do non-halophytes, but if transpiration rate is expressed on a leaf area basis, the rate can be higher than that of non-halophytes. The fact that a halophyte can transpire $1-2\frac{1}{2}$ times its weight of water daily would seem to indicate that salt marsh plants have no undue difficulty in absorbing water from their apparently unfavourable medium, and that transpiration proceeds at a rate not far different from that of non-halophytes. There is also some evidence[11] which indicates it is the effect of specific ions upon the transpiration rate that is more important than molecular substances such as excess sodium chloride.

OTHER IONS

Apart from sodium and chloride ions, relatively little work has been carried out upon other ions present in salt marsh soils. Some data are available for areas in Holland, Denmark and the Southern Hemisphere, but practically none for Great Britain. This is perhaps surprising when one considers the potential agricultural value of the marshes once they have been reclaimed. Indeed, it would be of the utmost value to follow the changes that occur, not only in the vegetation, but also in the soil chemistry and physics when a salt marsh is enclosed.

On the Norfolk marshes, changes in exchangeable calcium have been followed, but it was not possible to correlate them with either rainfall or tidal inundations. The data did indicate the existence of a horizontal gradient between communities in most of the soil layers but until further work has been carried out on other marshes it would be premature to make any generalization.

SOIL MOISTURE

The moisture content of salt marsh soils has been studied in some detail, but in view of its great variability it cannot be regarded as a factor that plays a part in determining zonation of the vegetation. In some cases a gradient may exist whereas in other cases it is absent or barely detectable. It is therefore apparent that further work on the soil moisture content would be very desirable. The nature of any vertical gradient would appear to depend on the geological structure of the marsh, and in particular on the nature and depth of the surface mud. Where there is a transition from clay to sand, there will be a marked gradient, particularly on high marshes where the soil water table is likely to be at some depth.

BIOTA

Animals are of great importance on a rocky coast (p. 76). On a salt marsh coast comparatively little is known about their role, though grazing by cattle and sheep can be very important on the grassy marshes (see p. 95), and before the incidence of myxomatosis, rabbit grazing undoubtedly affected the habit of some plants and the composition of certain communities.

PANS

The pans that form such a characteristic feature of salt marshes are worthy of study because they can well be compared with rock pools. Apart from their existence in upper or lower marshes (p. 110), they have been subdivided into hard and soft-floored pans[11] or into saline and less saline pans[17]. The salinity of the water depends on height and hence frequency of flooding, rainfall, whether there is layering or not, and the nature of the mud bottom. Layering will only occur if the pan is deep, but it may be quite significant (Fig. 5.8). After a dry period, if the pan becomes filled with rain water, there will be diffusion of salt outward from the mud so that the lower water layers are more saline than the upper. The oxygen content of the pan water depends upon the type and abundance of animal and plant life as well as upon the height of the pool in relation to tidal flooding. As one may expect, there is generally a rise in the oxygen concentration around midday (Fig. 5.8) as a result of photosynthesis. Remarkably little study has been undertaken of salt pans, both in regards to their flora and the conditions under which it exists. In view of the circumscribed nature of the habitat, salt pans are as excellent for field study as are rock pools.

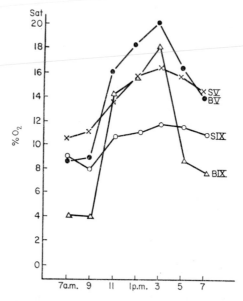

FIG. 5.8. *Diurnal variations in oxygen concentration in the diatom pool (pool* IX), *and in pool* V (Enteromorpha-Ulva). B, *bottom layers;* S, *surface layers (after Nichol).*

AUTECOLOGY

In so far as many of the species found on salt marshes are restricted to the salt marsh habitat, there is plenty of scope for autecological studies. This is an aspect of salt marsh ecology that has not received much attention, though valuable work has been done on the hybrid Cord grass, *Spartina townsendii*. Thus its germination and growth requirements, soil preferences and climatic limits are quite well

known. We also know that there is much dissemination by means of
rhizome fragments being carried around by the sea, that under certain conditions individual plants develop into clumps, the centres of
which subsequently die and become invaded by secondary growth[3],
that under certain soil toxic conditions "die back" occurs[12, 13], that
its great success may be correlated among other things with the

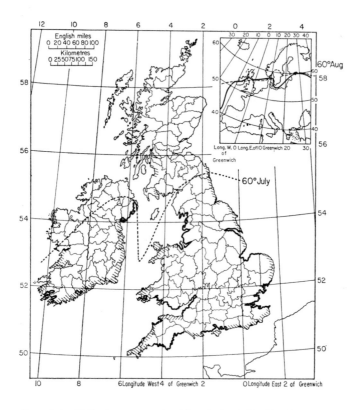

FIG. 5.9. Halimione portulacoides (L.) *Aell. Distribution in
British Isles and (inset) northern limits in Europe.* ■ = *extant.*
▨ = *probably extinct.* ▩ = *recorded in these vice-
counties but not seen by author or other persons other than
where full black (after Chapman).*

presence of two kinds of root, fine absorbing rootlets and deep, stout anchoring roots and quick-growing runners.

A study[5, 10] of Sea purslane (*Halimione portulacoides*) has shown that there are two main varieties, *latifolia* and *parvifolia*, which differ in their ecological requirements, the former being characteristic of creek banks and shingle borders and the latter of high sandy marshes. Both require good drainage conditions and var. *latifolia* seems to be susceptible to stock grazing. There is a close correlation between the 60° July isotherm and the northern limit of the species in Great Britain (Fig. 5.9) so that the northern limit could well be determined by temperature. Autecological studies are important because they help us to understand the limiting factors and behaviour within the habitat of a particular species. Only by combining field investigations with experiments under controlled conditions near the laboratory, can the autecology of any species be understood.

REFERENCES

[1] ARNOLD A., Die Bedeutung der Chlorionen für die Pflanzen. *Bot. Stud.*, Vol. 2. Jena (1955).

[2] BAUMEISTER W. and SCHMIDT L., Über die Rolle des Natriums in Pflanzlichen Stoffwechsel. *Flora*, **152** (1), 24–56 (1962).

[3] CALDWELL P. A., The spatial development of *Spartina* colonies growing without competition. *Ann. Bot.*, N.S. **21** (82), 203–214 (1957).

[4] CAREY A. E. and OLIVER F. W., *Tidal Lands: a Study of Shore Problems*. Blackie, London (1918).

[5] CHAPMAN V. J., A note upon *Obione portulacoides* (L.) Gaert. *Ann. Bot.*, N.S. **1** (2), 305–310 (1937).

[6] CHAPMAN V. J., Marsh development in Norfolk. *Trans. Norf. Norw. Nat. Soc.*, **14** (4), 394–397 (1938).

[7] CHAPMAN V. J., Studies in salt marsh ecology, I–III. *J. Ecol.*, **26** (1), 144–179 (1938).

[8] CHAPMAN V. J., Studies in salt marsh ecology, IV–V. *J. Ecol.*, **27** (1), 160–201 (1939).

[9] CHAPMAN V. J., The new perspective in the halophytes. *Quart. Rev. Biol.*, **17** (4), 291–311 (1942).

[10] CHAPMAN V. J., *Halimione portulacoides* (L.) Aell. in *Biological Flora of the British Isles. J. Ecol.*, **38** (1), 214–222 (1950).

[11] CHAPMAN V. J., *Salt Marshes and Salt Deserts of the World*. Leon. Hill, London (1961).

[12] GOODMAN P. J., Investigations into "die-back" in *Spartina townsendii* agg. II. *J. Ecol.*, **48**, 711–724 (1960).

[13] GOODMAN P. J. and WILLIAMS, W. J., Investigations into "die-back" in *Spartina townsendii* agg. III. *J. Ecol.*, **49** (2), 391–398 (1961).

[14] MONTFORT C. and BRANDRUP W., Physiologische und pflanzengeographische Seesalzwirkungen. II: Ökologische Studien über Keimung und erste Entwicklung bei Halophyten. *Jb. Wiss. Bot.*, **66** (5), 902–946 (1927).

[15] MONTFORT C. and BRANDRUP W., Physiologische und Pflanzengeographische Seesalzwirkungen. III. *Jb. Wiss. Bot.*, **67** (1), 105 (1928).

[16] MORSS W. L., The plant colonization of merselands in the estuary of the River Nith. *J. Ecol.*, **15**, 310–343 (1927).

[17] NICHOL E. A. T., The ecology of a salt marsh. *J. Mar. Biol. Ass. U.K.*, **20**, 203–261 (1935).

[18] NIENBURG W. and KOLUMBE E., Zur Ökologie der flora des Wattenmeeres, II. *Wiss. Meer. Kiel.* N.F. **21–22**, 77 (1931).

[19] PURER E. A., Plant ecology of the coastal salt marshlands of San Diego County, California. *Ecol. Monog.*, **12**, 81–111 (1942).

[20] STEERS J. A., *Scolt Head Island*. The Physiography and Evolution. Heffer, Cambridge (1960).

[21] STEINER M., Zur Ökologie der salzmarschen der Nordöstlichen vereinigten Staaten von Nordamerika. *Jb. Wiss. Bot.*, **81**, 94–202 (1934).

[22] WIEHE P. O., A quantitative study of the influence of the tide upon populations of *Salicornia europaea*. *J. Ecol.*, **23**, 323–333 (1935).

CHAPTER 6

Sand Dune Vegetation

OCCURRENCE

THE accumulations of sand that go to form sand dunes are almost entirely confined to coastal regions in Great Britain, though elsewhere far greater areas are occupied by dunes in the interior arid and semi-arid continental regions. Maritime sand dunes of Great Britain cover an area almost as great as that occupied by salt marshes. Like the marshes they are essentially confined to coastal plains, and are not to be found where there are steep cliffs just behind the beach. The habitat, particularly in its early stages, is characterized by special features, and in consequence the plants that occupy the early phases of sand dunes are restricted to certain species that can tolerate these conditions. The flora of the dunes as a whole contains a proportion of characteristic species, but is not so specialized as that of salt marshes. Some interesting species are, however, recorded in the dune flora, such as *Primula scotica* from Caithness and the Mediterranean ball rush (*Holoschoenus vulgaris*) from Somerset[34].

The names applied locally to sand dunes vary in different parts of the country. Thus in East Anglia they are known as "meols" or "meals", whilst in Cornwall and Devon they are called "towans" or "burrows"; in Wales they are known as "warrens" and in Scotland as "links". The maximum height reached by dunes in England and Wales is about 60 ft, but in the Culbin Sands they may reach an elevation of 100 ft. There appears to be no reason why these heights should not be exceeded, as they certainly are in other parts of the world.

FORMATION

There are two major phenomena that enable maritime dune formation to proceed. The first and most important is a supply of sand together with wind to move it, and the second is plant colonization. The supply of sand comes from the sand flats that are exposed at low tide, and on a windy day the movement of sand can not only be seen but felt. Blown sand is deposited wherever the wind drops, as in passing over a hillock or if it meets an obstacle, and the sand accumulates on the protected lee side. Plant colonization in the early stages assists in the further growth of dunes because plants represent obstacles, whilst the roots at the same time help to "fix" the sand already there although this function is not important. As the cover becomes more and more complete and other dunes form in front and cut off the sand supply, so the dune first gradually ceases to grow higher and is finally stabilized.

After dunes have been colonized and covered by plants, erosion may take place (see p. 187) should the vegetation cover become broken. When this happens, the wind can act on the exposed bare sand and secondary movement of sand then takes place. In the early stages the excavated area is known as a "blow-out", and, if not stopped, erosion proceeds until the whole dune has been removed, very often with the formation of a mobile dune. This has happened in the Culbin area of Scotland and also in some of the west coast dune areas.

DRIFT-LINE

Dune formation often begins on the drift-line where, amidst the mass of sodden flotsam and jetsam, plants can and do make their appearance[6]. Around these plants, small mounds develop, though whether any further growth occurs depends on how high the sand rises. We may therefore commence our study of sand dunes by a brief look at the drift-line vegetation.

Over a year more than one drift-line can be observed on a beach, but plants are generally restricted to the uppermost line, where there is the greatest stability. The drift-line occurs not only on the fore-shore, but, in the case of off-shore barrier islands and spits, it is also represented on the protected shoreward side where it rests at the base of the dunes or shingle ridges or else is evident on the highest marshes. The foreshore drift-line, which can be subject to storm tides, is poor in species, though these can be, and often are, the fore-runners of dunes. The plants are generally scattered, and there is no develop-ment into any form of closed vegetation. Most of the species are annuals, and it is noteworthy that they belong to about three families (Cruciferae, Chenopodiaceae and Polygonaceae). The principal fore-shore representatives are *Salsola kali* (Saltwort), *Cakile maritima* (Sea rocket), *Honkenya peploides* (Sea sandwort), *Agropyron juncei-forme* (Sand couch grass), *Atriplex littoralis* (Shore orache) and *A. hastata* (Hastate orache).

Sometimes these plants do not appear to be located in relation to the current drift-line, but if they are excavated it will be found that their roots are associated with a buried former drift-line. Although the species grow at the upper tidal limit, they cannot endure pro-longed immersion in sea water. Characteristically they have fleshy leaves and provision for water storage, either in the leaves (*Cakile*, *Honkenya*) or in special hairs (species of *Atriplex*), such water storage being regarded as one means of meeting the considerable osmotic pressures of tissues that result from the roots being in highly saline water. Thus Salisbury[34] records the following osmotic pres-sures in these plants:

Honkenya peploides	15·5–18·5 atm
Atriplex littoralis	37+atm
Euphorbia peplis	9–20 atm
Salsola kali	11–30·6 atm

In the non-halophytes the osmotic pressure of the sap is around 5–7 atm.

In the protected localities behind dunes and on marshes, the same species may occur, but others also enter into the community and very often are more abundant. Thus at Scolt Head in Norfolk, the drift-line between dune and salt marsh may possess the Shrubby sea-blite (*Suaeda fruticosa*), *Artemisia maritima* (Sea wormwood), *Beta vulgaris* ssp. *maritima* (sea beet), Danish scurvy-grass (*Cochlearia danica*), and Buck's-horn plantain (*Plantago coronopus*). Elsewhere in other parts of Great Britain Seakale (*Crambe maritima*), Northern shore-wort (*Mertensia maritima*) (usually associated with shingle), Woody nightshade (*Solanum dulcamara*), Sea radish (*Raphanus maritimus*), Shore knotgrass (*Polygonum littorale*), Ray's knotgrass (*P. raii*), Sea knotgrass (*P. maritimum*), and Babington's orache (*Atriplex glabriuscula*) belong to this community. In all localities one can find casuals that clearly come from some other habitat—dune or shingle, e.g. Sea heath (*Frankenia laevis*), Sea spurge (*Euphorbia paralias*), Curled dock (*Rumex crispus*), Matted Sea lavender (*Limonium bellidifolium*) and Sea campion (*Silene maritima*).

The species of Orache (*Atriplex*) are often the most abundant, though on salt marsh *Artemisia maritima* can form extensive areas. Whether the latter is a characteristic drift-line species, or is rather a denizen of the salt marsh, has yet to be settled. It is regarded as a nitrophile, and there is no doubt that the drift-line is very rich in nitrogen from the decaying organic matter.

Not only is the drift-line habitat extremely unstable, since there is the ever-present prospect of smothering from sand or a fresh supply of debris, but the soil water, particularly on the foreshore, does not depart very greatly from the composition of sea water. Up to the present, the drift-line community has not been subjected to serious study and, apart from *Suaeda fruticosa*, very little is known about the requirements of the individual species, or even about the nature of the environment. One interesting feature about it is that the working depth for the roots of different species is about the same[12] (Table 6.1).

The common Sea rocket (*Cakile maritima*) appears capable of tolerating some degree of sand covering, but it succumbs if the process is too frequent or the covering too great[6]: Sand couch grass

TABLE 6.1

(*After Gimingham*)

	Depth of longest root in inches		Length of longest lateral in inches		Position of longest lateral below surface in inches		
	Mean	Max.	Mean	Max.	Mean	Min.	Max.
Salsola kali	8·8	14·5	8·0	13·0	2·8	1·5	4·5
Atriplex glabriuscula	9·5	13·5	8·7	16·0	2·7	2·0	3·5
A. sabulosa (laciniata)	6·7	8·5	3·3	4·0	2·4	2·0	3·0
Agropyron junceiforme	8·2	10·0	6·3	12·5	1·5	1·5	2·0

(*Agropyron junceiforme*), on the other hand, is capable of thriving under such conditions.

The Mediterranean *Suaeda fruticosa* (Shrubby seablite) reaches its northern limit in Norfolk and South Wales. Experiments have shown[5] that it is not tolerant to water-logging, but apart from this factor two requirements are essential for its successful establishment. The first is the tide which brings the seed and the seed-bed material (debris). The second is a period of quiescence, when the drift-line is not disturbed, so that young plants do not become buried by sand or shingle before they are established. Once they are established, further burying stimulates them to send up new shoots (see p. 202). The conditions under which plants such as *Salsola* and *Cakile* will exist need to be determined and then experimental work undertaken to confirm them. The drift-line is a fertile field of investigation that quite clearly merits much further work.

DUNE CLASSIFICATION

Before describing the various stages of dune building and the plants associated with them, some brief mention must be made of dune classification. Various authors have attempted to classify dunes —mainly from a physiographic viewpoint. One simple classification[38] is as follows:

(a) *Accumulation forms*. In these dunes the vegetation becomes predominant and a successive series of new dunes arise in front of each other.

(b) *Fixation forms*. These refer to the older dunes in a series of ridges, which have been gradually deprived of their sand supply. The valleys or hollows that exist between such dune ridges are known as "slacks" or "lows" (see p. 151 et seq).

(c) *Remanié forms*. These result from erosion of the fixation forms as a result of wind attack if the vegetation cover is broken by some agency. If a dune undergoing erosion is stabilized, it represents a moderate remanié form, but in other cases practically the entire dune may be removed and in its place a mobile dune appears.

(d) *Parabolic dunes*. These can arise as above, or they may develop where the sand supply is particularly plentiful and the vegetation covering is inadequate, particularly in the centre of the dune as compared with the sides. In such cases the higher central part continues to grow and move forward. The continual moving of the sand over the top forms a sharp lee side, and gradually a parabolic dune is formed, i.e. a dune concave to the direction of the prevailing wind, the sides of which are held back by the vegetation covering. These dunes are the exact opposite of the crescentic dunes or barchans so typical of deserts, where there is no vegetation to control the two ends, which then move faster than the centre. Such dunes may later be broken through by a wind channel in the centre leaving two flanks on either side[44]. The orientation of the two flanks could lead one to think that wind was not involved in their formation. It has been pointed out[4] that records of wandering parabolic dunes in Europe are all of relatively recent date, and the question has been asked whether such dunes are the result of man's negligence or overexploitation. There is no doubt that elsewhere desert conditions have been induced by man (Egyptian desert and central Otago desert in New Zealand), and mobile coastal dunes may therefore be symptomatic of the same cause.

There is, however, another possible explanation. Mobile dunes may be associated with sinking shore-lines, when the sea increasingly brings about erosion of the fore-dunes. It is therefore worth noting that the present land sinking (south-east England and the Low Countries) commenced relatively recently (geologically speaking) (see p. 89 and Fig. 4.7).

Several authors[19, 36, 40] have proposed more elaborate systems of dune classification but these go beyond the scope of this book.

WIND AND VEGETATION

Emphasis has been laid throughout upon the importance of wind[44]. On the western coasts of England, Wales and Scotland, westerly winds blow steadily for most of the year. In the presence of drift-line vegetation these winds produce a succession of dune ridges which pass through the stages of vegetation development described in the next section. Elsewhere parabolic dunes are produced and the resultant dune mass must be interpreted in the light of the various stages of mobility and erosion, as well as whether they occur singly, overlapping each other or in laterally connected bands. Such dune complexes are well exemplified at Braunton Burrows[43] and Newborough Warren[25, 26, 27]. On other coasts the westerly winds are not important, and dune growth is dependent almost wholly upon local on-shore winds, especially those of storm periods. On the west coast, the prevailing westerly winds encourage the formation of parabolic dunes which move landward and in so doing generally break down and leave the flanks behind (see p. 164). Stabilization of such dunes, apart from the flanks, may take a long time to effect, and, because of the movement over a bare, damp sand substrate important relations exist between the slacks and dune vegetation (see p. 155). The flanks of eroded parabolic dunes will pass through vegetation phases comparable to those found on parallel dune ridges, though the embryo

dune phase will be missing. Because of the different stages of formation and decay the parabolic dunes have reached, it is much more
difficult to trace the vegetation succession in such areas.

The prevailing mobility of dune systems on the west coast has
meant that old concepts[4] based upon relatively stable dunes have had
to be extensively revised in such ever-changing areas. For some years
now, dune areas have been favourite locations for military exercises,
and whilst these activities undoubtedly have done much to keep
such dunes in a mobile condition, there is little doubt that on the
west coast the dynamic nature of the dunes is of very long standing
(see also p. 163).

DUNE VEGETATION

We may now turn to a study of dune formation in relation to the
vegetation cover. Here it is evident that the dune vegetation is
ultimately related to the two main types of dune, i.e. calcareous and
non-calcareous. In the former, the high proportion of calcium carbonate results in a flora that contains a calcicole or "chalk-favouring"
element, whereas in the latter, conditions become acidic and lead to
plants typical of heath formations.

Embryo Dune

The early stage of dune formation is known as the *embryo* dune
phase and is very often an Agropyretum junceiformi. Here small
mounds of sand accumulate on the foreshore around plants of the
drift-line, especially Sea rocket (*Cakile*), Saltwort (*Salsola*), Sea
sandwort (*Honkenya*) and Sand couch grass (*Agropyron junceiforme*).
As the mounds rise, the couch grass becomes more prominent and
Marram grass (*Ammophila arenaria*) is able to invade as the possibility
of tidal inundation decreases. The mounds gradually spread and
eventually fuse to give a small fore-dune. The dominant plant on the
fore-dune is commonly *Agropyron* because it is able to withstand
occasional wetting with sea water. It readily thrives with 1·5 per cent
salt in the soil and can temporarily tolerate up to 6 per cent. Apart
from its tolerance towards sea water, it is a valuable plant in dune

formation because it possesses extensive underground rhizomes which send up new aerial shoots. The aerial shoots assist in the accumulation of more sand, whilst the roots help to bind the sand that is deposited.

It has been found that the earliest tillers of *Agropyron* are markedly prostrate, and give rise to a rosette of shoots adpressed to the sand. When several such young plants are adjacent, a network of shoots is formed and these gather sand to form a low hummock. With increasing age and density, the prostrate habit of the shoots is replaced by an erect habit. Horizontal rhizomes then grow out to a distance of 2–3 ft from these patches, and in the succeeding year they produce a new rosette of tillers. In this manner a whole series of embryo dunes is gradually built up.

In the absence of sand couch grass, the fore-dunes are generally colonized by the Lyme grass (*Elymus arenarius*) or by Marram, either of which invades hummocks that have developed around the drift-line plants. The success of *Ammophila* invasion is, however, dependent upon there not being any frequent tidal flooding.

Yellow Dune

The embryo dune phase is succeeded by the *yellow dune* phase, so called because there is still much bare sand to be colonized. Studies of maps of rapidly growing areas, such as Scolt and Blakeney, can give a fair indication of the rate of growth of dunes to the yellow dune stage.

The increase in height through sand trapped by the *Agropyron* and other drift-line plants enables the marram grass to enter the community and form an Ammophiletum characteristic of this phase. Earlier entry by Marram grass is prevented by its reaction to salt, since it cannot tolerate more than 2 per cent in the soil. The erect shoots trap more sand, and indeed the more the sand covering, the more vigorous are the *Ammophila* plants. At the same time the horizontal rhizomes and the deep-going roots act as most effective sand stabilizing agents. Despite the deep roots the open *Ammophila* habitat is one in which drought conditions may prevail, especially in summer months. Structurally, the leaf possesses xeromorphic features, and in dry weather it also curls over so that water loss is still further reduced.

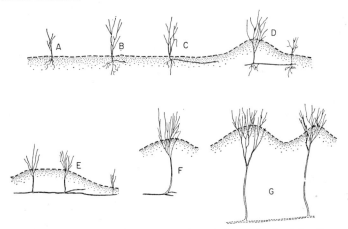

FIG. 6.1. *Diagrammatic representation of the mode of origin of a sand dune system caused by the growth of* Ammophila arenaria (*for explanation, see text*) (*after Greig-Smith* et al.).

It appears that the advent of the *Ammophila* can be by seed or by fragments of regenerating rhizome, rather like Cord grass (*Spartina townsendii*) (see p. 129). Generally it is likely that seedling establishment is sporadic but more observations are required. From the seedling or the rhizome fragment, a new horizontal rhizome appears (Fig. 6.1A–D). In the early stages the leafy shoots are generally unbranched and are not sufficiently dense to cause differential sand accumulation. When a shoot is overwhelmed by sand, one or more buds develop to produce a vertical shoot which develops leaves on reaching the surface (Fig. 6.1F). If sand accumulation continues, more shoots develop and the tussock habit, so characteristic of old dunes, is produced; the old rhizome then disintegrates (Fig. 6.1G), and is replaced by new adventitious roots nearer the soil surface[99, 14]. Indeed, a characteristic feature of many dune plants is their capacity to renew growth in response to sand covering. This can often be seen if a rooting system is carefully excavated.

It has been pointed out[6] that *Agropyron* and *Ammophila* on the embryo and yellow dunes respectively demonstrate how dominance can be achieved through unfavourable environmental conditions depressing or inhibiting potential competitors. The capacity of *Agropyron* to tolerate sea water enables it to dominate fore-dunes; the power of *Ammophila* to react vigorously to sand covering enables that species to dominate the yellow dune phase. Indeed, once the remaining bare sand has become covered by plants and there is no further supply of sand, the *Ammophila* tussocks commence to disintegrate. Short horizontal rhizomes are produced and these give rise to small, scattered leafy shoots that remain in the new vegetation. Whether the *Ammophila* actually becomes senescent or the response is to less favourable conditions has still to be established. It is a problem that should be capable of solution through experimental work. It has been suggested[39] that increased competition for water, lack of oxygen, or increased carbon dioxide in the soil atmosphere may be responsible. Alternatively, rate of growth may, normally, in the absence of sand covering, be so slow that it can no longer compete with other plants with a greater rate of growth.

Other species are associated with Marram, and as they have not been subjected to detailed study, they offer a fruitful field for investigation. Such species include the Lyme grass (*Elymus arenarius*), Sea sandwort (*Honkenya*), Sea convolvulus (*Calystegia soldanella*), Sea holly (*Eryngium maritimum*), Sea spurge (*Euphorbia paralias*), and Creeping fescue (*Festuca rubra* var. *arenaria*).

Some of the dune species spread into the community through vegetative growth, e.g. Sand sedge (*Carex arenaria*): others come from seed and produce a vertical root very rapidly and hence are soon anchored. This rapidity can be compared with much slower rooting establishment on low salt marsh (see p. 109). In the case of the Sea spurge (*Euphorbia paralias*), during the first 3–4 days after germination the root grows to a depth of 5–6 cm before the cotyledons have emerged, and within a fortnight the roots are down 10–15 cm into permanently moist sand.

The species (totalling about 26)[17] found in the early yellow dune phase or Ammophiletum can be regarded in the main as characteristic

dune plants which are rarely found elsewhere. The principal species
are as follows:

Agropyron junceiforme	*Ammophila arenaria*
Carex arenaria	*Honkenya peploides*
Eryngium maritimum	*Calystegia soldanella*
Euphorbia paralias	*Elymus arenarius*
E. portlandica†	*Festuca rubra* var. *arenaria*
Rhynchosinapis monensis*	*Thalictrum minus* ssp. *arenarium*
Viola tricolor ssp. *curtisii*	*Corynephorus canescens*

With increasing age, other species arrive, becoming ever more and
more abundant, until eventually the vegetation cover closes. Hepburn[17] noted over 250 species in dune localities with eighty or more
species widely dispersed on dune systems, though also occurring in
other habitats.

It is very evident from published lists of species from dunes in
different parts of the British Isles[3, 6, 8, 12, 13, 14, 16, 17, 22–27, 34, 35, 42, 43] that there is great diversity in the Ammophiletum. Apart from
those already mentioned other species, which are generally present
in such a community, include Wall-pepper (*Sedum acre*), *Erodium
cicutarium* ssp. *dunense*, Ragwort (*Senecio jacobaea*), and species of
Chickweed (*Cerastium*). Many additional species are only sporadic
and occur locally or are not present every year. This fact, coupled
with the great variability of the associated flora of older dunes, is
almost certainly due to accidental seeding, either by wind transport
or by human agency. An example of the latter can be observed in
places such as the ternery on Scolt Head Island, where the numerous
visitors are probably responsible for many of the casuals that have
been recorded. The erection of holiday huts on dunes often results in
a localized, associated flora introduced over the years consciously or
unwittingly by the hut occupants.

Moss Colonization

In the later stages of the Ammophiletum, particularly in depressions where the sand is fairly stable, mosses make their appearance

* West coast and Isle of Man.
† South and west coasts and Ireland.

and help in a minor manner to stabilize the sand. The principal species are *Tortula ruraliformis, Barbula fallax, Bryum pendulum* and *Brachythecium albicans*, though others may occur locally. In the case of *Barbula fallax*[10] there are regular growth increments with a heavy production of rhizoids at all subsurface levels. The net result is a cushion of some depth and sand-binding capacity. *Bryum pendulum*

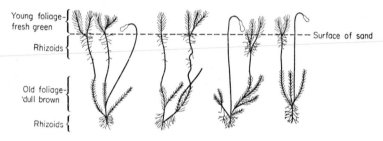

Young foliage—
fresh green

Rhizoids

Surface of sand

Old foliage—
dull brown

Rhizoids

FIG. 6.2. *Diagram of excavated shoots of* Bryum pendulum *Schp.*
(*after Gimingham*).

produces new shoots after burial, so that unless the sand is excessively mobile it readily becomes established (Fig. 6.2). Experimental work carried out by transplanting mosses to various dune sites or by burying them under known depths of sand[2] showed that no species appeared capable of tolerating a sand cover of 4 cm depth, but that species typical of the yellow dune phase were capable of emerging from under 3 cm. In the sand-covering experiments, marked powers of regeneration and recovery were also shown by *Pohlia annotina, Polytrichum piliferum* and *P. juniperinum* (Fig. 6.3). Despite this capacity to tolerate sand coverage, these last three species are generally restricted to the older stable dunes, and it may be that moisture requirement or some other factor prevents them from establishing themselves in the early dune states.

It has been pointed out[1] that dune mosses fall into three growth types, short turfs, mats and wefts (Fig. 6.4). Short turf mosses are essentially characteristic of the yellow dune phase whilst mats, represented by species such as *Brachythecium albicans, Eurhynchium praelongum*, are more abundant in the next stage—the grey dune phase, whilst on dune pasture one finds the wefts, such as *Hyloco-mium splendens* and *Hypnum cupressiforme*. Where there is abundant lime in the dune soil, *Camptothecium lutescens* will be present in quantity.

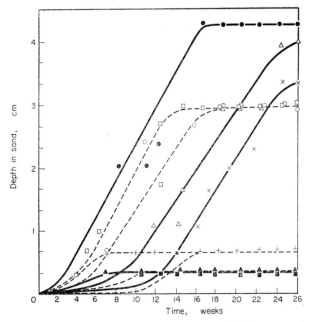

FIG. 6.3. *Time in weeks taken to recolonize half the area after burial under various depths of sand.* ●, Pohlia annotina; △, Polytrichum piliferum; ×, P. juniperinum; □, Tortula rurali-formis; ○, Brachythecium albicans; +, Rhytidiadelphus squarrosus; −, Bryum argenteum; ▲, Rhacomitrium canes-cens; ▧, Pleurozium schreberi (*after Brise* et al.).

Grey Dune

The yellow dune phase is succeeded by the fixed or *grey* dune phase, in which there is a complete vegetation cover. The species involved are extremely varied and it is not easy to provide any very generalized account. Some are strictly dune plants (see p. 143), but the great majority occur in other habitats. The name grey dune (an alternative is fixed dune) has been given to this stage because of the lichen invasion that occurs and gives a grey covering to the sand, the principal lichens being species of the genus *Cladonia*. The name could, however, well be applied to the greyish colour of such dunes when viewed from a distance, which is produced primarily by the glaucous green colour of the leaves of Marram.

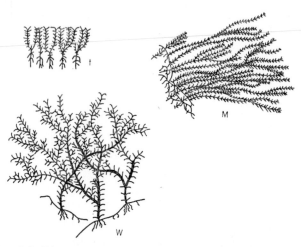

FIG. 6.4. *Diagrams of the three chief growth-form types repre-sented.* t, *short turf (viewed from side);* M, *mat (viewed from above)* W, *weft (viewed from side) (after Brise and Gimingham).*

Because there is such a great variation in the floras, dunes in different areas must be studied and lists of the species prepared. As Tansley[39] indicated, the plants are extremely varied and form, accord-ing to geographical situation, climatic region, and various physio-graphic, edaphic and particularly biotic factors, a considerable series of different communities. The final stage is either (a) grassland, especially on calcareous dunes (where grazing by rabbits or domestic animals takes place or the dunes are converted to golf courses, e.g. Southport, St. Andrews); (b) *Calluna* heath on non-calcareous dunes, particularly on the west and south coasts; (c) Forest, though natural forest does not occur on British dunes, probably because of the absence of suitable seed parents, or the restraining influence of human activities. The most successful trees on sand are species of pine or birch (acid dunes) and plantations are not uncommon in many parts of the British Isles. Such plantations provide an extremely effective means of stabilizing sand dunes and are planted for this purpose in many parts of the world. The great bulk of the British dunes terminate as grasslands, but Calluneta are recorded from Dorset[13], Walney Island[24], and in eastern Scotland[37], whilst at Newborough in Anglesey[27] *Calluna* is associated with *Salix repens* in the slacks (see p. 154).

Before the final stages are reached the *Ammophila* is gradually superseded by Creeping fescue (*Festuca rubra* var. *arenaria*) and Sand sedge (*Carex arenaria*), together with a host of associated plants including weft mosses and lichens. A feature of many of the phanerogams is their shallow rooting system, rather surprising in a habitat of this nature. The continual addition of plant remains brings about marked changes in soil colour. Originally this is white, if the sand has a high proportion of calcareous shell fragments, or yellow if it is largely composed of silica.

The grey dunes exhibit distinct seasonal aspects though these have not been widely studied. In the spring one can find a mass of ephemerals such as *Stellaria* spp., *Cerastium* spp., *Aira* spp. Later in the year taller plants, many of them perennials, take their place and give a splash of colour to the otherwise dull grey foliage of the grasses. The colour-providers include Lady's bedstraw (*Galium verum*), Restharrow (*Ononis repens*), *Thalictrum minus* ssp. *arenarium*, *Lactuca virosa*, Bird's foot trefoil (*Lotus corniculatus*), *Cirsium* spp. and Ragwort (*Senecio jacobaea*). Many of the species that occur are, as in the yellow dune phase, casuals, or else they are species with potential seed parents not too far away from the dunes. For full lists of species, reference should be made to the various accounts of dune systems that have appeared (see end of chapter). Among the lichens, which are essentially restricted to the grey dune phase, the most important genera are *Cladonia* and *Peltigera*, the former being particularly abundant and represented by about ten species. The entry of lichens into dune vegetation is dependent upon earlier moss colonization. Liverworts are generally rare, except in dune hollows where fresh water may be very near the surface or even form a pond.

Final Stages

With increasing age a greater proportion of non-maritime species enter the dune community, the exact nature of these species being determined to some extent by the acidity or alkalinity of the dune soil. Many of them can be regarded as "grass-heath" species which combine to give a dune pasture. In a comparison[34] of species lists for grey dunes at Blakeney (a non-calcareous dune region in eastern England) and in Co. Galway in western Ireland (a highly calcareous dune system), only seven were common to the two areas though each supported about forty species. If grazing is at all persistent or severe most of the maritime species disappear. The bracken will invade non-calcareous dune pasture if given an opportunity, and if not checked a closed bracken community can result. Such a community contains a few species not found on adjacent grass dune. The bracken will not, however, descend into damp hollows where there may be winter flooding. Once bracken is established on a dune system its further spread is almost wholly by vegetative means. On Braunton Burrows the mean rate of extension was found to be about 49 cm per year[43] so that its advance is slow but sure.

On acid soils heath vegetation develops, usually following on after the grassland stage (Walney) or direct from the Ammophiletum (Studland, Dorset). In such a heath both *Calluna vulgaris* and *Erica cinerea* are conspicuous elements. On the continent *Calluna* may be associated with *Genista littoralis*. Associated species in the heath stage are *Agrostis* sp., Sand sedge (*Carex arenaria*), Wavy hair-grass (*Deschampsia flexuosa*), Dwarf furze (*Ulex gallii*), and Gorse (*U. europaeus*). It is, however, impossible to provide a "typical" list because of the great local variations.

Dune scrub can be regarded as the fore-runner to indigenous forest, though in Great Britain even the scrub phase is not common. It consists of any of the spinous shrubs which can grow on light sandy soils. The Burnet rose (*Rosa spinosissina*) is a common species on calcareous dunes, whilst Bramble (*Rubus* sp.), *Ulex* (Gorse), Blackthorn (*Prunus spinosa*), other species of wild rose, and Elder (*Sambucus*) are also common components. There is only one shrub characteristically confined to the maritime dune habitat. This is the Sea buckthorn, *Hippophäe rhamnoides*, which is only indigenous on east coast dunes. It is very much more abundant on continental maritime dunes, where it is often associated with Privet (*Ligustrum vulgare*) and the two build up a form of macchia.

On the Dutch dunes the final stage is a low birch wood with *Hippophäe*, *Ligustrum* and *Berberis* into which the oak, *Quercus robur*, may eventually enter. In the Studland dunes, birch is to be found now and these trees may be the fore-runners of a birchwood. The final stage in northern Europe (and this would presumably apply also to Great Britain if the opportunity were available) is deciduous woodland which can be regarded as belonging to the Quercetum atlanticum in one or more of its many forms.

In other parts of the world, dune scrub as a fore-runner to dune forest is much more frequent, but in no part of the world has it received the amount of study it merits.

CRYPTOGAMIC VEGETATION

Sand dunes would not normally be regarded as a habitat in which many fungi could be found. Perhaps because of this relatively little work has been carried out upon them. When a list was made for the dunes of Scolt Head Island, it was found that there were no less than 15 Pyrenomycetes, 3 Discomycetes, 12 Fungi Imperfecti, 20 rust fungi, 5 smut fungi, 20 Agarics, 4 puff ball species, and the Stinkhorn, *Phallus impudicus*. Seven species of slime fungi (Mycetozoa) were also recorded. Whether this is typical of dune areas as a whole it is not possible to say, but it could be expected that the tall grasses, especially of the grey dune phase, would stop evaporation and keep the soil remains sufficiently moist for even agarics to grow satisfactorily. A number of the species found are of course parasites upon members of the phanerogamic vegetation (see also p. 183 for soil fungi). There is, however, also some evidence that open sand may be moister than that of grey dune, probably associated with no transpiration loss and a higher surface dew formation.

An interesting problem is presented by the development of the diatom flora of sand dunes. This has been studied by Round[31, 32] for Braunton Burrows and Harlech (we are only concerned here with the actual dunes, not the "slacks", for which see p. 153). On the dunes the diatom flora is restricted to the mosses, and it was shown that this epiphytic flora had been derived from the existing damp sand flora of the dune hollows or slacks.

SUCCESSION

The dune succession as described above is quite clearly a prisere, and since it develops on sand it is often known as a Psammosere. The principal communities of the succession are shown schematically on p. 151, though this "ideal" sequence is rarely found, except perhaps on some east coast dune areas. On the west coast, mobility of the dunes and the resulting interaction of dune and slack vegetation make for great complexity (see p. 155).

When grey dune or older dune pasture suffer a blow-out, provided the entire dune is not eroded away the blow-out may recolonize naturally and new dune builds up if there is still a source of sand. Under such circumstances one has an example of a cyclic process (see schema, next page).

The use of biological spectra has been referred to previously (see pp. 9, 10 and 103), and when such spectra are calculated for dunes and slacks, it is seen that the vegetation, like that of salt marshes, is essentially a hemicryptophyte flora.

Spectra for Newborough Warren (after Ranwell)

	Ph.	Ch.	H.	G.	H.	Th.
Dunes	4	11	40	5	0	40
Slacks	0	9	57	9	9	16

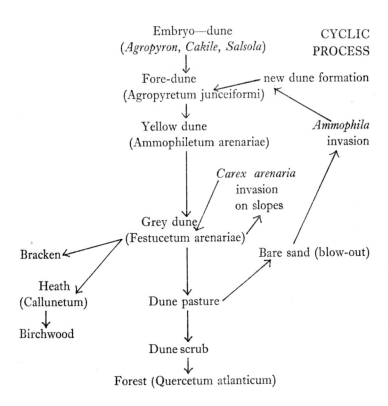

There is also a very high proportion of annuals (Therophytes) upon the dunes. These are primarily spring and early summer plants completing their growth and setting seed after the damp winter and before the onset of the dry summer.

DUNE SLACKS

One of the characteristic features of dunes are the damp or wet hollows, commonly called slacks, left between successive dune ridges

(Fig. 7.5), or which have been formed as a result of complete blow-outs. In such places the ground water may reach the surface throughout the year or only in the winter months, and this undoubtedly greatly influences the vegetation, not only as regards composition and distribution, but the plants themselves are often depauperate as compared with the same species elsewhere.

When water is present throughout the year, a pond of varying size is present with its attendant aquatic plants. In the water one finds species of Pondweed (*Potamogeton*), Shore-weed (*Littorella uniflora*) and, in some localities, Horned pondweed (*Zannichellia palustris*), whilst round the edges the vegetation does not vary greatly from that found around any inland pond. Where there is only standing water in the winter or where the soil is marshy, four or five species of rush (*Juncus*) can be found together with a variety of other marsh plants, including orchids. Such places usually have but a minor proportion of strictly maritime plants such as Sea milkwort (*Glaux maritima*), *Juncus balticus*, Sharp rush (*J. acutus*), Sea rush (*J. maritimus*), Sea club-rush (*Scirpus maritimus*), and Brookweed (*Samolus valerandi*), unless open to occasional flooding by the sea. A number of species of the moss genus *Hypnum* occur in such localities and it is here also that some hepatics, particularly *Riccia*, can be found, although in recent years *Riccia* has tended to disappear.

On Braunton Burrows three separate rush communities have been listed[43], the Juncetum maritimi, Juncetum acuti and Holoschoenetum vulgaris. There is also a damp pasture—*Carex nigra-Hydrocotyle* community and another community co-dominated by Buck's-horn plantain (*Plantago coronopus*) and Hairy hawkbit (*Leontodon leysseri*). The latter community forms a sparse soil cover and many of the associated plants possess a rosette habit or are creeping. The damp pasture is to be found in the most landward of the slacks or even landward of the last dune ridge. The composition varies greatly and, in some cases at least, differences are brought about by variations of level and flooding. Thus where there is prolonged flooding, *Hydrocotyle* is often the dominant plant.

Whilst most of the species to be found in dune slacks are common or reasonably common, there are a number of interesting varieties that have been recorded from various parts of the country. These include Coral-root (*Corallorhiza trifida*), Lesser twayblade (*Listera cordata*), *Cicendia filiformis* and Yellow bartsia (*Parentucellia viscosa*), whilst in the Caithness dunes there is *Primula scotica* and *Polygonum minus*.

Algae are to be found in this habitat, though very little work has been carried out on the algae of dune ponds. Myxophyceae, *Vaucheria, Chara, Mougeotia* and *Tribonema* have all been recorded, and Round[30, 31] has listed the diatom flora of such slacks. Because the water level fluctuates and the ponds may dry up, there is an absence of members of the Chlorococcales and Volvocales. In a Lancashire slack, the benthic (bottom-living) diatomaceous flora was well developed, and although the number of species was small, the actual number of individuals was very large. The samples from slacks at Harlech contained fewer species than either of those in Lancashire or Devon.

It appears that the damp sand flora is essentially a remnant of the pond flora, which is not surprising in view of the fluctuating water level, with the addition of a single variety of a species of *Nitzschia*. On the newly exposed floor of slacks, algae and mosses are commonly the first colonists.

On the west coasts of Great Britain, the damp soil of the slacks is colonized by a carpet of the Creeping willow, *Salix repens*, which forms a Salicetum repentis (Fig. 6.5). *S. atrocinerea* is rather less common in this type of habitat. If the surrounding dunes are stable, no sand is blown on to the *Salix* plants, and the surface soil remains wet, supporting a variety of marsh species together with mosses and liverworts. Peripheral growth of *S. repens* is very slow, so that its capacity to spread from damp slacks to the adjacent dunes is extremely limited. If sand is blown onto the *Salix*, hummocks are formed through which the shoots of the willow grow up. Since seedling establishment of *Salix* only occurs on moist ground, it is clear that the optimum habitat for entry into a dune system is quite different to the conditions required for optimum growth. With the production of hummocks, the soil becomes drier and the nature of the community changes.

F

It appears that *S. repens* cannot thrive in permanently water-logged habitats, and its lower limit in slacks is therefore set by the degree of water-logging. This is in contrast to a suggestion[34] that water deficiency determines plant limits in slacks, though this may be true for species other than *S. repens*. With the creeping willow, so long as the surface soil is not water-logged in the main growing season, the plants grow rather higher, whereas in the lower, temporarily wet areas, the plants remain dwarfed. Salinity may be a

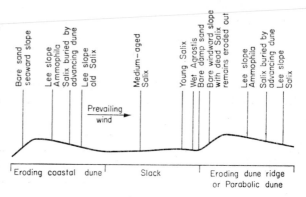

Fig. 6.5. *Distribution of dune and slack vegetation in a typical coastal region of Newborough Warren (after Ranwell).*

factor, especially in slacks nearest the sea, since the seeds germinate in 30 per cent sea water but rarely if the salinity is much higher.

In acidic dunes, the slacks eventually carry a vegetation dominated by *S. atrocinerea* and *Betula pubescens* (e.g Studland in Dorset) into which other species may enter. Thus Gresswell[16] reports the presence of the Larger wintergreen (*Pyrola rotundifolia* ssp. *maritima*) and Yellow bird's-nest (*Monotropa hypopithys*) living on the Lancashire dunes on the humus formed from decay of the willow leaves. Ranwell[27] also records the entry of *Pyrola* into the Anglesey dunes, where it is possible that a *Pyrola-Salix* community will develop. With the advent of still more sand, larger *Salix* dunes are formed and the associated flora becomes very similar to that of the Ammophiletum, the only essential difference being in the dominant.

Particular attention has recently been paid[27] to the Salicetum repentis of the dune slacks at Newborough Warren (Anglesey). The pattern of the vegetation suggested that cyclic changes occurred, and that the sequence depends on whether there is a mobile *Ammophila* dune associated with a wet slack (Fig. 6.6), or turf associated with a

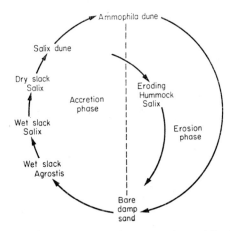

FIG. 6.6. *Cyclic sub-seral succession in the mobile dune-slack complex at Newborough Warren (after Ranwell).*

dry slack. In the former case it was estimated that the full cycle takes about 80 years to complete.

The final sequence in this area is extremely complex and although the main dune succession may appear simple, when one comes to analyse the slacks, and probably also the lows (see following), the story may be exceedingly complex. The mobility of the dunes on the west coast makes for this complexity, which is less evident on east coast dune systems where the spatial succession is in close approximation to the temporal succession.

LOWS

On the Norfolk coast, other depressions called "lows" have been described by the present writer[6]. These differ physiographically from dune slacks in that they are depressions enclosed by two laterals, usually with a break in the shingle laterals so that at high spring tides the sea has access. If the laterals are dune-covered such lows look very much like slacks. Because of the access of salt water, their flora is rather different from that of true slacks and it differs somewhat from the flora of adjacent dunes and salt marshes. The soil varies from bare sand to mud, the more sandy lows being adjacent to dunes. After flooding by the tide, water may remain in the low for some time and in the summer it is not uncommon to find salt efflorescence on the soil surface. Where there is a proportion of shingle in the soil, the typical species of the habitat are *Limonium bellidifolium*, Sea heath (*Frankenia levis*), and Shrubby seablite (*Suaeda fruticosa*), though this last-named is a relic from the drift-line. Where the soil is more sandy, dwarf and prostrate forms of Seablite (*Suaeda maritima* var. *macrocarpa*) and Glasswort (*Salicornia prostrata*, *S. appressa*) are predominant, though the erect species may also be present. Other plants of this habitat are Sea poa (*Puccinellia maritima*) and var. *parvifolia* of *Halimione portulacoides* (Sea purslane).

BIOTA

In conclusion, a few words may be said about the biota of the dunes. Birds play a part in that they are almost certainly responsible for the entry of scrub species, since most of them possess succulent fruits. Reference has already been made to the effect of grazing[33] and the subsequent perpetuation of a grass heath stage on old dunes. Browsing by rabbits produces a tussocky appearance to bushes of *Suaeda fruticosa*[6] near the dunes. When no grazing takes place[6, 28, 42, 43], dune grasses, especially *Festuca rubra*, and Sand sedge (*Carex arenaria*) become more luxuriant and many of the herbs drop out, presumably because of light competition. The changes essentially affect secondary species and there is no reversal of the ordinary dune succession. Ranwell[28] reports that at Newborough Warren (Anglesey), decrease in rabbit browsing brought about an increase in *Festuca rubra* and a decrease in *Agrostis tenuis*. The sharp reaction of the last-named species to grazing, together with evidence from other areas, suggests that at Anglesey the species is near the limit of its ecological range (see also effect of grazing on cliff vegetation, p. 219). Worms may be common in wet slacks and in the *Salix repens* zone at Newborough the biomass of worms per acre approximated to that of woodland. Worms and arthropods undoubtedly contribute to the aeration and fertility of these soils that suffer temporary water-logging.

One other example of plant–animal relationships is that of the cinnabar moth and the Ragwort, *Senecio jacobaea*[6]. When the caterpillars are abundant the *Senecio* plants are so decimated that very little seed is set. Fewer plants are available the subsequent year and they become completely destroyed. In the following years, the caterpillars have no food, and so the moth population decreases to the point when the *Senecio* can re-establish, and so the cycle continues.

REFERENCES

[1] BRISE E. L. and GIMINGHAM C. H., Changes in the structure of bryophytic communities with the progress of succession on sand dunes. *Trans. Brit. Bryol. Soc.*, **2** (4), 523 (1955).

[2] BRISE E. L., LANDSBERG S. Y. and GIMINGHAM C. H., The effects of burial by sand on dune mosses. *Trans. Brit. Bryol. Soc.*, **3** (2), 285 (1957).

[3] BRUCE E. M., The vegetation of the sand dunes between Embleton and Newton. *The Vasculum*, **17**, 94 (1931).

[4] CAREY A. E. and OLIVER F. W., *Tidal Lands: a Study of Shore Problems*. London. Blackie (1918).

[5] CHAPMAN V. J., *Suaeda fruticosa* Forsk. in *Biological Flora of the British Isles. J. Ecol.*, **35**, 293–302 (1947).

[6] CHAPMAN V. J., The plant ecology of Scolt Head Island in *Scolt Head Island*. Ed. J. A. Steers. Heffer, Camb. (1962).

[7] ELLISTON-WRIGHT F. R., Ecological studies, Braunton Burrows, in MARTIN, W. K., and FRASER, G. T., *Flora of Devon*. Arbroath (1939).

[8] FOTHERGILL P. G., The Blyth-Seaton sluice sand-dunes. *The Vasculum*, **20**, 23 (1934).

[9] GEMMELL A. R., GREIG-SMITH P. and GIMINGHAM C. H., A note on the behaviour of *Ammophila arenaria* (L.) Link, in relation to sand-dune formation. *Trans. Proc. Bot. Soc. Edin.*, **36** (2), 132 (1953).

[10] GIMINGHAM C. H., The role of *Barbula fallax* Hedw. and *Bryum pendulum* Schp. in sand-dune fixation. *Trans. Brit. Bryol. Soc.*, **1** (2), 70 (1948).

[11] GIMINGHAM C. H., Contributions to the maritime ecology of St. Cyrus, Kincardineshire. *Trans. Proc. Bot. Soc. Edin.*, **35** (4), 370 (1951).

[12] GIMINGHAM C. H., GEMMELL A. R. and GREIG-SMITH P., The vegetation of a sand-dune system in the outer Hebrides. *Trans. Proc. Bot. Soc. Edin.*, **35** (1), 82 (1948).

[13] GOOD R. D.'O., Contributions towards a survey of the plants and animals of the South Haven peninsula, Studland Heath, Dorset. *J. Ecol.*, **23**, 361–405 (1935).

[14] GREIG-SMITH P., GEMMELL A. R. and GIMINGHAM C. H., Tussock formation in *Ammophila arenaria* (L.) Link. *New Phyt.*, **46** (2), 262–268 (1947).

[15] GRESSWELL R. K., The geomorphology of the south-west Lancashire coast line. *Geog. J.*, **90**, 335–348 (1937).

[16] GRESSWELL R. K., *Sandy shores in south Lancashire*. Liverpool (1953).

[17] HEPBURN I., The vegetation of the sand dunes of the Camel Estuary, north Cornwall. *J. Ecol.*, **32**, 180–192 (1945).

[18] MCLEAN R. C., The ecology of the maritime lichens at Blakeney Point, Norfolk. *J. Ecol.*, **3**, 129–148 (1915).

[19] MELTON F. A., A tentative classification of sand dunes and its application to dune history in the southern high plains. *J. Geol.*, **48** (2), 113–145 (1940).

[20] MOORE S. J., The ecology of the Ayreland of Bride, Isle of Man. *J. Ecol.*, **19**, 115–136 (1931).

[21] OLIVER F. W., Blakeney Point Reports, 1913–1929. *Trans. Norf. Norw. Nat. Soc.*, Vols. of same years.

[22] OLIVER F. W. and SALISBURY E. J., *Topography and Vegetation of Blakeney Point, Norfolk*. Lond. Univ. Coll.

[23] ORR M. Y., Kenfig Burrows: an ecological study. *Scot. Bot. Rev.*, **1**, 209 (1912).

[24] PEARSALL W. H., North Lancashire sand dunes. *Naturalist*, p. 201 (1934).

[25] RANWELL D., Movement of vegetated sand dunes at Newborough Warren, Anglesey. *J. Ecol.*, **46**, 83–100 (1958).

[26] RANWELL D., Newborough Warren, Anglesey. 1. The dune system and dune slack habitat. *J. Ecol.*, **47**, 571–602 (1959).

[27] RANWELL D., Newborough Warren, Anglesey. 2. Plant associes and succession cycles of the sand dune and dune slack vegetation. *J. Ecol.*, **48**, 117–142 (1960).

[28] RANWELL D., Newborough Warren, Anglesey. 3. Changes in the vegetation on parts of the dune system after the loss of rabbits by myxomatosis. *J. Ecol.*, **48**, 385–396 (1960).

[29] RICHARDS P. W., Notes on the ecology of the bryophytes and lichens at Blakeney Point, Norfolk. *J. Ecol.*, **17**, 127–140 (1929).

[30] ROUND F. E., The algal flora of Massom's slack, Freshfield, Lancashire. *Arch. f. Hydrobiol.*, **54** (4), 462 (1958).

[31] ROUND F. E., Observations on the diatom flora of Braunton Burrows, N. Devon. *Hydrobiol.*, **11** (2), 119–127 (1958).

[32] ROUND F. E., A note on the diatom flora of Harlech sand dunes. *J. Roy. Micr. Soc.*, **77** 3/4, 130–135 (1959).

[33] ROWAN W., Note on the food plants of rabbits on Blakeney Point, Norfolk. *J. Ecol.*, **1**, 273–274 (1913).

[34] SALISBURY E. J., *Downs and Dunes*. Bell (1952).

[35] SKINNER E. A., Survey of the dunes between Meggies Burn and Seaton Sluice. *The Vasculum*, **20**, 122 (1934).

[36] SMITH H. T. U., Coast Dunes. Coastal Geog. Conf. 1954. Off. Naval Res. 51–56 (1954).

[37] STEERS J. A., The Culbin Sands. *Geog. J.*, **90**, 498–528 (1937).

[38] STEERS J. A., *The Coastline of England and Wales*. C.U. Press (1946).

[39] TANSLEY A. G., *The British Islands and their Vegetation*. C.U. Press (1939).

[40] VAN DIEREN J. A., *Organogene Dünenbildung*. (1934).

[41] WATSON W., Cryptogamic vegetation of the sand dunes of the west coast of England. *J. Ecol.*, **6**, 126–143 (1918).

[42] WHITE D. J. B., Some observations on the vegetation of Blakeney Point, Norfolk, following the disappearance of the rabbits in 1954. *J. Ecol.*, **49** (1), 113–118 (1961).

[43] WILLIS A. J., FOLKES B. F., HOPE-SIMPSON J. F. and YEMM E. W., Braunton Burrows: the dune system and its vegetation. *J. Ecol.*, **47** (1), 1–24, 249–288 (1959).

[44] LANDSBERG S. Y., The orientation of dunes in Britain and Denmark in relation to wind. *Geog. J.*, **122** (2), 176–189 (1956).

CHAPTER SEVEN

Sand Dunes—The Environment

THE principal feature of the dune environment is the sand that forms the dunes, because from it stem nearly all the other characteristics that make up the peculiarities of the habitat. The actual major physical and biological processes concerned in dune formation have already been outlined in the previous chapter, but there are some aspects, such as sand movement and soil formation, that need to be considered in more detail.

WIND AND SAND MOVEMENT

The material of which the dunes are built is composed of grains of silica in the case of siliceous dunes, and silica grains mixed with a varying proportion of shell fragments in the case of calcareous dunes.

The material, whether it be silica grains or shell fragments, varies in size and its distribution is therefore dependent upon wind velocity, the larger the grain or fragment the greater the wind velocity necessary to move it. Since size determines how far movement occurs, the actual proportion of the different sized grains in any part of a dune system depends on the mean average wind velocity. An experiment to demonstrate this phenomenon can easily be set up with the aid of a hair drier placed at varying distances from a heap of sand, the resulting wind velocities being measured by means of a portable anemometer. Table 7.1, which gives the figures for the different sized grains in the Southport and Blakeney dunes[13] provides an example of how the proportion of grains moved is related to the mean average wind velocity.

Grains in categories 1 and 2 generally roll, whilst those in the other size classes are often carried in the air. Grains of group 4 require a minimum wind speed of 1 m.p.h. before they will start to move. With the greater velocity of the prevailing westerly winds at Southport, it can be seen why there is a higher proportion of larger and heavier

TABLE 7.1

Proportion of Different Sized Grains in Dune Systems

	Grain size	Southport	Blakeney
		per cent	per cent
1	Over 1 mm	1·2	0
2	0·3 –1 mm	90·5	17·9
3	0·25–3 mm	3·0	68·9
4	0·2 –0·25 mm	3·0	8·9
5	>0·2 mm	2·0	4·1

grains. Since movement will only take place when the grains are dry, the time of exposure to both wind and sun is of considerable importance. As the dunes increase in age and become more closely clothed with vegetation, surface water loss is reduced, not only because of decreased surface evaporation, but also because the gradual and steady increase of humus increases the water-holding capacity of the sand and it therefore dries out less frequently as well as being less mobile.

It should be evident that in any duné area the annual incidence of gales and their direction, as also the direction of the prevailing winds, is of the greatest significance. Upon these rests the sifting process that is apparent, upon inspection, in all dunes, the coarser and heavier particles comprising the fore-dunes, the finer and lighter grains forming the bulk of the landward dunes. The construction of a *wind rose** is therefore almost a necessity in any ecological study of sand dunes.

On a very windy coast there will be a proportion of large grains in the dune and therefore water loss will be great, not only through drainage but also through evaporation. In addition there will be excessive sand movement so that the net result is a sand dune environment which is the least favourable for plants. As the dunes become older and more fore-dunes form, the size of the deposited particles on the hind-dunes decreases as only the lighter ones now reach them. A soil profile on an old dune should therefore yield an increasing proportion of larger particles with increasing depth. In calcareous dunes, shell fragments are commonly lighter than siliceous grains and hence are carried farther inland, but again the proportion of shell will be higher near the surface as the strata below represent the younger stages of the dune.

A clear understanding of sand movement and the effect of vegetation in relation to dune formation cannot be achieved without making actual field observations with a portable anemometer. If this is done it will be found that results comparable to the following are likely to be obtained: the wind velocity will increase with height above the dune surface but it will also vary depending on the location (windward face, crest, leeward or in a slack) (Fig. 7.1). The effect of vegetation is to increase the difference between surface and upper velocities. Thus over bare dunes the velocity at the surface may be half that at 2 ft above, whilst with sparse Marram the surface velocity may be one-quarter that at 2 ft above. The mere presence of the vegetation therefore lowers the surface wind velocity considerably. For example, Salisbury[13] records a wind velocity of 8·3 m.p.h. at 2 in. on bare dune whilst in adjacent Marram it was 1·7 m.p.h. at the same height. In the case of marram grass the individual tufts can have, as may be expected, a considerable effect upon wind velocity. Thus a wind velocity of 4·4 m.p.h. in front of a tuft can drop to 2·3 m.p.h. behind the tuft. Figures such as these indicate the great importance of aerial shoots as obstacles leading to sand accumulation.

* Term applied to a diagram that shows the percentage of winds coming from different compass points over a year.

Unless the root systems are extremely extensive they are not nearly so efficient a protection against sand removal as are the shoots.

DUNE MOVEMENT

The brief background of sand grain movement and the factors controlling such movement given above enable us to progress to a consideration of the movement of dunes as a whole.* So far as coastal dunes in Great Britain are concerned, the rate of movement appears to vary considerably, obviously depending on mean wind

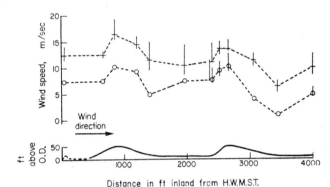

Distance in ft inland from H.W.M.S.T.

FIG. 7.1. *Wind speeds recorded at 5 cm (0———0) and 1 m +———+) above the ground surface on profile T1–T4 during a south-west gale of 40 knots (20 m/sec) at Newborough Warren. The verticals on the curves show the range of speeds recorded at individual sites. The point where the dotted lines cut the verticals is the estimated average speed at the site (after Ranwell).*

velocities, the degree of vegetation cover and degree of protection by other windward dunes. Maximum dune movement at Morfa Harlech is around 3·7 m/annum, at Morfa Dyffryn 6·1 m/annum. Much lower values have been recorded for Great Crosby dunes (1·1 m/annum) and Norfolk dunes (1·5 m/annum), whilst at Freshfield higher values (5·5–7·3 m/annum) represent the situation[8].

* More detail will be found in KING, C. A. M., *Coasts and Beaches*. Arnold (1959).

One of the more detailed studies of dune movement has been carried out over a period of 3 years by Ranwell[8] on sand dunes at Newborough Warren in Anglesey. It has already been noted that wind velocity varies with topography (Fig. 7.1) so one can anticipate that the movement of different parts of a dune system will also vary. Using stakes placed firmly in the sand and making careful measurements Ranwell was able to show that the rates varied from zero to 65 ft per annum, the maximum rates being on the leeward side up to the crest, since it is in this region that the sand is most mobile. There is no doubt that movement takes place also on the windward side but as sand is continually being added here from the beach it is less obvious. In the slacks behind the dunes there is little or no sand movement (Fig. 7.2). Where dune movement of the nature described

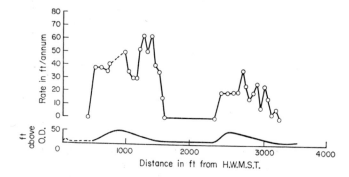

Fig. 7.2. *Rates of inland movement of different parts of a dune section in Newborough Warren (after Ranwell).*

above is taking place the windward side of the dunes is steeper than the landward. This contrasts with the kind of profile found on shingle beaches, where, as a result of wave action and water percolation, the lee side may be much steeper than the seaward side (see p. 198).

In any dune system the fluctuations in movement, and the effect of such fluctuations upon the dune profile, can be considerable, especially over a single gale period, and it is therefore the annual changes that are the more meaningful. The amount of sand annually deposited on an accreting lee slope may amount to 2–3 ft, whilst on very mobile dunes the windward slope may decrease in height by a comparable amount as a result of erosion. During a gale great changes can occur and variations in level of $1\frac{1}{2}$ ft are not impossible. Some indication of the extent of short period changes is provided in Fig. 7.3 showing the height of sand at certain pole sites over a period of years. The very rapid changes of an eroding vegetated dune

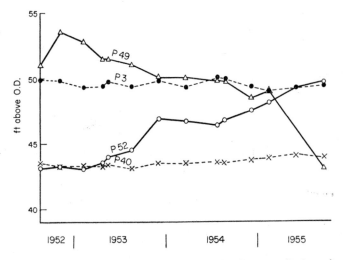

FIG. 7.3. *Short-period changes in sand level at a selection of different pole sites on the dune transects at Newborough Warren. P49, a vegetated crest site changing from accretion to erosion. P3, a non-vegetated crest site. P52, a rapidly accreting vegetated lee slope site. P40, a slowly accreting vegetated lee slope site (after Ranwell).*

(p. 137) and of a vegetated accretion lee site (p. 141) show how, on the one hand, a dune can be eroded away to a remanié form, and on the other hand how the Marram (*Ammophila*) and other plants must be able to respond to considerable smothering. Whilst figures for the majority of fore-dune and yellow-dune species are not available, it seems that in the case of *Ammophila* seedlings an accretion rate of 6 in. per year is the maximum they can tolerate with a further maximum of 1–2 in. at any one time (i.e. any one gale). It is unlikely that other species would tolerate greater rates.

When sand accumulates behind tufts of Marram, it is the leeward side of the tuft that receives the stimulus and the new shoots grow out (see p. 140) on this side so that the tuft gradually moves in the same direction as the dune. In some respects this is similar to the movement of shrubby seablite up a shingle beach (see p. 201). The data obtained from the Newborough dunes is of the greatest importance in our understanding of the dynamics of dune systems. However, dune systems vary substantially and for this reason data from other dunes is greatly to be desired. Much of it can be obtained by simply driving poles marked in feet and tenths of a foot into the dunes at strategic places.

TEMPERATURE

On the fore-dunes and in the yellow dune phase, where there is open soil, the soil temperatures may reach values as high as 60°C in summer. Sand is a poor conductor of heat and therefore the soil temperature drops very rapidly with depth, even in the first 5 cm. Dune temperatures also exhibit a daily rhythm which is very much more pronounced on the sparsely vegetated yellow dunes, where heat can be absorbed and lost more rapidly than on grey dunes (Fig. 7.4). These particular temperature records also show that at night the surface temperature can fall below the dew point, so that dew then forms on the surface and drains down into the sand. This is a different phenomenon to that of internal dew formation when the internal dune temperatures are below the dew point (see pp. 178 and 207).

The surface sand temperature is affected not only by the degree of plant cover and the amount of sunlight received but also by the rainfall and exposure to wind. All of these factors need to be taken into account when considering diurnal and seasonal temperature fluctuations.

SOIL FORMATION

Whilst development of the sand to form a soil must commence

from the moment of establishment of the first plants, it is evident that, until the dune becomes stabilized, the rate of soil development is going to be very slow. A variety of processes are involved in soil formation. These include leaching, which removes chemicals from the surface layers to lower layers, removal of nutrients by the roots

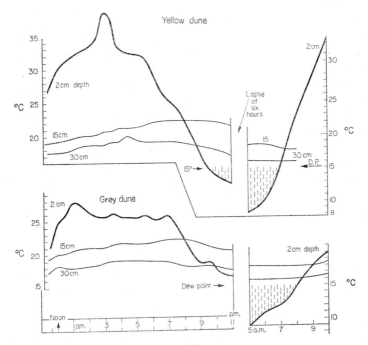

FIG. 7.4. *Dune temperatures showing daily rhythm. Note the fall below the dew point in the surface temperature at night and the more marked extremes in the yellow dune than in the maturer soil of the grey dune (after Salisbury).*

of plants and replenishment of these nutrients together with humus at the surface from dead and decaying plant material.

In the early stages of dune development, removal proceeds at a greater rate than replenishment. Pits dug in the sand generally show a uniform profile which may suggest that little redistribution of nutrients is taking place, whereas in fact the very reverse is the case. With increasing stabilization of the dunes the degree of leaching increases because there is no steady supply of new sand, but this leaching will depend to some extent on the vegetation cover, the less the cover the greater the leaching. If trees are either planted on dunes or arrive naturally, their roots will tap the lower soil layers and remove nutrients, and in the case of dune afforestation it is likely that in the first 15–20 years the drain on the soil can be very severe. Subsequently, downward leaching from the litter will tend to restore the balance[17, 18].

Effective studies of dune soils can only be carried out if it is possible to give a date, even if only approximate, to the various dune ridges. One obvious way of doing this is by a study of old maps[16], which may show when a dune system was or was not present. It is now also possible to arrive at dune dating by making use of the ^{14}C technique in which the amount of ^{14}C present provides a measure of the age. This is based upon the half-life disintegration period of the ^{14}C atom, and the proportion that is generally present in living material as compared with the amount present in occluded soil organic matter.

WATER RELATIONS

Since sand dunes can be regarded as edaphically dry habitats, the moisture content of the dunes and also the behaviour of the water table is of paramount interest. Digging down into the sand of maritime dunes soon shows that the subsurface layers are moist, this moisture being derived mainly from the process of internal dew formation (see p. 178) as well as from rain. The dry character of the habitat is therefore more apparent than real, and provided plants can rapidly put out long roots (see p. 142) water should not be a major limiting factor. Indeed, it seems evident that on young dunes it is the mobility of the sand and possible damage from sea spray that are more restrictive.

In those systems where the nature of the water table has been studied it appears to be dome-shaped, a feature common to isolated granular deposits where drainage is maximal at the margins (Fig. 7.5).

Since the water table is close to the surface in the slacks the sand there remains moist and stable, though wind velocities in such places are also much less (p. 163), and would generally be insufficient to move the grains. Although the water table over the dune system as a whole tends to be dome-shaped, minor variations can occur. Thus at the transition from slacks to dunes the water table, especially in

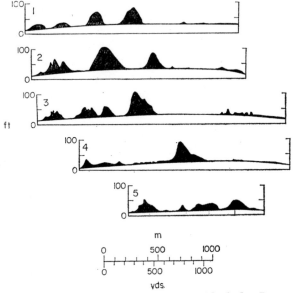

FIG. 7.5. *Profiles across the dune system with slacks, Braunton Burrows. Heights, obtained by survey, are given in feet O.D. The sand above the water table of June 1952 is shown in black (after Willis et al.).*

winter, undergoes a distinct rise (Fig. 7.6). This is probably associated with the greater accumulation of water in the dune under winter conditions together with the greater depth of soil in which water can accumulate.

The importance of the water table in the slacks in relation to the type of vegetation has already been mentioned (see p. 152). The control of Creeping willow (*Salix repens*) by water-logging is one aspect of this, whilst another is the relationship of wet plant associes, e.g. *Juncus maritimus*, *Agrostis-Juncus articulatus*, and *Littorella-Samolus*, with slacks where the water table is never more than 1 m below the surface. Where the table descends to 1–2 m one finds dry slack associes dominated by *Salix repens* or *Festuca-Calluna*. If the water table descends still deeper true slack communities become replaced by dune communities.

Whether one is investigating fore-, mid- or rear-dunes, it will be found that the water is fresh so that the roots of the plants are always in fresh water, and the only problem associated with excess salt is related to the amount deposited by wind-borne spray (see

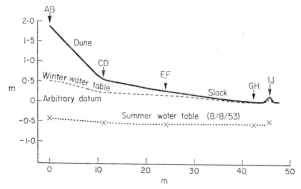

FIG. 7.6. *The free water table levels at the junction between dune and slack on Newborough Warren (after Ranwell).*

p. 182). The dune water table can be regarded as potentially subject to four major types of change: (a) seasonal, (b) regular periodic, (c) daily rhythmic, (d) irregular.

Where the *seasonal* change has been studied[9], it has been shown that there is a distinct three-phase pattern. In the winter, the water table is high and maintained by the winter rains. In the spring there is a fall in the water table which continues into the summer. This is associated with generally drier weather, but is probably more largely affected by the increasing transpirational demands of the plants. With the decrease in vegetative activity in autumn, and often an increased rainfall with reduced surface evaporation (air temperatures

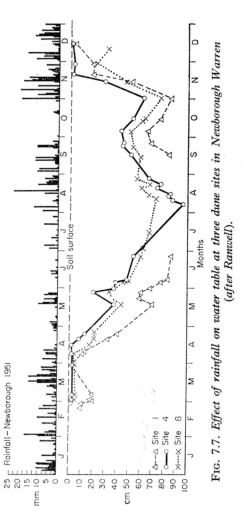

FIG. 7.7. *Effect of rainfall on water table at three dune sites in Newborough Warren (after Ranwell).*

being lower), the water table commences to rise again. This type of behaviour is shown irrespective of the vegetation, though at Newborough the degree of change varied between the different types of vegetation. The water table movement in this particular dune system ranged from 70 to 100 cm. In the Winterton dunes on the east coast the range is about half this amount, and this can be correlated with the much lower rainfall there. There is, as one might anticipate, a correlation with monthly precipitation, and this is well shown for

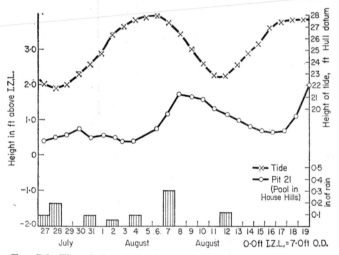

Fig. 7.8. *The relation of the change of water level in dunes (House Hills) on Scolt Head Island to that of the tide. The maximum height in the dunes is reached 48 hours after the highest spring tide (after Chapman).*

three dune sites at Newborough (Fig. 7.7). There the effect of the August rainfall is particularly obvious, also that of the later October dry period.

Periodic changes can occur in the water table of some dunes, especially if they are near the shore and the dunes are built upon shingle ridges. In these cases the changes are associated with the behaviour of the tides, the onset of spring tides bringing about a gradual elevation of the dune water table, with a subsequent fall during the neap tide period. Movements such as this only occur where the dunes have developed on shingle ridges (Blakeney, Scolt) which facilitate the influence of the tides (Fig. 7.8) (see p. 207). In dune systems based upon sand, periodic movements related to the tides have not been reported.

Sand movement, whether by accretion or erosion, at the surface of the dunes is important because it can determine changes in the depth at which the water table occurs. To some extent this sand movement is responsible for the apparently *irregular* fluctuations of the water

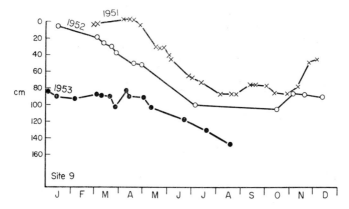

Fig. 7.9. *Sand accretion and the free water table at Newborough. The three curves show the depths of the free water table in centimetres below the soil surface in conditions of steadily increasing sand accretion from 1951 to 1953. The accretion from 1951 to 1952 was 8 cm and from 1951 to 1953 was 20 cm at this site (after Ranwell).*

table because they are associated with wind of gale force rather than heavy rain. Some indication of the extent of this phenomenon is shown in Fig. 7.9 for a site where rapid accretion was taking place. The mean increase in depth of the water table between 1951 and 1953 was of the order of 70–80 cm. *Daily rhythmic* movements have been recorded from the dunes at Newborough where the table fell 2–3 cm per day in summer and rose again after sunset. This is clearly a transpirational effect, and since the fall is generally greater than the rise in this period the overall result is the summer lowering of the water table (Fig. 7.7).

The water table in the slacks may be very close to or even above the surface, but in the dunes there is usually a considerable depth of sand above the water table. This sand contains moisture available to the plants so the dune ecologist is greatly interested in the amount

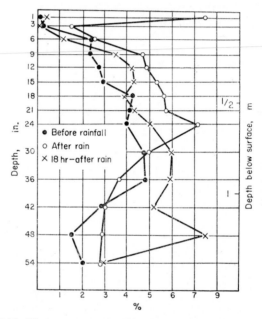

FIG. 7.10. *Water contents of yellow dunes before and after rain in summer, Blakeney Point, Norfolk. The surface water contents are here represented as such, but in fact are averages for the top inch of sand (after Salisbury).*

present. Normally moisture is expressed on a dry weight basis, but as Salisbury[13] has pointed out, if one takes equal volumes of sand from young and old dunes and determines dry weight, that of the old dune will be less because it contains more humus which is lighter than sand. For sand dune soils therefore, the moisture content is more accurately expressed on a volume basis. The moisture content can quite obviously vary with season but it can also vary with age of the dunes, because older dunes with their greater amount of humus retain more water. So far as seasonal variation is concerned, the water content will be highest in winter and lowest in summer, but at any

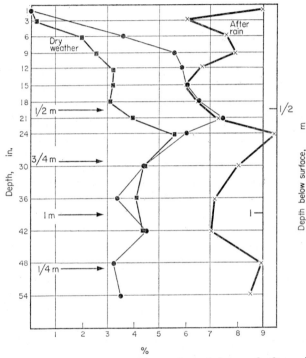

FIG. 7.11. *Water contents of grey dunes before and after rain. Early phase of grey dune in summer, Blakeney Point, Norfolk. Compare with Fig. 7.10 (after Salisbury).*

time it increases sharply after rain. In the Blakeney dunes 4 per cent moisture by volume has been recorded in the spring but by the summer it has fallen to 1 per cent or less. In medium-aged and old dunes at Rye, Salisbury[13] records that the moisture content ranged from 4·6 to 7·7 per cent by volume after rain.

The variation in moisture content that can occur with age of dunes can be seen from Figs. 7.10 and 7.11 for yellow dune and young grey dune at Blakeney.

Figure 7.10 shows that in yellow dunes the water content increases with depth and then falls off at about 0·75 m down. The effect of excess water from rain is evident at the surface and 18 hours later the high peak is seen to have percolated down to below 1 m. In the grey dunes (Fig. 7.11) the water content, which is greater than that of the yellow dunes, normally reaches a maximum at about 0·5 m below the surface, but this kind of profile is very dependent upon the amount of organic matter present in the surface layers. If it is considerable the surface layers will tend to have higher values than shown here. It has been demonstrated[10] that a considerable increase in water content of surface soil takes place between dunes with open vegetation (yellow) but that little change occurs in the water content of soil at the 1 ft depth.

Further work will be necessary in order to show whether this is a universal feature or not. In so far as open vegetation permits of sand movement and consequent covering or removal of litter whereas closed vegetation promotes the accumulation of litter, it is probable that the phenomenon is widespread. After rainfall, however, the organic matter generally in the sand of grey dunes results in higher values throughout the profile as compared with the yellow dune phase. The effect of the organic matter in retaining this extra moisture, even though it be only a few per cent, is reflected in the greater root development of the plants wherever such organically rich layers may occur (Fig. 7.12).

The moisture content of sand dunes is obviously low, and if one considers it in relation to known transpiration rates of plants some interesting results emerge. The kind of observations which have been carried out are not difficult, and comparable results could no doubt be obtained with the aid of quite a simple potometer for the transpiration experiments. Salisbury[13] has shown that if you take a plant such as Hare's foot (*Trifolium arvense*), it can have a total leaf area of 10·57 cm² and that such a plant will transpire 1 ml of water per day. The root system of such a plant will be distributed through a column of sand of about 95 cm³ volume, so that if the water content of that sand is 4 per cent by volume, the plant will have exhausted the entire water supply in 4 days. Plants of *Trifolium*, however, can be found

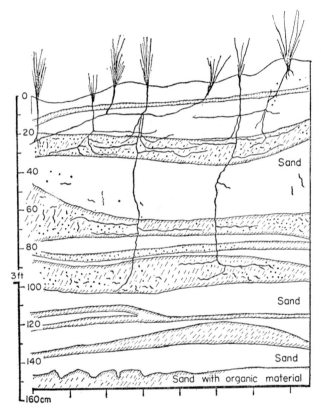

FIG. 7.12. *Semi-diagrammatic representation to scale of the root system of the Marram grass* (Ammophila arenaria) *in the vertical section of a dune on the Norfolk coast about 25 ft² in extent (about 2·5 m²). Yellow sand is shown white and layers of dark sand, containing considerable organic material, by diagonal shading. Roots, shown as black lines or as black dots where cut across, are seen to be most numerous in the originally enriched and therefore moister strata (after Salisbury).*

growing apparently unharmed in sand and not showing signs of
wilting even after 6 weeks of no rain. Similar calculations can be
made for other dune plants which show that they ought to wilt
within 1–4 days without rain. The explanation of their survival is
provided by the process of internal dew formation which regularly
replaces the water used by the plants. Field studies have shown that
even in June the internal temperatures of dunes drop below the dew
point between midnight and around 5.30 a.m. with a minimum value
around 1.30 p.m., so that during this period dew will be steadily
deposited within the dunes. A further demonstration of the phenomenon can be provided by actually determining the increase in water
content between the end of the day and towards the end of the following night. Table 7.2 gives data illustrating this phenomenon for two
different sites.

TABLE 7.2

*Increase in Water Content (by weight) at Different Depths as a
Result of Internal Dew Formation (after Salisbury)*

	Site A	Site B
	per cent	per cent
3 in.	+0·18	+0·41
12 in.	+0·13	+0·64
36 in.	—	+1·86

SOIL ACIDITY

Apart from sand movement and water content, two other important
features of the dune habitat are the carbonate and humus contents of
the soil, both of which play a major part in determining the pH
(acidity) of the soil. Humus will accumulate so long as plants colonize
the dunes, but the amount of carbonate present depends on whether
shell sources are in the proximity or not. Table 7.3 lists values for
carbonate and pH in a number of dune systems.

TABLE 7.3

Percentage of Carbonate (C_aCO_3) *and pH of Dunes*

Locality	Percentage of $CaCO_3$	pH
R. Camel (Cornwall)		
Shore	53·9	8·3
0–5 cm—fixed dune	55·6	8·4
0–5 cm—blow out	68·8	8·5
0–5 cm—blown sand 1 km from		
shore	51·7	8·0
Southport	2–3	7–7·4
Ayreland of Bride (I. of Man)	0·75	6·9
Blakeney	Under 0·5	6·8
Dogs Bay, Galway	75	8·1
Rosapenna, Donegal	48	8·3
Holme, Norfolk	2–3	—
Walney, Lancs.	—	6–6·5
St. Cyrus	1·75	7·6 mean
Isle of Harris	48–70	7·2–7·6
(Luskentyre banks)	(mean 58·6)	
South Haven (Dorset)	·037	6·8 (young) to 4·4 (old)

As may be expected, non-calcareous dunes are more acid (have a lower pH), and this is reflected in the ultimate character of their vegetation which is essentially acid grass heath (see p. 148). The average pH value for surface soils of young dune systems is just above neutral (7·4–8·0) with a regular tendency to become more acid with age. In the dunes on South Haven Peninsula, where it has been possible to date the various ridges[16], the gradation of pH with age is quite evident (Table 7.4), especially since in this siliceous dune system the sand becomes highly acidic.

Whilst sand dunes become more and more acidic with increasing age, when individual profiles are examined it is found that they regularly become more alkaline with increasing depth, a phenomenon which has been reported from several dune systems (St. Cyrus, Newborough, South Haven).

These gradations in pH may depend upon the mobility or otherwise of dune systems, because at Newborough Warren[9] there is apparently no change of pH in successive ridges. This can be accounted for in the mobility of the dunes which would not give organic matter the opportunity to collect and so the surface layers would not become more acid.

In dunes composed of sand containing a high proportion of carbonate, there is generally a gradual leaching out of the carbonate with increasing dune age. This has been very well demonstrated for

TABLE 7.4

Variation of pH with Age, South Haven Dunes (Dorset)

pH	Dune type	Age
		years
7·0–6·6	Fore-dune	0– 20
5·5–5·0	Dune grassland	0– 50
5·5–4·8	Late dune grassland	50– 80
4·6–3·9	Dune heath	80–110
4·5–3·9	Dune heath	110–230
4·5–3·6	Dry heath	240–350

dune systems by Salisbury[12] (Fig. 7.13) and Gorham[5]. At Newborough[9] also the carbonate content decreased with distance from the sea but in the wet slacks here, and possibly similarly in other dune areas, one can get local areas of high carbonate where molluscan shells have accumulated. In regions of high wind, where blown sand may be an important factor even at the grey dune phase, the gradual leaching out of the carbonate may not occur. This, at least, appears to have been the case at Luskentyre on the Isle of Harris. Gimingham[4] and his co-workers suggest that this dune system differs from those at Southport and Blakeney in that sand deposition can take place over all areas except the final dune pasture. It is evident, therefore, that further work on the carbonate content of dune soils is still

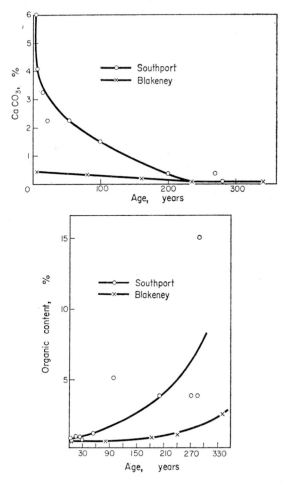

Fig. 7.13. *Carbonate and humus content of dunes at Southport and Blakeney Point. The diagrams show the regular variation of these contents with increasing age of the dunes. The soil changes are bound up with the occupation of the dunes by vegetation, which both induces the changes and indicates responses to them (after Salisbury).*

necessary. Further work is also essential in order to demonstrate the effectiveness of the downward leaching.

The other factor which can affect pH is that of the humus. Here Salisbury[12] has shown that on the Southport and Blakeney dunes there is a steady increase in the humus content with increasing age (Fig. 7.13). This is perhaps to be expected because increasing vegetation cover should bring about more and more litter. However, this is apparently not always the case because on the St. Cyrus dunes the organic matter showed no significant increase until the vegetation became closed, and then the increase was only in the surface layers. Where the dune ridges are separated by slacks, and if such slacks carry a vegetation of Creeping willow (*Salix repens*), there will be a considerable increase in the organic matter from the decaying leaves and roots of the *Salix*.

MINERAL NUTRIENTS

The proximity of coastal dunes to the sea might lead one to think that the soil, particularly the surface layers, would have a higher than normal sodium content. This does not appear to be the case, and all investigators who have looked into the matter have reported low sodium chloride values, so that if spray is carried onto the dunes, as it certainly is in cases, then the salt must be rapidly leached down into the lower layers. The amount of aeolian (wind-borne) salt carried and deposited on the leaves of plants may be sufficient to inhibit some plants growing in areas of maximum deposition. The principal zone of deposition appears to be the windward slope and crest of the fore-dune and the crest of the rear-dune. On the coastal dunes of North Carolina the relative distribution of the grasses *Uniola* (tolerant) and *Andropogon* (relatively intolerant) can be explained on the basis of such salt spray distribution. No attempt appears to have been made to see whether any of the British dune plants respond in this way to salt spray incidence.

In a detailed investigation of the fertility of the dune soils of Braunton Burrows, it was found[15] that none were deficient in respect of minor nutrients, but that all were deficient in the major nutrients (nitrogen, phosphorus, potassium). Because of this low fertility it has been suggested that the growth of dune plants may be limited to some degree. The major nutrients, being very soluble, are probably leached out at an early stage in dune formation, though there may not be very much nitrogen and phosphorus from the start. Some support for early leaching is available from analyses of dune sands[5] at Blakeney and of water in slacks at Sandscale[6] which showed the slack waters, representing the water table, to be rich in soluble salts and calcium. In the case of experiments at Braunton Burrows it was found that the addition of the three major nutrients caused the grasses to assume dominance. A very similar phenomenon occurs on coastal cliffs in the presence of bird populations where, unless there is extensive rabbit grazing, grasses become overwhelmingly dominant (see p. 214). It is, therefore, highly probable that the sparse growth and open character of the vegetation in the early stages of dune development is at least partly associated with low nitrogen and phosphorus.

On the Norfolk dunes Gorham[5] found that potassium, phosphate and ammonia nitrogen increased with age of the dune, but that nitrate nitrogen decreased. The latter may be related to the combined effect of absorption by plants and leaching, and presumably the demand is so great that even the breakdown of litter is not adequate to maintain the supply.

SOIL MICROBIOLOGY

Relatively little attention has been paid to the biological properties of dune soils, i.e. the microfauna and flora, and even less to the ecology of the soil microflora that accompanies the plant communities. In communities with distinct dominant species, such as Marram (*Ammophila*), Sand sedge (*Carex arenaria*), or Creeping fescue (*Festuca rubra*), these plants can influence the flora as a whole through their own root microflora and also by the effect their litter and humus may have upon the adjacent soil microflora. A good example of this occurs on acid sand heaths carrying *Calluna*, because the acid heath humus brings about a depression of the bacterial population but increases the fungal population. The micro-organisms of the soil are also very important in so far as they materially contribute towards the general maturation of the habitat. Whilst at present we know practically nothing about the micro-organisms associated with the dune habitats and their dominant species, even when we do we shall want to know how the microflora and fauna varies with age of dune and depth of soil, and what is the nature of the differences between the flora of the rhizosphere (portion of the soil subject to the plant root system) and that of the root surface.

Studies that have been carried out on the soil fungal population of dunes* have shown that there appear to be three common soil genera, *Penicillium*, *Cephalosporium* and *Coniothyrium*, both in respect of number of species and frequency, and that *Penicillium nigricans* is the most widespread species in British dunes[1]. The available information indicates that the fungal population is a rich one, but very few of the species can be considered as restricted to dunes. Indeed, many can only be regarded as casuals, and quite a few are to be found associated primarily with rabbit pellets. There is apparently no marked seasonal variation, but more work on this aspect is really required. However, a very distinct difference is evident as between the floras of acidic and alkaline dunes. Brown[1] compared two such dune systems (Sandwich and South Haven) and found that one yielded ninety-five species and the other ninety-nine, but only twenty-eight were common to the two areas. In general the number of species and the frequency of their occurrence decreased with increasing depth of the soil (Table 7.5). The principal exception to this was found in the fore-dunes, but one can perhaps account for the greater numbers at the lower depths here by postulating their association with pockets of buried organic matter (drift). There was also some evidence of certain fungi being associated with specific stages in the phanerogamic succession. A similar phenomenon has also been reported in respect of mycorrhizal infection. All this work is of the very greatest interest, but it is evident that further studies of a similar nature on other dune systems are greatly to be desired.

* See also p. 149.

Whilst a considerable volume of work has been carried out on the British sand dune systems, it is also evident that it has been largely restricted to certain regions, and there is therefore plenty of scope for additional studies on any of the numerous dune areas that have so far received no attention. It is true that comparable work has been done on many continental and Scandinavian dune systems, and this mostly serves to confirm the results that have already been described.

TABLE 7.5

No. of Fungal Species isolated at Different Depths on Sand Dune Soils (after Brown)

Soil depth (in.)	0–0·5	1·0	3·0	6·0	12·0
Sandwich (alkaline)					
Open sand	11	—	—	—	—
Fore-dune	10	14	12	7	14
Semi-fixed yellow	29	22	14	12	9
Fixed grey	20	17	13	14	12
Dune pasture	22	22	13	16	11
South Haven, Studland (acid)					
Open sand	9	—	—	—	—
Fore-dune	6	10	11	11	4
Semi-fixed grassland	20	13	10	14	8
Semi-fixed heath	25	21	17	14	20
Heath	22	22	14	14	12
Pteridium heath	23	20	15	16	10

DUNE BUILDING AND MAINTENANCE

Sand dunes in certain places form an essential feature of the natural coast protection system. This is particularly true in Norfolk when a major breach in the dunes can lead to disastrous flooding of the farmland behind, as happened in 1938 and 1953. Maintenance of the dune system is therefore of great practical importance, and, should it be breached, methods of rebuilding are equally vital. Much attention has been given to this problem in different parts of the world since Great Britain is not the only country that may depend on dunes to protect a part of the coast-line. Maintenance and repair of dune systems is essentially a job for the civil engineer, but since he makes use of plants it will not be out of place if some reference is made here to the principles involved. The agriculturist may also be concerned when a dune system becomes mobile and starts invading and swamping good agricultural land, as has happened with the

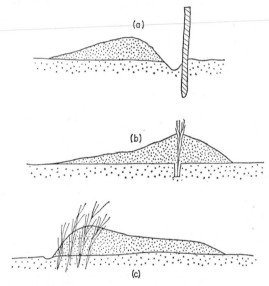

Fig. 7.14. a, *Effect of solid obstacle.* b, *Effect of an inflexible open obstacle.* c, *Effect of a flexible obstacle, for example, a bunch of Marram grass (after Cockayne).*

Culbin sands. The immediate stabilization of such mobile dune areas is therefore also very important.

It has already been seen that the development of coastal dunes results from sand meeting an obstacle (a plant), so that the effect of various types of obstacles upon sand drift is very important[2]. If the obstacle is solid then the wind is reflected and an eddy is formed which scoops out the sand at the base of the obstacle and forms a mound in front (Fig. 7.14a). If the obstacle is low, e.g. buried paling or groyne, the mound increases in height until it is level with the top. No eddy can now occur and the sand is blown over the obstacle and collects on the leeward side as the wind velocity drops (see p. 162). Now that the eddy has ceased, sand falls into the scooped-out hollow, and as sand is also accumulating on the leeward side the obstacle is gradually buried. If the obstacle is flexible and open, e.g. tuft of Marram or Lyme grass, the sand is deposited first in the centre of the tussock and then it commences to accumulate on the lee side (Fig. 7.14b). If the obstacle is rigid and open, e.g. a brush fence, the wind is checked in its passage through it but as it is not reflected there is no eddy. As a result sand accumulates on both sides until the fence is finally buried (Fig. 7.14c).

Whether one is building new dunes, repairing breaches or immobilizing mobile dunes, it is important to get plants established as quickly as possible because plant cover brings about sand stabilization. The actual stabilization of dunes is based upon certain principles which can be briefly enumerated as follows:

1. Elimination of sand movement by providing a cover to the sand. This may have to be artificial at first but a closed vegetation cover, preferably pasture or forest, is the ultimate objective.

2. Anything that can lead to secondary exposure of a bare sand surface should be prevented. Burning, over-grazing, excessive trampling by animals or human beings, can damage the plant cover and expose sand and then with undercutting the whole dune can erode away.

3. It is useless to try and establish on mobile sand plants that cannot survive sand covering. Sometimes the sand movement may be too great even for a plant such as Marram, and in these cases it is necessary to break the force of the wind by putting in brush fences or covering the sand surface with brushwood.

4. The most effective cover is given by trees because they have a long life, improve the soil with their litter, and they require little attention and are not likely to be damaged other than by fire. Adequate attention must therefore be given to fire risk and also to

the felling programme. The best type of tree for this purpose is a softwood, and there are a number of pine species that grow very well on the poor soil of sand dunes.

5. The most satisfactory way of establishing plants is through planting rather than sowing. Marram is the grass usually planted and where areas are extensive it can now be done by machinery, as at Muriwai in New Zealand. In other parts of the world different dune grasses may be used. If a plant such as Tree lupin (*Lupinus arboreus*) is to be used, it is best sown and then one must select the best time of year for sowing, which is when the sand is wet and not likely to travel, to give the seedlings a chance to become established.

6. The movement of sand should be stopped as near the source as possible. On a beach, new dune should be formed as close to high water mark as possible. In the case of mobile dunes, one should not try and stop the advancing edge: measures have to be taken first at the source of the sand. When that has been stabilized, attention can then be given to the advancing edge.

7. Since wind velocities are greatly affected by irregularities in the dunes, gullies and embayments should not be allowed to develop in coastal dunes. The smoother and more regular the sea frontage, the less chance of erosion. Similarly, in interior dunes it is most desirable to build up hollows between hills. Because of the impact of surface irregularities on wind behaviour, great care must be taken to see that no isolated artificial mounds of sand are produced.

8. The initial fences must be located in relation to the prevailing or dominant winds depending on which type is of major importance in sand movement.

9. If the land is sinking in relation to sea level, erosion may be a continual menace unless the sand supply is very large, but if not dunes may need artificial building up from time to time.

If the sand is not too mobile, it can be successfully stabilized by planting with Marram or sowing with lupin. In the former case, the Marram should be planted in rows at right angles to the incident wind, and plants in successive rows should alternate so as not to create wind channels. Lupin can be sown by scattering seed, but it is better to lay lupin branches on the sand and let the seed pods burst naturally. If the sand is highly mobile, it can be stabilized by burying brush fences at right angles to sand movement and planting in the leeward ridge dune that is formed.

When a fore-dune has to be repaired or a new dune created, there is a recognized process which should aim at producing a dune with a wide base, a low summit and relatively flat slopes. The general method is to establish two fence rows about 7 ft apart and $2\frac{1}{2}$ ft high. When the sand reaches the top, two more fences, each a little to the seaward of the first pair, are set up. When these are nearly covered the sand can be planted, or if the dune is still not high enough a third set of fences can be put in (Fig. 7.15). The front of the dune is best

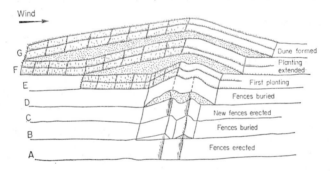

FIG. 7.15. *Stages in building of new fore-dune (after Steers).*

planted in squares whilst rows can be used on the leeward slope. When the Marram is established lupin can be sown. Later, under the lupin, grass and clover or trefoil can be sown or young pine trees can be planted. Legumes are desirable plants to introduce at an early stage because of the nitrogen they add to the soil through the nitrifying bacteria in the root nodules. At this stage the dune has been stabilized and should form an effective part of the coast protection. Pines that can be used successfully include *Pinus maritimus*, *P. austriaca*, *P. radiata* and *P. corsica*, whilst in wetter slacks birch, poplars, alder and willows are readily established.

This brief account of the process of dune building and stabilization will, it is hoped, serve to show how information gained from an ecological study of a particular habitat and the various communities it bears can be successfully applied to a major physiographic problem.

REFERENCES

[1] BROWN J. C., Soil fungi of some British sand dunes in relation to soil type and succession. *J. Ecol.*, **46** (3), 641–664 (1958).

[2] CHAPMAN V. J., The stabilization of sand-dunes by vegetation. *Proc. Conf. Biol. & Civil Engin.* (Inst. of Civil Engineers), 1948. 142–157 (1949).

[3] EASTWOOD D. J., FRASER G. K. and WEBLEY D. M., Microbiological factor in the Culbin Sands afforestation scheme. *Nature, London,* **165,** 980 (1950).

[4] GIMINGHAM C. H., GEMMELL A. R. and GREIG-SMITH P., The vegetation of a sand-dune system in the Outer Hebrides. *Trans. Bot. Soc. Edin.*, **35** (1), 82–96 (1948).

[5] GORHAM E., Soluble salts from dune sands from Blakeney Pt. in Norfolk. *J. Ecol.*, **46,** 373–379 (1958).

[6] GORHAM, E., The chemical composition of some waters from dune slacks at Sandscale, north Lancashire. *J. Ecol.*, **49** (1), 79–82 (1961).

[7] NICHOLSON T. H., Mycorrhiza in the Gramineae. II. Development in different habitats, particularly sand dunes. *Trans. Brit. Mycol. Soc.*, **43** (1), 132–145 (1960).

[8] RANWELL D., Movement of vegetated sand-dunes at Newborough Warren, Anglesey. *J. Ecol.*, **46** (1), 83–100 (1958).

[9] RANWELL D., Newborough Warren, Anglesey. I. The dune system and dune slack habitat. *J. Ecol.*, **47** (3), 571–601 (1959).

[10] ROBERTSON E. T. and GIMINGHAM C. H., Contributions to the maritime ecology of St. Cyrus, Kincardineshire. *Trans. Proc. Bot. Soc. Edin.*, **35** (4), 370–412 (1951).

[11] SALISBURY E. J., The soils of Blakeney Point: a study of soil reaction and succession in relation to plant covering. *Ann. Bot.*, **36,** 391–431 (1922).

[12] SALISBURY E. J., Note on the edaphic succession in some dune soils with special reference to the time factor. *J. Ecol.*, **13** (3), 322–328 (1925).

[13] SALISBURY E. J., *Downs and Dunes.* G. Bell (1952).

[14] WEBLEY D. M., EASTWOOD D. J. and GIMINGHAM C. H., Development of a soil microflora in relation to plant succession on sand dunes, including the rhizosphere flora associated with colonizing species. *J. Ecol.*, **40** (1), 168–178 (1952).

[15] WILLIS A. J. and YEMM E. W., Braunton Burrows: mineral nutrient status of the dune soils. *J. Ecol.*, **49** (2), 377–390 (1961).

[16] WILSON K., The time factor in the development of dune soils at South Haven Peninsula, Dorset. *J. Ecol.*, **48** (2), 341–360 (1960).

[17] WRIGHT T. W., Profile development in the sand dunes of Culbin Forest, Morayshire. I. Physical properties. *Soil Sci.*, **6,** 270–283 (1955).

[18] WRIGHT T. W., Profile development in the sand dunes of Culbin Forest, Morayshire. II. Chemical properties. *Soil Sci.*, **7** (1), 33–42 (1955).

CHAPTER EIGHT

Shingle Beaches

FORMATION

WHILST shingle beaches occur from place to place around our coasts, in most cases the stones and pebbles are so mobile that vegetation is quite unable to become established. The large shingle beaches, where portions have become stabilized and bear vegetation, are relatively few, and are to be found mainly on the south and east coasts of England. Stones varying size form the basic material of which they are composed. Quite a proportion of these stones are derived from glacial deposits and have come from cliff erosion.

In other cases they have been brought down by rivers, especially where there is an adjacent high upland. A third source of material is the off-shore sea bed. The shingle from any one of these sources may be built up to form a beach in the immediate vicinity, or the material may be transported along the coast (see p. 194) to form a shingle beach some distance away. Some of these shingle beaches subsequently acquire a partial covering of sand dunes (e.g. Blakeney, Scolt Head Island) and so it is necessary to consider both habitats (see Chapter 6) in order to obtain a comprehensive picture.

The main factors responsible for beach building are fourfold: first, there is the beach material and here size and quantity is important; secondly, the strength and direction of the waves, which in turn are influenced by the third factor, the wind, and finally there is the extent of the tidal rise and fall. On some beaches, e.g. the Chesil in

Dorset, the structure may also be determined to some extent by water percolation (see p. 197).

In the construction of shingle beaches, the most important factor is that of wave action. The size of the waves is, of course, determined by wind velocity and duration, associated with the distance or *fetch* over which the waves are generated, the greater the fetch the larger the waves. Waves can approach the beach either directly or obliquely. In either case they can throw up material, but if oblique they can also bring about beach drift as well as generate long-shore currents that will produce movement of material. Dependent upon the degree of wave action, there may be mass transport of water that in shallow depths can result in landward movement of material on the sea bottom.

The tides are obviously less important than wave action, though abnormal high tides can have a major effect on a shingle beach, particularly in raising its elevation and causing landward movement. Associated with the tides there are the tidal currents, which can move the lighter material on the sea bottom. These currents exist during ebb and flow periods and are non-existent at slack, low and high water.

LONG-SHORE MOVEMENT

Long-shore movement of beach material takes place either at the upper limit of the waves or else in the surf and breaker zone. In the

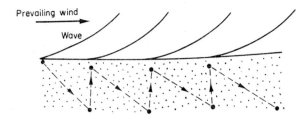

FIG. 8.1. *Diagram illustrating beach drift with waves caused by prevailing wind approaching obliquely. The broken line represents successive movements of a pebble (after Steers).*

former case the swash moves pebbles obliquely up the beach and the backwash takes them down vertically (Fig. 8.1). The angle of wave incidence is therefore important, though movement is also greater on a more steeply shelving coast. In the surf and breaker zone, it is mostly smaller material in suspension that is moved, such movement also being contributed to by any long-shore tidal and wind currents. The actual rate of beach material movement can be followed by the use of marked pebbles. On the beach proper paint can be used, whilst below low water stones tagged with radio-active barium or lanthanum have been employed successfully, the course of movement being followed by means of detectors. Movement does not take place in deep water, but in shallow water stones may travel from 90 to 600 yd over a period of 4 weeks[5].

Long-shore growth of shingle beaches, especially when they form a spit or off-shore barrier island, normally takes place in one direction depending on the prevalence of the factors mentioned above. From time to time, however, storms come from the opposite direction to the winds and waves that promote normal growth. When this happens the growing point can be turned at right angles and a lateral is formed. It is not uncommon, therefore, for spits to show a series of such laterals with a hook at the end (Fig. 4.1). At the growing point, movement can be considerable and this is reflected in the changes over the years. Under such conditions any vegetational growth is likely to be of an ephemeral nature.

BEACH MATERIAL

It should be evident that, in general, shingle beaches normally develop at right angles to the incident waves[5, 6] and that the "pile-up" to form our shingle beaches is due to the action of direct on-shore waves. On the beach itself it is usual to find the coarsest stones on the crest. This is because the beach profile is often such that it allows the waves to break close in-shore at high tide, and the energy liberated by these waves moves the larger material. This is particularly true of storm waves operating at high tide periods. These are, in fact, the principal beach builders and profile moulders.

On some beaches, such as the Chesil in Dorset, the stones show a gradation in size from large ones at the Portland end to small ones at Abbotsbury. At the former place the beach is 200 yd wide and 43 ft above high water, and the stones are 2–3 in. in diameter. At the latter, the width is 170 yd and the height is about halved and the stones are only about ½ in. in diameter. This gradation of material has resulted in argument concerning the origin of the beach and whether it has grown from the east or the west. There is no doubt that in relation to its physiography the waves at the Portland end have more energy and have therefore built a wider and higher beach with the coarser materials.

WAVE ACTION

It is not necessary in this little book to embark on a detailed discussion of waves and wave action, but in so far as shingle beaches are concerned it should be noted that waves are either constructive or destructive[6]. The former have an elliptical motion, and when breaking or spilling the wave front is not at a steep angle (Fig. 8.2b). The energy contained in such waves resides mainly in the swash, which therefore carries pebbles up the beach. Destructive waves have a plunging motion and a steep front when breaking (Fig. 8.2a), and because they plunge more vertically downwards their energy is mainly contained in the backwash, so that the beach is combed down and a steep head bank is formed around high tide mark. The two kinds of beach profiles are shown in Fig. 8.2c, AB representing the profile formed by destructive waves and CD that formed by constructive waves. In Fig. 8.2d, we see the effect of destructive waves upon the beach profile CD that has been built up. At low tide the backwash removes material below E resulting in a new profile. As the tide rises, more and more material is removed by the backwash (e.g. FB). At or near high water, the top of the beach at C will be cut back and the final stage will be a beach profile resembling the curve AB. In Fig. 8.2e, we follow the effect of constructive waves on a profile formed after a series of destructive waves as above. Here the swash carries up more pebbles than the backwash removes, and a

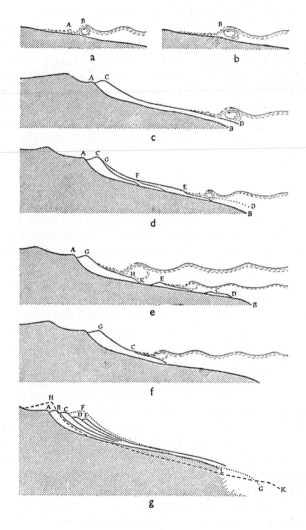

FIG. 8.2. *Beach profiles and wave action. For explanation, see text (after Lewis).*

small ridge CD is formed. As the tide rises, this ridge travels up the rising shore (e.g. E) until around high water the final ridge AGHK is produced. In a series of tides from neaps to springs, a new ridge will develop at each new high tide. In Fig. 8.2f the same beach is seen on a falling tide when material is still being added to the beach, so that there is a slight ridge at C which may travel slowly down the beach as the tide recedes. In Fig. 8.2g, AL represents a beach profile resulting from destructive waves at spring tides. If a period of constructive waves sets in, then ridges such as B, C, D, E will be formed, falling in height as successive tides decrease. If these are then followed by another series of spring tides a new major ridge F would be formed with the profile FLG. If, however, destructive storm waves are at work they will cut down all these ridges, carrying the shingle below low water mark and result, at low water, in the profile represented by HLK. It should be sufficiently clear now that the profile of shingle beaches is likely to be extremely variable and therefore inhospitable to vegetation of any kind.

Storm waves at high tide, and particularly at spring high tides, are of paramount importance because at such times pebbles can be thrown right over the beach. It is indeed through the action of such storms that shingle beaches gradually move landwards, and, if salt marsh had previously developed behind, old marsh mud can be exposed on the foreshore. Such landward movement is not a regular process along the whole length of the beach and is generally represented by shingle fans on the landward side. These may remain mobile or they may become stabilized by vegetation and new fans develop elsewhere. Whilst movement for any given storm is therefore represented by specific points of mobility, over a long period the whole beach exhibits landward movement.

On a large, high beach such as the Chesil the development of shingle fans on the landward side is associated with the percolation of sea water, which takes place under storm conditions, and which is of course easy with shingle. As drainage water percolates out on the landward side, usually between fans, shingle is removed and small ravines are formed. On the Chesil these ravines are known as "cans" and together with their two side buttresses they form a "camm"[11]

(Fig. 8.3). These camms are quite important physiographic features in relation to the distribution of the vegetation, particularly of Shrubby seablite (*Suaeda fruticosa*) (p. 201). The shingle forming the back and walls of a camm is usually just at the angle of repose (34°) for shingle of that size.

Whilst the main beach material is clearly shingle or pebbles, in certain areas either material is mixed with sand so that dune plants become associated with the shingle plants in the same way as they do when dunes on a shingle ridge erode away (see p. 204). This kind of phenomenon can be seen at the Ayreland of Bride in the Isle of Man, where there are low dunes lying on shingle, and shingle ridges can be seen in the dune lows of Winterton Ness[16].

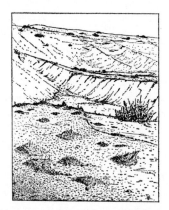

FIG. 8.3. *Shingle ravines on the Chesil Bank as seen from the terrace. Sketch by Mr. T. G. Hill (after Oliver and Salisbury).*

On the Norfolk coast the shingle is commonly associated with sand, but as a result of landward movement the beach may rest on salt marsh mud (see p. 87), though in other localities it lies on a sand base. Where a shingle beach protects salt marsh, one can expect to find some salt marsh plants at the lower levels on the landward side. It has been suggested that a true shingle beach flora only develops where there is pure shingle overlying a sand base. Even here, however, the presence of drift-line plants adds a complicating element.

Indeed it can be argued that there are no true shingle species, and that all those plants which do occur have come in from other habitats.

TYPES OF BEACH

Shingle beaches can be placed in one of five different categories. The first type of beach, which is associated directly with cliff, has been called a *fringing beach*[18] and generally carries only drift-line vegetation. The second type of shingle beach is the *spit* which is represented by Hurst Castle spit, Calshot, Northam and Blakeney Point (Fig. 4.1).

Very comparable to the spit, but differing from it in that it unites two areas of upland, is the shingle *bar*. The outstanding example of this type is the seven-mile-long Chesil Beach in Dorset. The fourth type of shingle area is represented by a place such as Dungeness where a whole series of parallel shingle ridges have been thrown up. This forms what is known as a *cuspate foreland*. The inner ridges soon become isolated from the sea and in the absence of drift and seeds they remain sterile for a long period. Finally, there are shingle *off-shore barrier islands* represented by the numerous examples on the Norfolk coast and with a major development in Scolt Head Island. Of these various types of shingle beach only Blakeney, Scolt and the Chesil have had any detailed botanical examination. Therefore any other shingle beach that carries vegetation provides, at present, a significant field for study.

Blakeney Point, Scolt Head Island, Dungeness and the Chesil are such major physiographic features that geomorphologists[6, 7, 8, 15] have devoted considerable attention to their origin and development. At Blakeney and Scolt Head, growth westwards has been interrupted by the formation of laterals formed as described above. Between the laterals, salt marsh has developed, and on the shingle, sand dunes have formed and in some cases have subsequently been eroded away.

At Dungeness, Lewis and Balchin[8] have argued that the various heights of the successive groups of ridges are related to past changes in land–sea levels. Whilst this may indeed be the correct interpretation one must express the hope that future physiographers will have a

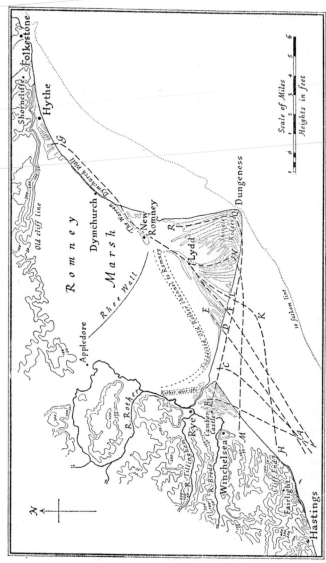

Fig. 8.4. Dungeness, showing lines of probable previous shingle beaches. AB is the oldest and BNQR the stage not very different from that of the present day (after Lewis).

further look at the problem here and elsewhere, in particular making use perhaps of ^{14}C methods for dating ridges. After a careful study of the ridges, Lewis[7] has worked out the probable course of development (Fig. 8.4). Early successive beaches are thought to have existed along the lines AB, AC, AD, AE, AF and then later a change of direction took place, represented by HK, MN and BQ. At present Dungeness is growing outwards as a result of on-shore waves from the south-west and from the east forming shingle beaches on two sides.

The account given above of the nature of shingle beaches and the factors involved in their formation does not pretend to be exhaustive. There are other facets and details that could be elaborated, and for those who are interested reference should be made to King's[5] book—*Beaches and Coasts*.

VEGETATION

The vegetation of shingle beaches is not rich floristically, but in the light of their mobility this is not surprising, nor has it been studied in any great detail except at Blakeney, Scolt and the Chesil. On all these areas, the Shrubby seablite, *Suaeda fruticosa*, which can grow to a height of 4 feet, is a most important plant[1, 13]. In all three areas, the *Suaeda* originates as a drift-line plant (p. 136), the seeds being brought with the flotsam and jetsam. When the seeds germinate, long tap roots rapidly grow down and enable the plants to become established.

Once plants have established, sooner or later they become overwhelmed by a shingle fan (p. 197); the now horizontal shoots put out new roots and new vertical shoots (Fig. 8.5). This process is repeated again and again as each succeeding shingle flow increases the amount of shingle over the original spot, so that the *Suaeda* appears to mount the shingle beach (Fig. 8.6), though really the beach is very slowly being moved landwards.

As the shingle becomes deeper and deeper, the older parts of the plant decay. Also since each line of *Suaeda* establishes during the same quiescent period and it is the same storms that generally bring about the overwhelming process, the plants appear to move up as a zone (Fig. 8.7).

The response of *Suaeda* to shingle covering is not the only factor controlling its growth. Thus, experiments have shown that the seedlings are very susceptible to water-logging of the roots though the adult plants are not so sensitive.

Fig. 8.5. *Prostrated branch of Shrubby seablite* (Suaeda fruticosa) *rejuvenating in the shingle from lateral buds; to show habit. One-third natural size (after Oliver and Salisbury).*

On a relatively low beach, such as Blakeney, where there may be some mobility on the landward side, the plants of *Suaeda* are more common in the bays between successive shingle fans, since it is noticeable that successive shingle flows tend to move along the same lines. The shingle on the Blakeney beach is sufficiently mobile for it to be thrown right over the beach. When such thrown shingle encounters lines of *Suaeda* bushes, a heaping up of the shingle occurs (Fig. 8.7).

Apart from the shrubby seablite, a number of other species occur on the more stable portions of shingle beaches. More than sixty species have been listed for the main beach and laterals at Blakeney, of which at least twenty are very rare and a further sixteen rare.

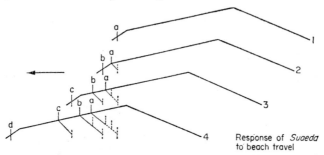

Response of *Suaeda* to beach travel

FIG. 8.6. *Diagram illustrating the mode of ascent of Shrubby seablite* (Suaeda fruticosa) *from the place of establishment on the lee fringe up to the crest of a travelling beach. Four profiles* (1, 2, 3, 4) *in the travel of the beach are shown and four* Suaeda *plants* (a, b, c, d) *successively establishing at each stage are considered. The existing portions of the* Suaeda *are represented by continuous lines, the parts which have disintegrated by broken lines. The direction of travel is from right to left (after Oliver and Salisbury).*

Among the more important and common species are Sand couch grass (*Agropyron junceiforme*) (drift-line plant), Sea couch grass (*A. pungens*) (dune plant), Creeping fescue (*Festuca rubra*) (dune plant), Yellow horned-poppy (*Glaucium flavum*), Sea sandwort (*Honkenya peploides*) (drift-line and embryo dunes), Curled dock (*Rumex crispus*), Wall-pepper (*Sedum acre*), Groundsel (*Senecio vulgaris*), Sea campion (*Silene maritima*), Sowthistle (*Sonchus oleraceus*) and Field milk-thistle (*S. arvensis*). Sea sandwort is normally found where the shingle is mixed with sand and nearly all the above species are associated with the drift-laden portion of the beach. An interesting plant found only locally but characteristic of shingle beaches, is the Northern shore-wort (*Mertensia maritima*).

This is found at Blakeney and on shingle beaches in northern England and Scotland, as well as in Ireland.

On the landward side where the shingle abuts on to salt marsh both at Blakeney and Scolt, one can find Sea purslane (*Halimione*), Sea aster (*Aster*), Sea wormwood (*Artemisia*), Sea poa (*Puccinellia*), Sea plantain (*Plantago maritima*) and Sea lavender (*Limonium vulgare*). Where sand is mixed with shingle, either because it is blown there or because former dunes have been removed by erosion (see p. 137), plants of Sand sedge (*Carex arenaria*), Sea convolvulus (*Calystegia soldanella*), Lyme grass (*Elymus*), Sea holly (*Eryngium*) and Ragwort (*Senecio jacobaea*) may occasionally be found. Nearly all these plants have a lower growth habit than their counterparts in the other habitats that they normally occupy.

On the laterals at both Blakeney and Scolt Head, where conditions

FIG. 8.7. *Profile of Blakeney Main Beach showing how the* Suaeda *bushes cause a heaping up of the shingle. Only two of the* Suaeda *zones are represented (after Oliver and Salisbury).*

are very much more stable, a wider variety of plants can be found. Species additional to those listed above are Rock sea lavender (*Limonium binervosum*) (a plant which will not tolerate covering by sand or shingle), Darnel poa (*Desmazeria marina*), Sea pink (*Armeria maritima*), Thyme-leaved sandwort (*Arenaria serpyllifolia*), Sea heath (*Frankenia laevis*) and Buck's-horn plantain (*Plantago coronopus* var. *pygmaea*). These stable laterals frequently exhibit a distinct zonation. This zonation may be related to inundations but is more likely to be related to gradations of salinity in the soil water or decrease in the amount of soil. It must, however, be admitted that at the present time no work has been carried out on such zonations, and until it has been, it is probably premature to suggest possible factors.

The lowest zone on these stable shingle laterals of the Norfolk coast is dominated by Shrubby seablite (*Suaeda fruticosa*), but associated with it one finds Sea purslane (*Halimione portulacoides*), Sea poa (*Puccinellia maritima*), Scurvy-grass (*Cochlearia*), Matted sea lavender (*Limonium bellidifolium*), Annual glasswort (*Salicornia stricta*) and Seablite (*Suaeda maritima* var. *flexilis*)—the whole group being strongly representative of the salt marsh flora.

At Blakeney[12] there is a zone above this with Sea couch grass (*Agropyron pungens*) and Creeping fescue (*Festuca rubra*), the latter being the dominant. The zone next above is found in both localities, and can well be termed the *Limonium binervosum* zone. Associated with the lavender, there is sea pink, sea heath, sea poa, and the dwarf form of buck's-horn plantain. On the crest, Fiorin (*Agrostis stolonifera*), Wall-pepper (*Sedum acre*), Sea campion (*Silene maritima*) and some of the species from lower down form the final cover. Should the lateral have a curved tip, the elbow of the bend is commonly higher than the crest of the lateral, and on the elbow additional species such as Bird's-foot trefoil (*Lotus corniculatus*), Sheep's sorrel (*Rumex acetosella*), Ribwort (*Plantago lanceolata*), Lady's bedstraw (*Galium verum*), Crested hair-grass (*Koeleria gracilis*) are to be found. These are all species of gravelly heaths and light inland soils, and their presence indicates more or less complete freedom from strictly maritime conditions. Such zonation as has been described above is essentially a static one. A comparable zonation can be found on the Chesil, but of course there are no laterals. The crest of the Chesil is dominated by the Sea pea (*Lathyrus maritimus*), which is not present in Norfolk, and there may also be much *Geranium purpureum*.

Information about the vegetation of the other main shingle areas is very scanty, and no detailed accounts have appeared. Golden samphire (*Inula crithmoides*) is reported as occurring on stable shingle at both Dover, Hamstead and Hurst Castle. At Dungeness the ridges, known as "fulls", generally bear Curled dock (*Rumex crispus*), and Sea campion (*Silene maritima*) in the younger stages, whilst later a whole collection of herbs and grasses cover them, so much so that some areas have been incorporated as pasture. If no grazing takes place, a scrub develops with bramble, gorse, hawthorn, blackthorn and elder. Whether such a scrub would ever give way to a

forest climax it is not possible to say: theoretically it should, but it
has never been suggested nor does the available information indicate
that it is likely. The hollows between ridges, which are known as
"lows" or "swales", are bare in the early stages and later may carry
marsh plants such as Marsh arrow-grass (*Triglochin palustris*).

The ridges at Winterton Ness are less obvious than those at
Dungeness, and there is a considerable amount of sand mixed in the
soil. According to Steers and Jensen[16], the youngest ridges are
characterized by a covering of the grass *Corynephorus canescens* with
two species of the lichen genus *Cladonia*. Older ridges, which are
farther inland, are still dominated by *Corynephorus* but plants of
Sand sedge (*Carex arenaria*) are evident, and this becomes more and
more abundant with increasing distance from the sea.

Mosses and lichens have been studied at Scolt[2, 3], Blakeney[9, 14]
and on the Chesil[19]. As may be expected they are confined to the
stable areas of shingle, namely near and on the crest of the beaches.
At Blakeney there is some difference between the moss species (nine)
that occur on the more mobile main bank in comparison with those
on the more stable laterals. On the Chesil the most important species
are *Bryum capillare*, *Ceratodon purpureus* and *Hypnum cupressiforme*.
Because of the stony substrate, lichens are really more important than
mosses. Since there are lichens that tolerate immersion in salt water
(p. 37), it is not surprising to find *Verrucaria maura* and *Placodium
lobulatum* occupying the lowest part of the beach where there will be
occasional submergence. On the stable laterals of Scolt and Blakeney,
crustose lichen species form the characteristic element at the lower
levels, whilst below and on the crest where there are grasses, the
non-crustose *Cladonia furcata*, *C. pungens* and *Cetraria aculeata* give
a greyish colour to the ground. The nature of the habitat does not, of
course, provide encouragement for any growth of algae.

FACTORS

Substrate

When we turn to consider the factors of the environment, it will
be evident from what has been said that the seaward side of the

beach is substantially different from the landward. There will clearly be variations in the soil environment and also the microclimate, as between each of these. Unfortunately at present no information is available and a detailed study of the environment of shingle beaches is greatly to be desired. Any humus present comes essentially from the drift, and on old laterals at Blakeney it can amount to 3·1 per cent of the soil, sufficient to give a hydrogen ion concentration slightly on the acid side of neutral.

Water Table

When pits are dug into the shingle, standing water can be encountered at not too great a depth. In many cases this water is fresh, or at the most brackish. Values have been recorded from the Blakeney beach at 5 cm depth with a chloride content of 0·07–0·44 per cent. Lower down at 5–9 ft, which was equivalent to the level of the adjacent salt marsh, the chloride in the water did not exceed the same range. The whole question of fresh water in shingle beaches has been carefully examined by Hill and Hanley[4], though further work would be desirable in order to substantiate their conclusions. Figure 8.8 shows a composite profile of the Blakeney main beach derived from digging a series of pits. The position of the water table in relation to the soil surface is also shown. There is no doubt that in such shingle beaches the water table fluctuates in relation to the tides (see also p. 172). There will be irregularities of movement but they can be associated with irregularities in tide heights, since the tides only rarely conform to their exact predicted heights (Fig. 7.8).

The water that is present is regarded as coming essentially from three different sources. Because of the nature of the substrate, rain water penetrates rapidly and comes to lie on top of any underlying salt water table, if there is one (and further work here would be desirable). Ordinary dew forms and water from this source also readily runs down between the shingle. There is, however, the special process known as internal dew formation (see p. 178) which

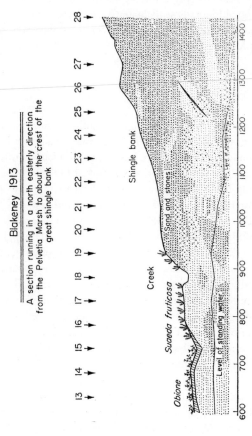

FIG. 8.8. *Section of part of Blakeney Beach to show structure (after Hill and Hanley).*

is probably responsible for much of the water, and which keeps the stones moist to just below the surface (this cannot be capillarity as the rise is often too high above the water table).

From the above account it will be seen how relatively scanty is our knowledge of shingle beaches, and it is clear that in the case of cuspate foreland and fringing beaches in particular there is scope for plenty of study, both descriptive and experimental.

REFERENCES

1 CHAPMAN V. J., *Suaeda fruticosa* Forsk *in* Biological Flora of the British Isles. *J. Ecol.*, **35**, 303–310 (1947).

2 DUCKER B. F. T., The Bryophytes of Scolt Head Island, in *Scolt Head Island*. Ed. J. A. Steers. Heffer, Cambridge. (1960).

3 ELLIS G. A., The Lichens, in *Scolt Head Island*. Ed. J. A. Steers. Heffer, Cambridge (1960).

4 HILL T. G. and HANLEY J. A., The structure and water content of shingle beaches. *J. Ecol.*, **2**, 21–38 (1914).

5 KING C. A. M., *Beaches and Coasts*. Arnold (1959).

6 LEWIS W. V., The effect of wave incidence on the configuration of a shingle beach. *Geog. J.*, **78** (2), 129–148 (1931).

7 LEWIS W. V., The formation of Dungeness Foreland. *Geog. J.*, **80** (4), 309–524 (1932).

8 LEWIS W. V. and BALCHIN W. G. V., Past sea-levels at Dungeness. *Geog. J.*, **96** (4), 258–285 (1940).

9 McLEAN R. C., The ecology of the maritime lichens at Blakeney Pt., Norfolk. *J. Ecol.*, **3**, 129–148 (1915).

10 OLIVER F. W., The shingle beach as a plant habitat. *New Phyt.*, **11**, 73–99 (1912).

11 OLIVER F. W., Some remarks on Blakeney Pt., Norfolk. *J. Ecol.*, **1**, 4–15 (1913).

12 OLIVER F. W. and SALISBURY E. J., Topography and vegetation of Blakeney Point. *Trans. Norf. Norw. Nat. Soc.*, **9** (1913).

13 OLIVER F. W. and SALISBURY E. J., Vegetation and mobile ground as illustrated by *Suaeda fruticosa* on shingle. *J. Ecol.*, **1**, 249–272 (1913).

14 RICHARDS P. W., Notes on the ecology of the bryophytes and lichens at Blakeney Pt., Norfolk. *J. Ecol.*, **17**, 127–140 (1929).

15 STEERS J. A., *The Coastline of England and Wales*. C.U. Press. (1946).

16 STEERS J. A. and JENSEN H. A. P., Winterton Ness. *Trans. Norf. Norw. Nat. Soc.*, **17** (4), 259–274 (1953).

17 TANSLEY A. G., *Types of British Vegetation*. C.U. Press. (1911).

[18] TANSLEY A. G., *The British Islands and their Vegetation.* C.U. Press (1939).

[19] WATSON W., List of lichens from Chesil beach. *J. Ecol.*, **10,** 255–256 (1922).

CHAPTER NINE

Coastal Cliff Vegetation

THE vegetation that is to be found above high water mark on coastal cliffs around the British Isles has been the least studied of all maritime vegetation types. One reason is probably that it does not normally form the clearly demarcated communities that are to be found on salt marshes, sand dunes and shingle ridges. Whilst undoubted maritime species occur, there is a considerable admixture of non-halophytes and the transition from what may be termed true maritime to non-maritime is not readily observable. Cliffs of any nature are also dangerous places on which to work, and in many cases, unless the investigator is also an experienced rock climber, effective study of the plant cover is not possible. Relatively few areas of coast have therefore been subject to investigation, but there is a classical work on the subject in the series of papers by M. E. Gillham[1-6]. Vegetation changes over a period of years emerge from the series of papers on St. Kilda by Petch[11], Poore and Robertson[12], and McVean[10], whilst accounts have also been published on Ailsa Craig in the Firth of Clyde[16], on Cornish cliffs[8], on Sussex cliffs[15], and on the cliffs of Clare Island and western Eire[13].

CHARACTERISTIC PLANTS

Tansley[14], in his monumental work on the vegetation of the British Isles, considered that the only plants which could be regarded as characteristic of cliffs were Seakale (*Crambe maritima*), Rock samphire (*Crithmum maritimum*), Sea beetroot (*Beta vulgaris* ssp.

maritima), Fennel (*Foeniculum vulgare*), Wild cabbage (*Brassica oleracea*), Stock (*Matthiola incana*) and Sea spleenwort (*Asplenium marinum*). To this list Petch[11] added the following as characteristic cliff-dwelling plants on St. Kilda: Long-leaved scurvy grass (*Cochlearia anglica*),* Scentless mayweed (*Matricaria maritima* ssp. *inodora* var. *salina*), Sea pink (*Armeria maritima*), Sea campion (*Silene maritima*) and Dark green mouse-ear chickweed (*Cerastium tetrandrum*). It seems evident that some of the species, e.g. *Armeria maritima, Silene maritima, Plantago maritima*, though occurring elsewhere, e.g. salt marsh, shingle, are nevertheless characteristic species of sea cliffs. Indeed, it is not surprising to find salt marsh and other species finding a niche in rock face communities. The general sequence most likely in any suitable place at low levels, is first of all for mats of vegetation to occur in which halophytes are predominant.

With increasing height or distance from the sea these mats are replaced by submaritime grassland or heathland, or in Scotland, by a community with pronounced alpines such as Least willow (*Salix herbacea*) and Rose-root (*Sedum rosea*). In some places, perhaps surprisingly, one may even find woodland plants, e.g. Wild angelica (*Angelica sylvestris*), Lady fern (*Athyrium felix-foemina*), Broad buckler-fern (*Dryopteris austriaca*), which may be present as relics of former woodland or, perhaps more likely, because of reduced competition.

SPECIAL FEATURES

Maritime cliffs are often the haunt of sea birds, either as nesting areas or as "sitting out" places. If the bird population is considerable and the area repeatedly used, then the amount of bird droppings can exert a considerable influence upon the plant life. Indeed, vegetation altered in this way by intense animal occupation has been termed zooplethismic, and any account of coastal cliff vegetation must pay particular attention to examples of such vegetation. Apart from bird populations, which, around the coastal cliffs of Great Britain, essentially comprise colonies of gulls, puffins, fulmars, storm petrels,

---

* Dr. Gillham (personal communication) considers that *C. officinalis* is more characteristic of cliffs.

shearwaters and others, there is no doubt that sheep-grazing also has exerted as much effect on the vegetation as it does on the grassy salt marshes of the western coasts (see p. 95). Until the advent of myxomatosis, rabbit populations were also highly significant, not only because of the grazing but also because their burrows were used by the puffins and shearwaters. In certain isolated places, such as Skokholm, where the virus has not penetrated, rabbits still remain a most important factor[3].

Some of the best coastal cliff vegetation is to be found on the offshore islands around the coast, and indeed much of the published work relates to the Pembrokeshire Islands, St. Kilda and Ailsa Craig. Here, whilst one may observe the effects of animal grazing from introduced domestic animals, there are places where no grazing occurs and then one can see the difference between grazed and ungrazed vegetation (see p. 216).

As with other types of plant communities it is possible to compile biological spectra based on Raunkaier's Life Form System. So far this has only been done for the Pembrokeshire Islands[7] where the spectrum is as follows:

Nph.	Ch.	H.	G.	Hh.	Th.
2·5	6·0	45	11	7	28·5

It will be evident that there is a close similarity to the kind of biological spectrum found for salt marshes (see p. 103) with Hemicryptophytes as the dominants and Therophytes as the next most important group. The absence of tree vegetation is essentially related to the impact of grazing and the susceptibility of British native trees to the effect of salt spray. However, in other parts of the world trees may form a component of the sea cliff vegetation. In northern New Zealand the Christmas tree or Pohutukawa (*Metrosideros excelsa*) is the characteristic tree of coastal cliffs, though it will also occur on maritime volcanic lava and maritime sand dunes.

PLANT COMMUNITIES

A number of communities have been described from coastal cliffs and a brief account of these will follow. The height at which these communities commence above mean high water mark depends very largely on the exposure of the coast to wind and wave action. The more exposed the coast the higher up the cliff face the vegetation will begin. In Cornwall Hepburn[8] records it as commencing about 6 m above M.H.W.M., though in sheltered coves the plants may descend to high tide level. Tansley[14] recorded Rock samphire (*Crithmum*), Sea beet (*Beta*) and Sea purslane (*Halimione*) at a height of 6 ft on the Sussex cliffs with Sea poa (*Puccinellia maritima*), Sea lavender (*Limonium vulgare*) and *Spergularia marginata* at 10 ft. In most places it is the Sea pink (*Armeria*) that descends closest to sea level.

In areas where grazing is not a pronounced feature, one of the most extensive communities is the Festucetum rubrae. Gillham[1] believes that it is indeed the climatic climax for the majority of exposed coastal regions in Great Britain. In those places where there is no grazing or trampling, the *Festuca* grows luxuriantly with leaves up to 30 cm long. Under such conditions other plants are not able to compete and very few species are associated with the dominant. The same situation has also been recorded from sand dunes (see p. 156). On Grassholm, off the Pembrokeshire coast, Gillham recorded only eight species in the Festucetum. Similar dense *Festuca* is recorded[12] on the Island of Dun off St. Kilda and on sea stacks off the west coast of Eire. The extreme competition provided by the fescue is not only through nutrients but also in respect of light, since the species likely to be associated with it in such a habitat are the low-growing maritime ones, e.g. the sea pink, sea plantain and sea campion. On Fair Isle, Red campion (*Melandrium rubrum*) grows well in the fescue swards, probably because being a woodland species it is shade-tolerant. Where there is some grazing, additional species enter and one may find from sixteen to twenty-two species or more. At the same time the Festucetum as a community is not so ubiquitous, and other communities are also to be found covering rather greater areas than in ungrazed places. When grazing becomes even more intense, a still greater variety of species are able to enter and one may find up to fifty species present. The effect of grazing is illustrated very well in Table 9.1 (p. 218) for three islands off the Pembroke coast.

Another very widespread community in exposed places is the so-called "Plantago sward"; this covers large areas with smooth, shining sheets where there is heavy grazing by sheep and/or rabbits, and where conditions farther inland favour the development of moorland rather than grassland. The soil of this community becomes soaked regularly in spray during the winter gales. The existence of the Plantaginetum relative to exposure and spray means that it plays a large part in western Ireland and also on the coastal cliffs of Scotland, whilst on St. Kilda, where the winter spray can be terrific, the community occurs up to a height of 600 ft above sea level. The dominant is generally Sea plantain (*Plantago maritima*) but in places *Festuca* may become almost co-dominant. Other species found in this sward include Buck's-horn plantain (*Plantago coronopus*), Ribwort (*P. lanceolata*), Sea pink (*Armeria maritima*), Dark green mouse-ear chickweed (*Cerastium tetrandrum*),* Early hair-grass (*Aira praecox*), Sea pearlwort (*Sagina maritima*)* and Creeping fescue (*Festuca rubra*)*.

In the presence of heavy grazing, this community probably represents the plagioclimax (see below) on cliffs of western Ireland and the western and northern Scottish coasts, where the climate generally favours the development of peat. In the southern portion of its range the community, as one might expect, is floristically much richer. This has been referred to by those who have compared the same sward in western Ireland with that on St. Kilda. Poore and Robertson[12] record the community as occurring on 3 ft deep peat on St. Kilda, the peat being formed under the prevailing climatic conditions from the remains of the plants. Since the Festucetum rubrae appears to be the climatic climax in the absence of grazing, one must regard the Plantaginetum maritimi as either a post-climax or more properly as a *Zooplethismic* or deflected climax (plagioclimax) brought about by grazing. Thus on St. Kilda the probable succession is regarded as bare $- - - - - \rightarrow$ Armerietum $- - - - - \rightarrow$ Festucetum (grazed) $- - - - - \rightarrow$ Plantaginetum maritimi.

* These were originally recorded as *Cerastium vulgatum*, *Sagina procumbens* and *Festuca ovina*, but Gillham (personal communication) considers the species are more likely to be those above.

The transition from the "Plantago sward" to adjacent communities can be extremely sharp, often a matter of 2–3 ft. On the islands off the Welsh coast, the Plantaginetum is more commonly dominated by Buck's-horn plantain (*Plantago coronopus*) rather than the Sea plantain (*P. maritima*), and the community does not occupy extensive areas, occurring mainly on rock outcrops, ledges and in shallow depressions. The presence of *P. coronopus* rather than *P. maritima* is probably the result of very severe grazing, because in places where grazing is less severe *P. maritima* may become co-dominant or even locally dominant. When, however, grazing is completely removed, *P. maritima* is not able to compete with the lush growth of Creeping fescue (*Festuca rubra*), though a succulent form of *Plantago coronopus* can do so.

Another fairly widespread community is that of the Armerietum maritimae (see also p. 96), which is generally associated with a soil that is drier than that of the "Plantago sward" and which also has a higher mineral content. In places *Festuca rubra* may become a co-dominant. On St. Kilda, Lundy Island, and also on the Pembroke-shire Islands, this community is highly favoured by the puffins and shearwaters and may often be riddled with their burrows; indeed these birds are responsible for the hummocky nature of the community. The sea pink is a plant that is tolerant of salt spray and salt in the soil, and it also reacts much better to grazing than does fescue, nibbling of the leaves stimulating growth rather than inhibiting it. The presence of this community is therefore indicative of heavy grazing associated with excessive salt spray. Patches of almost pure *Armeria* allied with Cliff sand-spurrey (*Spergularia rupicola*) will also be found on ledges of cliffs exposed to heavy spray. On the Cornish cliffs, Hepburn[8] records the sea pink as being most abundant at the lower levels, where it is associated with Rock samphire (*Crithmum*), *Spergularia rupicola* and the Sea spleenwort (*Asplenium marinum*), whilst higher up it occurs with the Sea campion (*Silene maritima*). *Plantago coronopus* and English stone-crop (*Sedum anglicum*) are two other species to be found on rock ledges and in clefts at these higher levels.

As Gillham[4] has pointed out, it is clear that there are three main ecological factors leading to dominance of the Armerietum. The first of these is climatic in that *Armeria* is more resistant to salt spray than all its competitors (except perhaps Sea rocket), and it therefore occurs at the very edges of cliffs and on ledges all the way down (Belt A, Fig. 9.1). Because it is more resistant to grazing and burrow-

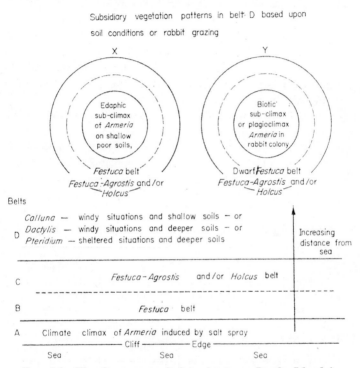

FIG. 9.1. *The three types of Armerietum on Lundy Island in relation to adjacent communities (after Gillham).*

ing under maritime conditions, it dominates bird and rabbit colonies. This community is biotically determined, and it is therefore a sub-climax, or plagioclimax, which will proceed to a later stage (Festucetum) (see p. 214) if the grazing is removed (Y, Fig. 9.1). The third factor is the edaphic one, and because *Armeria* is more tolerant of

H

shallow, poor soils it dominates exposed eminences where much of the soil has been eroded away. Should the soil improve, then the *Armeria* would be replaced by other plants so that again it must be regarded as a sub-climax (X, Fig. 9.1).

In protected areas, Yorkshire fog (*Holcus lanatus*) can take over and form patches or occupy considerable areas in which it is dominant or is the sole species. This grass also tends to develop in areas associated with gulls[4]. It persists in spite of a dense rabbit population because it is one of the species avoided by that mammal. It is, however, intolerant of trampling, and under such conditions it tends to disappear. It flourishes best in depressions where conditions are the most mesophytic available, and it will occur on cliffs with Fiorin (*Agrostis stolonifera*) where flushes of fresh water run down. Algae such as *Hormidium* and *Cladophora* can also occur in this type of community[1]. Another grass community associated with shelter is that of the Agrostidetum which may be dominated either by Com-

TABLE 9.1

Effect of Grazing on Agrostidetum tenuis (after Gillham)

Grazing intensity (av. no. rabbit pellets per $\frac{1}{2}$ m²)	No. of plant species	Percentage of grass cover	Percentage of cover by *Agrostis* and *Festuca*
None	2	100	100
	3	100	96
0–10	4	100	95
	4	100	75
5–100	21	91	62
	16	75	68
300–500	23	54	50
	24	56	48

mon bent-grass (*Agrostis tenuis*) or *A. stolonifera*, the latter species being encouraged in the presence of a seagull population. The *Agrostis* sward, which can be regarded as sub-maritime grassland, will withstand heavy grazing in protected places or alternatively it will tolerate strong winds if there is little grazing, but when the two factors are combined it then gives way to other species (Table 9.1).

On the sea cliffs of north Cornwall, as soon as the slope eases the maritime species are replaced by an *A. setacea* community with stunted herbaceous plants and in which only Sea pink (*Armeria*), Sea campion (*Silene maritima*), Sea plantain (*Plantago maritima*) and *Spergularia* among the halophytes, can compete. The *Armeria* zone does not in fact extend much beyond 300 m from the edge of the cliffs. Both *Armeria* and *Agrostis* do, however, occur clothing the seaward faces of the stone walls which are nearest the cliff edge.

Where there is a heavy bird population, particularly of puffins, a local community dominated by the Sorrels, *Rumex acetosa* or *R. acetosella*, is to be found. This is a strictly Zooplethismic community and is associated with the high guano (bird manure) deposits. The type of vegetation is very similar to the sheep "lair" flora of cliffs described by McLean[9] and by Gillham[5]. Such places are very rich in nitrogen, the soil is dark and tends to be moist and well pulverized. In these places the plants found are coprophilous* and quick-growing. Characteristic species are Annual poa (*Poa annua*), Chick-weed (*Stellaria media*) and Buck's-horn plantain (*Plantago corono-pus*). Chickweed is another species that may become locally dominant in the presence of considerable animal resting populations. Such Stellarieta have been recorded from seal breeding grounds on North Rona[10] and also on the Pembroke island of Middleholm where birds commonly roost[6].

The above represent the communities that can most properly be termed maritime. Others have been described from the off-shore islands, but it is likely that they are really non-halophytic. Included among these is the Molinietum of St. Kilda dominated by Purple moor-grass (*Molinia caerulea*) and the bracken community of the Pembrokeshire Islands. On the cliff faces themselves, cracks with

* Dung "loving".

water trickles or small caves are likely to have Sea spleenwort (*Asplenium marinum*) as a dominant associated with mosses and the liverwort *Marchantia*. On the cliffs of Ailsa Craig, where birds congregate, Vevers[16] has reported dwarfed plants of Elder (*Sambucus nigra*) and the Tree mallow (*Lavatera arborea*), together with typical maritime herbs such as *Spergularia*, *Silene* and *Puccinellia maritima*. *Erodium maritimum* (Marine crane's bill) can form pure patches on the tops of cliffs, and *Silene maritima* may do the same where there is shelter on the Pembrokeshire Islands. Here, too, on moderately exposed cliff faces, *Plantago coronopus*, Scentless mayweed (*Matricaria maritima* ssp. *inodora* var. *salina*) or *Holcus lanatus* (Yorkshire fog) are to be found, and with increasing shelter Scurvy-grass (*Cochlearia officinalis*), or Cow parsnip (*Heracleum sphonydlium*) or *Agrostis tenuis*. *Holcus*, *Agrostis stolonifera* and Pennywort (*Hydrocotyle vulgaris*) are species restricted to the fresh water flushes on such cliff faces. On the island of Grassholm, where there is no grazing, Gillham[1] has recorded a Sedetum on rocky areas that are not too exposed, and also small communities dominated either by species of *Atriplex* or *Spergularia*.

Among the lower plants, lichens are common on the exposed rock of cliff faces. Those that have been recorded as particularly abundant are the yellow *Xanthoria parietina*, *Ochrolechia parella* and *Ramalina siliquosa*, whilst at the lower levels are to be found the more strictly maritime *Lichina* and *Verrucaria* (see p. 37). In those areas frequented by birds, the fresh water alga *Prasiola* is a common soil-dweller, though it tends to be absent where there is no vegetation so that the soil bakes hard in the summer.

ENVIRONMENT

As a habitat, coastal cliffs exhibit certain environmental features which undoubtedly play a part in determining the nature of the vegetation. Among such features are wind and sea spray, the latter affecting not only the exposed parts of the plants but also the salinity of the soil. At very low levels, splash from storm waves may inhibit growth of many species. The soil is normally shallow and hence is easily subject to drying out, and this not only reduces the moisture but also increases the salt content. The stability of both soil and vegetation is obviously directly related to the angle of slope. The geological strata, particularly if rich in chalk, as on the south coast and in Norfolk, will determine the presence or absence of certain species. The biotic influence, e.g. birds, rabbits, sheep, is paramount in some areas, and there is little doubt that the type of community is determined in such places by the intensity of grazing.

Whilst the nature of the major factors is quite obvious, there is very little data available. Information about wind intensity and the proportion of on-shore gales can be obtained from meteorological records, and these serve to indicate their importance. In the case of the Pembrokeshire Islands, it has been shown that the greatest damage (caused by wind-carried spray) is derived from winter gales of over 46 m.p.h. A wet windy spring keeps the soil cool and also the air temperature, with the result that vegetation growth is retarded as compared with similar plants some little distance inland or under protection. One would indeed welcome some information on soil temperatures as compared with adjacent inland soils. Relatively small changes in contours of the land can bring about considerable variations in wind velocity and direction, and can well determine minor fluctuations in vegetation distribution and times of flowering (Fig. 9.2). This relationship has been so little studied that it is well worthy of more attention.

So far as salt in the soil or salt deposit on the leaves is concerned, the plants of coastal cliffs can be divided into those that are highly salt tolerant, those that are salt tolerant, and those that are not salt tolerant. In the first group, one finds species such as the Sea pink (*Armeria maritima*), the Sea plantains (*Plantago maritima, P. coronopus*), Rock samphire (*Crithmum maritimum*), the Cliff sandspurrey (*Spergularia rupicola*), the Tree mallow (*Lavatera arborea*) and plants of the drift-line and shingle that encroach into the habitat, e.g. *Beta*, Sea radish (*Raphanus maritimus*), Golden samphire (*Inula crithmoides*), Babington's orache (*Atriplex glabriuscula*), *Silene maritima*. Species belonging to the second group include Scurvy-grass (*Cochlearia officinalis*) and Danish scurvy-grass (*C.*

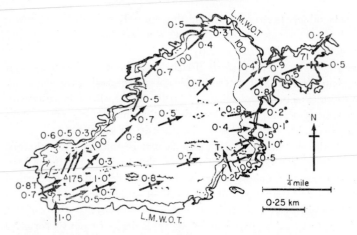

Fig. 9.2. *Map showing variations in direction and speed of a west-south-west wind of 16 m.p.h. (25·9 km.p.h.), i.e. force 4 on Beaufort scale, at the wind indicator on the lighthouse (after Gillham). (Crown Copyright reserved).*

danica), Dark-green mouse-ear chickweed (*Cerastium tetrandrum*), *Festuca rubra*, *Holcus lanatus* and English stone-crop (*Sedum anglicum*). The third group naturally contains the great majority of plants. Because of the shallow nature of the soil it is often very difficult to secure soil samples and in many cases the roots of the plants descend into rock cracks where there is the minimum of any soil. From such little information as is available it is clear that the salt content varies enormously, and is, of course, dependent upon amount of surf, height above wave splash, normal rainfall, presence of fresh water draining down through cracks in the rock, and protection by crags from rain and splash.

The effect of height in relation to the incidence of spray is well illustrated by figures (Table 9.2) for soils from the St. Kildan islands of North Rona (low cliffs) as compared with Hirta (high cliffs).

For those who have the opportunity there is plenty of scope to obtain further information about the salt habitat of the coastal cliff-dwellers—not only in the different communities but also in respect of seasonal variations.

TABLE 9.2

Mg Cl/100 g Soil

North Rona		Hirta	
Festucetum rubrae	82–493	"Plantago sward"	321
Armerietum	423	Zooplethismic grassland	149
Rumicetum	257	Molinietum	134

Biota

Birds and mammals play a very great part in determining the nature of the vegetation and their influence falls under three heads: treading and burrowing, dunging and grazing.

Trampling and burrowing may inhibit the growth of vegetation, though not to the major extent associated with excessive grazing. Over-dunging also eliminates many species and if extreme, results in bare ground. Where there is a large puffin colony on the cliff top, a bare area is found at the cliff edge and the few species that occur behind the bare zone have a specialized growth form (Fig. 9.3). The bare zone is not to be found with shearwater colonies, but in some roosts where gulls are particularly abundant the plant species are few, the plants minute and closely adpressed to the ground.

The Sea campion (*Silene maritima*) is apparently very intolerant of trampling, but on the other hand it is greatly stimulated by guano and so is abundant in bird colonies, unless there is grazing towards which it is not particularly tolerant. Where the birds or mammals use recognized paths across the vegetation one finds that the usual plants disappear and are replaced by species such as *Poa annua*, *Agrostis tenuis* and *Plantago coronopus*, which are able to tolerate trampling.

Puffin, shearwater and rabbit burrows may be very frequent in certain areas. In such cases one can observe secondary successions on the material extruded from the burrows. If the soil is friable and the burrows face the dominant winds (gale winds direction) undercutting of the vegetation takes place, and as a result it is only deep-rooted species such as *Armeria* and the Sorrels (*Rumex acetosa* and *R. acetosella*) that can survive. The presence of numerous burrows must exert an effect upon the soil. Thus it has been shown[6] that they lead to much greater fluctuations in soil moisture content as com-

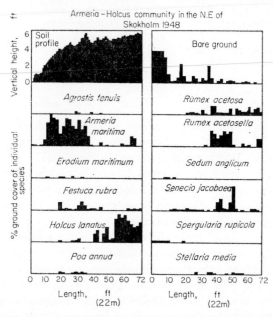

FIG. 9.3. *Belt transect showing the percentage ground cover of the chief species of the puffin colonies and the marginal strip of bare soil at the cliff edge where the birds congregate in large numbers. The profile of the transect is shown top left and the per cent bare soil top right. The per cent ground cover of the individual species is shown below (after Gillham).*

pared with unburrowed areas. During extended periods of dry weather, the soil above and around burrows is likely to dry out more than it would otherwise be expected to do. It is evident that the presence of burrows enables rain water to penetrate the soil more readily, especially if the soil is of a peaty nature, because peat has a "blotting-paper" action which normally stops much rain water from penetrating to lower levels.

It appears that soil temperatures adjacent to burrows can rise to higher day temperatures and this results in a hastening of growth in the spring. Here then we have a factor that can partially offset high winds and spray that may keep temperatures low (see p. 221). Although it has not been studied in any great detail, it appears that light penetrating into a burrow can bring about an alteration in the direction of growth of underground rhizomes of some species.

Bird dung (guano), much more so than mammal dung, can exert a profound effect upon the vegetation of cliffs.* The flora of guano-rich areas is a restricted flora and for any major region it tends to exhibit a marked uniformity. Minor differences within the basic framework of this coprophilous (dung-rich) community occur because there is a difference in the habits of the various bird species. Thus in the case of the shearwaters they defaecate in the burrows during the daytime but outside at night. The floors of the burrows as a result become very rich in nutrients. Puffins, on the other hand, defaecate in one of three places: the first is what may be called their "standing ground", the second is at the burrow entrance, and the third is in a specially enlarged portion of the burrow, which is termed the "defaecation chamber", that may be marked above ground by a darker green of some plants. With increasing concentration of the surface dung the normal vegetation is eventually replaced by a Rumicetum (see p. 219), but if it becomes too concentrated even the sorrels cannot survive and bare ground ensues. The stages in transition to the Rumicetum depend upon whether or not there is grazing and we must now turn our attention to this factor.

In the absence of grazing a luxuriant and species-poor Festucetum rubrae develops. In the presence of grazing, and depending upon its intensity, other communities appear determined by the response of species to grazing. A study of the plants found in cliff vegetation shows that they can be classified into:

* Tree mallow (*Lavatera arborea*) is very resistant to bird pressure and on Breton cliffs[17] is the last major species to be ousted.

(a) "Rabbit avoided", e.g. *Holcus lanatus, Poa annua, Stellaria media.*

(b) "Rabbit resistant", e.g. *Agrostis, Festuca, Armeria, Plantago.*

(c) Non-resistant, e.g. *Beta, Crithmum, Asplenium marinum,* which are therefore restricted to inaccessible places.

The effect of increased grazing on species-poor submaritime *Festuca* grassland is first to bring about a rise in the number of species as the more resistant halophytes enter. Later there may be a decrease as taller plants such as *Holcus* (rabbit avoided) take over and eliminate others through light competition. The general effect of grazing on maritime vegetation is shown at Y in Fig. 9.1 which illustrates zonation around a large rabbit warren on Lundy Island. The phenomenon

TABLE 9.3

	Heavy grazing. Open Plantaginetum with *Ceratodon purpureus* (moss)	Medium grazing. Closed Agrostidetum +Plantago and *Silene maritima*	Slight grazing. Pure closed Agrostidetum
Total no. of species	7	8	3
Percentage cover of grasses (*Agrostis, Festuca, Poa annua*)	8	80	96
Percentage cover *Agrostis*	3	73	92
Percentage cover of herbs	47	19	3
Percentage cover of *Plantago*	41	8	0
Percentage cover of mosses	25	0	0
Percentage bare soil	30	1	1
Av. ht. of sward (cm)	$<\frac{1}{2}$	1	2

in reverse is illustrated in Table 9.3 which shows the change that occurs in a *Plantago coronopus* sward when grazing is removed.

Sand dunes, salt marshes and coastal cliffs form habitats in which grazing experiments can be readily carried out. Wire-netting fences

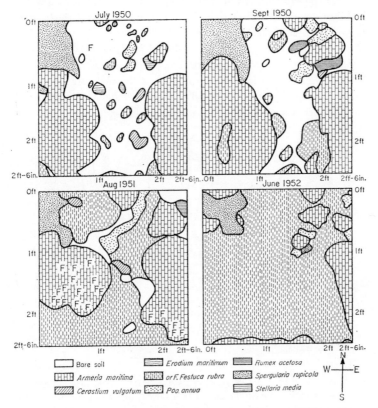

FIG. 9.4. *Four quadrats of the vegetation within a rabbit-proof enclosure on Skokholm Neck to show the change from an open Armerietum to a closed Festucetum 2 years after the cessation of grazing (after Gillham).*

placed in strategic localities can yield a wealth of information (Fig. 9.4). When such enclosures were erected on the Island of Skokholm the Armerietum (plagioclimax) gradually gave way to a tall growth of *Festuca rubra* (Fig. 9.5). Height increases in some of the plants can be quite considerable. Thus fescue can increase from ½ cm to 35 cm, sorrel from 2 to 20 cm and buck's-horn plantain from ½ to 35 cm.

Since the sea pink is well fitted to withstand wind and spray, its inability to compete when there is no grazing with a relatively non-aggressive grass such as *Festuca rubra* high-lights the profound effect of the grazing factor. In more sheltered localities, *Agrostis tenuis* becomes an aggressive competitor, but later it is generally over-run by *Calluna* because the *Agrostis* provides sufficient extra protection to the *Calluna* shoots so that wind damage to *Calluna* is repaired and the *Agrostis* is ousted through competition for light.

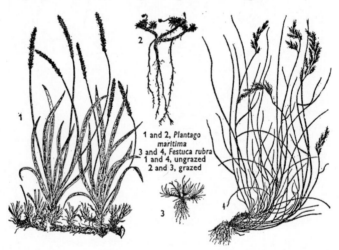

1 and 2, *Plantago maritima*
3 and 4, *Festuca rubra*
1 and 4, ungrazed
2 and 3, grazed

FIG. 9.5. *The effect of grazing on the growth form of* Plantago maritima *and* Festuca rubra (× 0·22) (*after Gillham*).

It has been pointed out by Gillham[3] that the elimination of grazing could have effects upon other members of the biota. Thus the increased growth of Yorkshire fog and bracken could well result in restricting wheatears to cliffs, because the tall vegetation makes unsuitable foraging ground. In the absence of rabbits, burrows could well collapse and this would reduce or eliminate those birds, e.g.

wheatears and shearwaters (puffins can construct their own burrows), that are dependent upon ready-made homes.

One major objective of ecological studies on coastal cliffs must be an understanding of the successions and the impact upon the communities of the major environmental factors of wind, salt spray and the biota. Such objectives have only been achieved in the British Isles for the Pembrokeshire Islands, and the hypothetical scheme proposed by Gillham, which effectively summarizes her findings, is reproduced below.

Successions depending upon the alteration of grazing

Conditions of severe exposure

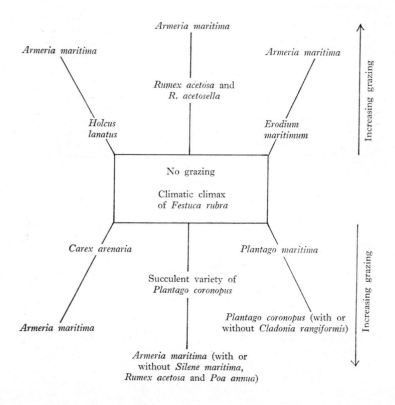

Hypothetical successions involving the islands as a whole

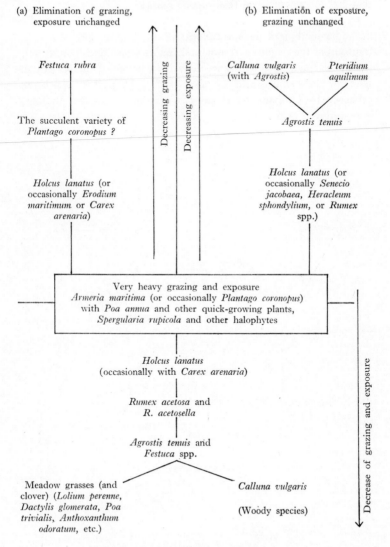

(a) Elimination of grazing,
     exposure unchanged

(b) Elimination of exposure,
     grazing unchanged

Festuca rubra

Decreasing grazing

Decreasing exposure

Calluna vulgaris
(with *Agrostis*)

*Pteridium
aquilinum*

The succulent variety of
Plantago coronopus ?

Agrostis tenuis

Holcus lanatus (or
occasionally *Erodium
maritimum* or *Carex
arenaria*)

Holcus lanatus (or
occasionally *Senecio
jacobaea, Heracleum
sphondylium*, or *Rumex*
spp.)

Very heavy grazing and exposure
Armeria maritima (or occasionally *Plantago coronopus*)
with *Poa annua* and other quick-growing plants,
Spergularia rupicola and other halophytes

Holcus lanatus
(occasionally with *Carex arenaria*)

Rumex acetosa and
R. acetosella

Agrostis tenuis and
Festuca spp.

Meadow grasses (and
clover) (*Lolium perenne,
Dactylis glomerata, Poa
trivialis, Anthoxanthum
odoratum*, etc.)

Calluna vulgaris

(Woody species)

Decrease of grazing and exposure

(c) Elimination of both grazing and exposure

REFERENCES

[1] GILLHAM M. E., An ecological account of the vegetation of Grass-holm Island, Pembrokeshire. *J. Ecol.*, **41,** 84–99 (1953).

[2] GILLHAM M. E., Ecology of the Pembrokeshire Islands. III. *J. Ecol.*, **43** (2), 172–205 (1955).

[3] GILLHAM M. E., Some possible consequences if rabbits should be exterminated by myxomatosis on Skokholm Island, Pembrokeshire. *North West Nat.*, 30–34 (March 1955).

[4] GILLHAM M. E., Some effects of the larger animals on the flora of Lundy. *Trans. Devon. Ass. Adv. Sci. Lit. & Arts.*, **87,** 205–229 (1955).

[5] GILLHAM M. E., Ecology of the Pembrokeshire Islands. IV. *J. Ecol.*, **44** (1), 51–82 (1956).

[6] GILLHAM M. E., Ecology of the Pembrokeshire Islands. V. *J. Ecol.*, **44** (2), 429–454 (1956).

[7] GOODMAN G. T. and GILLHAM M. E., Ecology of the Pembroke-shire Islands. II. *J. Ecol.*, **42,** 296–327 (1954).

[8] HEPBURN I., A study of the vegetation of sea cliffs in north Cornwall. *J. Ecol.*, **31,** 30–39 (1943).

[9] McLEAN R. C., An ungrazed grassland on limestone in Wales with a note on plant dominions. *J. Ecol.*, **23,** 436–442 (1935).

[10] McVEAN D. N., Flora and vegetation on the islands of St. Kilda and North Rona in 1958. *J. Ecol.*, **49** (1), 39–54 (1961).

[11] PETCH C. P., The vegetation of St. Kilda. *J. Ecol.*, **21,** 92–100 (1933).

[12] POORE M. E. D. and ROBERTSON V. C., The vegetation of St. Kilda in 1948. *J. Ecol.*, **37** (1), 82–97 (1949).

[13] PRAEGER R. L., Clare Island survey. X. Phanerogamia and Pterido-phyta. *Proc. Roy. Ir. Acad.*, **31,** 40 (1911).

[14] TANSLEY A. G., *The British Islands and their Vegetation*. Cambridge (1939).

[15] TANSLEY A. G. and ADAMSON R. S., A preliminary survey of the chalk grasslands of the Sussex downs. *J. Ecol.*, **14,** 1–32 (1926).

[16] VEVERS A. G., The land vegetation of Ailsa Craig. *J. Ecol.*, **24** (4), 424–445 (1936).

[17] GÉHU, J. M. and GÉHU-FRANCK, J., Récherches sur la végétation et le sol de la Réserve de l'ile des handes (Ille-et-Vilaine) etdequel-ques ilots de la cote Nord-Bretagne. *Bull Lab. Mar. Dinard* Fasc. **47,** 19–57, (1961).

Index